"This is a pleasing and compelling exploration of spirituality as manifested in the life of William Ward, the indispensable printer for the justly-famed Serampore Trio. Not only did he print, he wrote. Not only did he publish, he was a theologian. Not only was he doctrinally aware, he was spiritually deep. Not only was he spiritual, he was an activist. Not only did he have and hold strong convictions, he was a peacemaker and strategist. As the author notes early in this book, 'this work focuses on the beliefs that animate the life—the convictions that made Ward tick—and then asks the question, "What kind of man did these beliefs produce?"' Matthew Reynolds poses the question well and answers it with an instructive fullness that will benefit lay men and women, pastors, missiologists, and young people. Covering an impressive latitude of roles played by Ward, Reynolds brings to light his work as 'preacher, evangelist, mentor, mission administrator, missiologist, theologian, historian, draftsman, author, college professor, pastor, husband, father, counselor, peacemaker, and friend.' This is a great read about a great man pursuing a great calling."

TOM J. NETTLES
Senior Professor of Historical Theology, SBTS

"The name of William Ward has been familiar to readers of Baptist history for over two hundred years due to his close missionary association with William Carey. With Carey and Joshua Marshman, Ward formed what has been called the Serampore Trio, a wonderful mission partnership in the early nineteenth century. Yet, despite this and unlike the way Carey's story has been remembered, next to nothing has been written specifically about the life of this winsome Christian. In this year of our Lord, 2023, the bicentenary of Ward's stepping into Glory, it is only proper to correct this deficiency. I am thrilled that Matthew Reynolds' robust study of Ward's thought and piety, which began its existence as a doctoral thesis, is going to be available to a much wider audience. May this wider reading lead to both a better understanding of the Serampore mission and also a new appreciation of Ward as a Spirit-filled believer and missionary."

MICHAEL A.G. HAYKIN
Chair & Professor of Church History, SBTS

"Matthew Reynolds walked the streets, learned the language, and spent time scouring dusty texts where William Ward lived, unpacking this missionary giant's theology and spirituality. I have known Matthew as a friend, pastor, colleague, and scholar, and I commend the research of this man of piety as he guides us in understanding and assessing the spirituality of Ward. Through careful analysis of personal journals and records of public ministry, we see that Ward's role in the Serampore Trio went well beyond pressing ink to paper. Before he was a printer, God pressed theological truths on Ward's heart. These treasured doctrines manifested love, humility, prayer, and usefulness in his spirituality. Furthermore, Reynolds' well-researched text shows how Ward's spirituality impacted the unity and peace of the broader Serampore missionary community. I heartily endorse this text for missionaries seeking to know, remember, and emulate a faithful missionary and for the renewed attention on this pioneer missions community."

JOSHUA BOWMAN
Assistant Professor of Missions & Theology,
Cedarville University

"If remembered at all, William Ward is known as the industrious and efficient administrator of the Serampore Mission. In the shadow of William Carey, few are aware how the evangelistic zeal, missiological clarity, and pastoral concern of this unlikely missionary fueled the mission's success. In addition to his skill as printer and editor, Ward was a vibrant itinerant evangelist, discipled new converts, invested in the spiritual growth of the young men and women of the mission, and labored to cultivate a gospel culture of generosity and peace that sustained the missionary team. Through careful examination of Ward's journal and correspondence, Reynolds sheds new light on the deep evangelical piety that animated this humble and remarkably 'useful' man."

RYAN GRIFFITH
Vice President for Strategic Initiatives and
Associate Professor of Church History,
Southwest Baptist University

"No hero of the faith stands alone. Every David has his Jonathan. And though William Carey has been famously awarded the title, 'Father of Modern Missions,' the gentle-hearted 'amiable manners' of William Ward kept the Serampore Trio together for the sake of the mission. Reynolds' fabulous study of Ward's piety reveals the blessing of spiritual friendships and warm-hearted camaraderie in Great Commission service. For its depth of historical research and breadth of spiritual refreshment, any scholar or Great Commission servant would find this peaceful spirituality of William Ward to be illuminating and inspiring."

E.D. BURNS
Professor of Spirituality & Missiology, Asia Biblical Theological Seminary; Author of *A Supreme Desire to Please Him: The Spirituality of Adoniram Judson*

"*The Spirituality of William Ward* by Matt Reynolds is a well written account of one of the 'Serampore Three.' With compelling scholarship, much from original sources, this is a fascinating history of one of the key figures on one of the first teams of the modern missionary movement.

Matt has captured brilliantly the impact of a godly life when lived with humility, grace and disciplined, intense focus. He accomplishes this by painting a picture of the unique challenges and complexities confronting the missionaries of the day. Climate, health, a dizzying cultural context and the control of governments both local and colonial enable the reader to feel the full weight of the pressures working against Gospel advance in that era.

Yet, Ward worked as a tireless printer, administrator, evangelist and Christlike peace maker who brought together a diverse group of God-lovers from many different backgrounds and ethnicities to labor for the work of the God's kingdom in that place. Against that dynamic and ever challenging backdrop, the life lived by Ward provides a memorable account of how one person's robust and resilient faith against all odds could have such a profound impact. We desperately need more men and women like Ward in our day!

If a thoughtful practitioner or interested student of mission history wants to know how the challenges of cross-cultural ministry were confronted and conquered in a previous era, this is a must read. Matt has given us a masterful work of enduring quality and sound historical perspective. We owe him a deep sense of gratitude. To God be the glory!"

JOHN LOVE
Regional Leader of a mission
in Southeast Asia

"One of the towering figures in modern Protestant missions was William Carey, a key pioneer of mission and Bible translation in Bengal. Carey famously walked alongside two other colleagues as the 'Serampore Trio,' Joshua Marshman and William Ward. Those with at least a passing familiarity with the story of early Baptist missions in India will often recall Carey as a translator; if they know anything about his colleagues at all, they would see Marshman as an evangelist and debater, and remember William Ward primarily for his expertise as a printer. While it's certainly true that Ward engaged in painstaking, brilliant work in designing typeface for multiple languages and scripts, in this volume, Matthew Reynolds opens the door to the almost hidden knowledge of the depth of character and spiritual life exemplified in the life of William Ward. The extensive quotations from Ward's own writing gives voice to this fascinating figure, and enables readers to see him as a significant figure in his own right, rather than simply being a 'supporting actor' in Carey's overall story. It is clear from this account, too, that rather than Ward's Reformed theological leanings being of the type implied in John Ryland, Sr.'s reported 'When God pleases to convert the heathen, he will do so without your aid nor mine' rebuke to a younger William Carey, but rather like that of the more recent John Piper, who wrote that his Reformed theology 'does not make missions unnecessary, it makes missions hopeful.' The emphasis here on Ward's spiritual life and vision for mission make this not only a scholarly work of biographical history, but a work of *applied* history, enabling the reader to draw lessons for missional practice and spiritual life."

MATTHEW FRIEDMAN
Adjunct Professor,
Asbury Theological Seminary

The Spirituality of William Ward

STUDIES IN BAPTIST HISTORY

THE SPIRITUALITY OF WILLIAM WARD

Unsung hero of the Serampore Mission

MATTHEW M. REYNOLDS

The Spirituality of William Ward

Copyright © 2023 Matthew M. Reynolds All rights reserved.
This book may not be reproduced, in whole or in part, without written permission from the publishers.

Studies in Baptist History, Volume 2

H&E Academic, West Lorne, Ontario
www.hesedandemet.com

Frontispiece: Portrait of W. Ward, engraved from a drawing by Thomas Overton in 1820 for Stennett, *Memoirs of The Life of the Rev. William Ward, Late Baptist Missionary in India* (London: Simpkin and Marshall, 1825).

Paperback ISBN 978-1-77484-122-8
eBook ISBN 978-1-77484-123-5

I dedicate this book to God, my Father in Christ. From its inception, it has felt that this endeavor has hung on a thread. But time and time again, God has orchestrated circumstances in just such a way as to make continued progress—and ultimately completion—possible. To him be all the glory.

CONTENTS

List of Abbreviations xiii
Foreword xv
Preface xix

Introduction 1
1. The Life of William Ward 9
2. The Essence of Ward's Spirituality 63
3. "When brothers dwell in unity":
   Ward's Spirituality in Relationships 123
4. "A soft answer turns away wrath":
   The Peacemaking Effect of Ward's Piety 171
6. Conclusion 227

Appendix 1: The Lost Devotion of Question Meetings 231
Appendix 2: The Winsome Wit of Ward 237
Timeline 247

Bibliography 251
Index 267

List of Abbreviations

BMS	Baptist Missionary Society
CLRC	Carey Library and Research Centre
LMS	London Missionary Society
PA	*Periodical Accounts* of the Baptist Missionary Society
PBMS	Particular Baptist Missionary Society
SFA	*Serampore Form of Agreement*

Foreword

Amongst the curiosities on display, the Carey Museum showcases a copy of the marriage agreement of William Ward and Mary, the widow of fellow Baptist missionary John Fountain. This document gives important insights into Ward's character. In October 1799, Mary had arrived at Serampore to marry John, but he died eight months later, leaving her giving birth in the care of the Mission. But Mary and John Jr. needed a husband and father. Ward, being eligible, was the most obvious candidate. His Journal records that their marriage was "intended for some time, but circumstances hindered it."[1] He noted that suitable accommodation for the couple only became available in April 1802. So, finally, on a sultry Monday evening on May 10, William Carey performed their wedding ceremony at Mission House.

Though the text of the covenant (as per Ward's own choosing) was plain and sober, he notes how gifts of *mishty* (sweetmeats) and fruit made sure the night finished on a celebratory note. The document reveals that among the seventeen witnesses were the residential missionaries and their wives, Carey's eldest sons, besides several European and Bengali enquirers and converts.[2] This list shows Ward's remarkable generosity and inclusiveness, his all-embracing love for the Bengali community, and his fondness of Felix and Wm Carey Jr., whom he had mentored so patiently.

---

[1] Entry May 10, 1802. *Ward's Journal*, 230–231. mss, CLRC, Serampore.

[2] Among the European witnesses were, Wm Carey, Joshua Marshman, Felix Carey, David Moon, I. Ferguson, I. Fernandez, William Carey-Junr. Hannah Marshman, Ann Brunsdon, Ann Grant, C. Rumour [Carey's future wife]. Bengalis: Shri Krishna Chandra [Pal], Shri Pitambar Singho, Shri Kamalakanta Sharma, Shri Pitambar Mitra, Shri Ramakanta, Shri Samadas. The names are all given (some with different spelling) in Ward's Journal.

The Spirituality of William Ward

Besides Krishna Pal (Serampore's first Bengali convert), Ward would have especially loved the presence of Pitambar Singh. "Old Pitamber" was of the writer's caste, who in December 1801 had walked 30 miles to Serampore to enquire about one of Ward's tracts, and choose a new way of life. When he was baptized a few weeks later, Ward especially rejoiced over him. In Singh, as in other new converts, Ward had found his life's purpose. The wedding shows Ward's "warm hearted evangelical piety" that Matt Reynolds notes as the key principle to understand him: a spirituality that expresses itself into a desire for true Christian communion, the union of all believers, no matter their background. As Matt's investigation shows, this passion is evident throughout Ward's life.

Matt has extensively walked the Indian Road, and lived among some of South Asia's most neglected communities. He and his family sat down with people, absorbing their culture and language, while tirelessly seeking to present the living water in Indian bowls. When I learnt in 2016 he planned further studies, I was delighted to hear of his desire to investigate William Ward's life. Matt has been gifted with a warm personality, a fine pastoral heart, and a deep desire to expound evangelical truth. As a practitioner, he is uniquely placed to bring Ward out from under Carey's shadow and let him speak. On his visit to our Archives at Serampore College, we were both overjoyed to uncover rare (and dusty!) copies of Ward's writings. We continued our conversations over email while the Reynolds moved back to Kentucky. Over the years we puzzled over obscure entries in Ward's *Journal*, using the transcript which is deposited in our Archives. With this publication, the wish for an authentic biography of Ward, by its transcriber E. Daniel Potts, has at least partially been fulfilled.

Foreword

At the start of Matt's investigation, it is appropriate to hear afresh Ward's prayer of hope for our suffering world, that sums up his practical spirituality:[3]

Let ... [the Christ filled faith] be universally embraced,
its spirit imbibed, and its precepts obeyed,
and wars will cease to the ends of the earth—
ignorance and superstition will be banished—
injustice and oppression removed—
jails, chains, and gibbets, rendered unnecessary—
pure morality, flowing from the religion of the heart,
will diffuse universal happiness,
and earth become the vestibule of heaven.

Peter de Vries
Carey Library and Research Centre
Serampore College, India
May 2023

---

[3] William Ward, *A View of the History, Literature, and Mythology of the Hindoos*, 3rd edn. (London: Black, Kingsbury, Parbury, and Allen, 1820), III, Pt II, 297.

Preface

Having lived in Kolkata with my family for extended periods of time during various teaching and preaching stints, it has been a peculiar privilege to write this book on a missionary hero who, two hundred years before, walked the same streets and ministered among the same people. Many have assisted me along the way, and I am deeply grateful to all.

I am most grateful to my wife, Shannon, for her encouraging words, helpful suggestions, keen interest, longsuffering patience, and, in general, for bearing with me in love throughout the entire project. She is a true helpmeet to me.

I am thankful for our daughters, Noël and Halle, for their smiles and laughter, for lightening the mood, and always bringing me down to earth. I gratefully acknowledge my parents, Marvin and Jeannie Reynolds, for their constant interest and encouragement in this endeavor.

As this work was originally a dissertation, I gratefully acknowledge the counsel and guidance of my doctoral advisor, Dr. Michael A.G. Haykin. His enthusiasm for church history is contagious, and I am thankful for the privilege of writing on a Baptist subject under the tutelage of such a renowned Baptist scholar. I am also grateful for his recommendation of my dissertation to Chance Faulkner for publication through H&E Publishing so that a wider readership may become acquainted with a member of the Serampore Trio that has long been overlooked. Thank you Chance for your interest in Baptist History and your willingness to publish a work on William Ward, a figure in Baptist History who is truly worthy of publication but whom few have ever read.

The Spirituality of William Ward

As with any writing effort, this work required hours upon hours spent in solitude. But I thank God that I have not been alone on this literary journey. In the research for this book, I have been greatly assisted and encouraged by two other Serampore scholars, Peter de Vries and Sam Masters. Both supplied me with copious primary sources related to Serampore and William Ward that greatly expedited my research and writing. In this modern-day Serampore Trio, I am by far the least, but it has been an honor and a joy to collaborate with them to bring new works to light that commend William Ward and his work to a twenty-first century audience.

Matthew Reynolds
Louisville, Kentucky
May 2023

Introduction

History tends to remember the pioneers. This is understandable, for they enter the story first. They blaze the trail that others follow. In the case of Protestant missions, this honor goes to William Carey (1761–1834) who is often considered the "father of modern missions."[1] Consequently, numerous biographies have been written about him in his own day and ours.[2] But Carey's life work took place in the context of a bustling mission comprised of numerous other missionaries sent out by the Baptist Missionary Society (BMS), Asiatic missionaries of mixed native and European ancestry, and native Indian evangelists and pastors. And at the center of this missiological orbit was not Carey alone, but a fellowship of three—the famed Serampore Trio—consisting of Carey and two other seldom-mentioned colleagues, Joshua Marshman (1768–1837) and William Ward (1769–1823). These enjoyed an amazing twenty-three years of harmonious service together in the Serampore Mission and rarely did anything without consulting each other.

Yet, sadly, when the Serampore Mission story is told, it is often only Carey's name that is remembered. This is tragic

---

[1] Sam Masters notes that the first use of this epithet is toward the end of the second volume of John Clark Marshman's (1794–1877) seminal history of the Serampore Mission, *The Life and Times of Carey, Marshman, and Ward*. Samuel Everett Masters, "'Will Anyone Say The Lord Is Not Among Us?' The Serampore Mission And Its Covenant" (PhD diss., The Southern Baptist Theological Seminary, 2020), 6; John Clark Marshman, *The Life and Times of Carey, Marshman, and Ward* (1859; repr., Serampore: Council of Serampore College, 2005), 2:477.

[2] For an exhaustive list of biographical works on William Carey from the nineteenth, twentieth, and twenty-first centuries, see www.wmcarey.edu/carey/bib/ from the Center for Study of the Life and Work of William Carey, D. D. (1761–1834) website of William Carey University in Hattiesburg, Mississippi, U.S.A.

not only because it is historically myopic, but also because it deprives the church of a realistic view of missions and ministry. For, anyone who has served overseas as a missionary—or on the staff of a church in a sending country—can testify to the challenges of serving with a team full of strong-minded individualists and dreamy visionaries. With such a team, much may be discussed and even started, but lacking gifted administrators and genial peacemakers, the mission will at best have difficulty maintaining and finishing what it starts, and at worst, will fracture and dissolve over personality conflicts and intractable disputes.

The Serampore Mission might well have ended in such a manner, shortly after it was begun, had it not been for the presence and impact of William Ward. Thankfully, however; between a plodding Carey and a polemic Marshman, Ward's irenic influence often made for peace and a way forward in the Mission during times of disagreement and conflict. Ward's administrative gifting provided for the maintenance and smooth running of the mission. And Ward's printing prowess ensured that Carey's translations, and Joshua Marshman's educational reforms were recorded in print and disseminated to a wide audience in Bengal and beyond.

Ironically, though Ward was the member of the Trio that penned the original history of the Serampore Mission, history has largely forgotten William Ward.[3] In 1978, when Mary

---

[3] William Ward is the author of the mission Journal that ran from 1799–1811 which were sent to England, edited by Andrew Fuller, and then recorded in the *Periodical Accounts*. After 1811, similar historical material was recorded and preserved by Ward in *Circular Letters. BMS Missionary Correspondence; William Ward; Transcript of Diaries in 2 Books Comprising 4 Volumes; Book 1 (Vols. 1 & 2) 1799–1805; Book 2 (Vols. 3 & 4) 1806–1811*, microfilm; reel 44, publication No. 5350 (London: Baptist Missionary Society Archives), 1981; *Periodical Accounts Relative to the Baptist Missionary Society. Baptist Missionary Society Archives, 1792–1914*, microfilm, reels 1-9 (London: Baptist Missionary Archives, 1981); *Monthly Circular Letters Relative to the Missions In India, Established By a Society In England, Called the "Baptist Missionary Socie-*

Introduction

Drewery's *William Carey, Shoemaker and Missionary* was published, E. Daniel Potts, author of *British Baptist Missionaries in India*, complained to former Serampore Archive Librarian, S. K. Chatterjee, "It's a pity that Hodder and Stoughton would publish yet another biography on Carey ... and refuse to publish [my] one on Ward."[4] Similarly, eminent Carey scholar A. Christopher Smith lamented that though Ward was integral in the running of the Mission, he slipped from the memory of succeeding generations almost as soon as he was laid to rest.[5] This lacuna would be understandable were there little in the way of primary sources concerning Ward, but, on the contrary, there is more primary source material either penned by or connected with Ward than by Carey himself.[6]

Following Ward's death in 1823, only two full-length memoirs of William Ward have ever been written. The first, written two years after his death, is by Samuel Stennett, a

---

ty" (Serampore: Mission Press, 1811).

[4] Peter de Vries, email message to author, November 3, 2016, regarding E. Daniel Potts' unpublished biography of William Ward. "I have not had access to this biography for this thesis until recently."

[5] A. Christopher Smith, *The Serampore Mission Enterprise* (Bangalore, India: Centre for Contemporary Christianity, 2006), 46.

[6] This is largely due to the foundational role that Ward's Journal played in public relations in the Trio's day as well as the fact that this same document has been the primary source for every historian since writing on Carey or anything related to the Serampore Mission. This primacy is asserted by Potts in E. Daniel Potts, "William Ward's Missionary Journal," *The Baptist Quarterly* 25, no. 3 (July 1973): 111. Following Ward's Journal which ends October 30, 1811, Ward's *Circular Letters* (begun in December 1807) continued to serve as the official and primary conduit of news between the Serampore Mission and the Society in England. Potts, "William Ward's Missionary Journal," 113. In addition to these key historical works, Ward also drafted the *Serampore Form of Agreement*, the principles originally adopted by the Mission to govern its work in Serampore and outlying mission stations. Other key works include his *A View of the History, Literature, and Religion of the Hindoos*; *Brief Memoir of Krishna Pal, the First Hindoo, in Bengal, who broke the Chain of the Cast, By embracing the Gospel*; and *Reflections On The Word of God For Every Day In The Year: In Two Volumes*, a daily devotional along the lines of Spurgeon's later, more famous *Morning and Evening*.

former classmate of Ward's at Ewood Hall.[7] Stennett enjoyed a "long cherished friendship" with Ward, and his work is based on knowledge acquired through friends of "circumstances not yet made public, and a number of original letters."[8] Though other, shorter memoirs of Ward have been written, many draw from Stennett's work, and to date, there is no better single biographical work on Ward.[9]

In part, this work on the *The Spirituality of William Ward*, is a humble attempt to correct this historical omission. But it is not a biography of William Ward. As mentioned above, such a biography was written by E. Daniel Potts but was never published.[10] This is rather a work about the spirituality of William Ward. As such, while containing much that is biographical, this work focuses on the beliefs that animate the life—the convictions that made Ward tick—and then asks the question, "What kind of man did these beliefs produce?"

The Spirituality of William Ward plumbs the depths of Ward's Journal, his personal *Reflections on the Word of God*

---

[7] Christopher Smith notes that Stennett and Ward were classmates at Ewood Hall. A. Christopher Smith, "William Ward, Radical Reform, and Missions in the 1790s," *American Baptist Quarterly* 10 (1991): 240nn1-2. Samuel Stennett, *Memoirs of the Life of the Rev. William Ward, Late Baptist Missionary in India; Containing A Few Of His Early Poetical Productions, and Monody to His Memory* (London: Simpkin and Marshall, 1825).

[8] Stennett, *Memoir*, v–vi.

[9] Though Stennett does not always reveal the intended recipients of Ward's letters that he reprints, the letters he includes are of a more personal nature than those photographed in BMS Archives which are of a more official nature. *BMS Missionary Correspondence; William Ward; Transcript of Diaries in 2 Books Comprising 4 Volumes; Book 1 (Vols. 1 & 2) 1799–1805; Book 2 (Vols. 3 & 4) 1806–1811*, microfilm; reel 44, publication no. 5350 (London: Baptist Missionary Society Archives, 1981).

[10] Since the writing of the dissertation on which this current work is based, a copy of Potts' biography was obtained by Peter de Vries and given to the author. It is an academically meticulous work and excels in delivering historical detail. It lacks, however, sympathetic treatment of Ward's theological influences and convictions or his piety. Perhaps with permission from his estate, this biography will yet be published, but even if it is, there is great need for a comprehensive biography that provides theological and spiritual insight into the person of William Ward instead of merely recording the events of his life and ministry.

Introduction

For Every Day of the Year, and other pertinent primary sources to understand the times and theology that shaped Ward's spirituality, the strands of spirituality that were most prominent in his life, and the impact of his spirituality on the lives and times within his sphere of influence.

In the first entry of his missionary *Journal*, Ward writes, "Blessed be God that I have seen this land and that I am now on board a vessel, which will, I trust, carry me to India, to print the New Testament. 'Unto me, who am less than the least of all saints, is this grace given, that I should [print] amongst the Millions in India, the unsearchable riches of Xt.'"[11] And so he did. Over the next twenty-three years, Ward would print the New Testament in twenty different languages.[12] But when he finally rested from his labor on

---

[11] William Ward, Journal MSS, Lord's Day, May 26, 1799, 1.

[12] Quoting from the funeral sermon that Joshua Marshman preached on March 23, 1823 at Calcutta's Union Chapel, Ward's memoirist, Samuel Stennett writes, "The Twentieth version of the New Testament in the languages of India [which was] printed under his eye, had advanced to the book of Revelation at the time of our beloved brother's removal." Samuel Stennett, *Memoirs of the Life of the Rev. William Ward, Late Baptist Missionary in India; Containing A Few Of His Early Poetical Productions, and Monody to His Memory* (London: Simpkin and Marshall, 1825), 231-232. Mention of the same number is found in Marshman's the printed version of his funeral sermon from the same text. Joshua Marshman, *Divine Grace the Source of All Human Excellence* (Serampore, 1823), 39. Another number, namely, forty, is often heard in connection with *translations* accomplished at Serampore. In a resolution passed by the British and Foreign Bible Society at the time of Carey's death, it is mentioned, "The subsequent extent of his talent as well as of his diligence and zeal, may be judged of by the fact, that, in conjunction with his colleagues, he has been instrumental in giving to the tribes of Asia the sacred Scriptures, in whole or in part, in between thirty and forty different languages." John Clark Marshman, *The Life and Times of Carey, Marshman and Ward* (1859; repr., Serampore: Council of Serampore College, 2005), 2:480-481. Similarly, Carey biographer, George Smith records that "writing in 1904 on the centenary of the British and Foreign Bible Society, Mr. George A. Grierson ... head of the Linguistic Survey of India, sums up. ... 'The greathearted band of Serampore missionaries issued translations of the Bible or of the New Testament in more than forty languages.'" George Smith, *The Life of William Carey, D. D.: Shoemaker & Missionary*, rev. ed. (London: J.M. Dent & Sons, 1909), 178. The slightly larger number forty-four is recorded by Carey biographer, Deaville Walker: "By 1832 complete Bibles, New Testaments or separate books of Scripture had issued from the mission press in forty-four languages and dialects." F. Deaville

The Spirituality of William Ward

March 7, 1823, it was not his work as a printer which received first mention in the loving memoir recorded in the funeral sermon presented by his colleague, Joshua Marshman). Instead, Marshman remembered the, "natural sweetness of disposition and ... depth of judgment which distinguished him throughout his whole life. That mildness and gentleness of temper which insensibly endeared him to all with whom he had intercourse." His was a nature, "formed ... for kindness and friendship," such that he attracted, "the affections of almost all who came near him."[13] Such was the legacy of William Ward, the oft-forgotten member of the

---

Walker, *William Carey; Missionary Pioneer and Statesman* (London: Student Christian Movement, 1926), 285. Today, the William Carey Museum at Serampore College displays a list of forty-five translations and has on display approximately thirty-five fragments of Bible translations! Other discussions of the number of translations can be found in Marshman, *Life and Times*, 2:254–255, Smith, *The Life of William Carey* (London: John Murray, 1885), 238–239 and rev. ed. (London: Dent & Sons, 1909), 177–178, and S. Pearce Carey, *William Carey D.D., Fellow of Linnaean Society*, 8th ed. (Hodder and Stoughton, 1923), 410, 412. Smith lists thirty-four translations, "made and edited" by Carey with six more translations, "edited and printed," by Carey in his first work and thirty-six and eight respectively in his revised edition. According to Serampore historian, Peter de Vries, the list of thirty-five Carey translations assembled by S. Pearce Carey is most often used which includes the following Indian languages and dialects: "Bengali, Oriya, Hindi, Marathi, Sanskrit and Assamese—whole Bibles. Panjabi NT and OT up to Eze. xxvi. Pashto and Kashmiri New Testaments, and Old Testaments up to 2 Kings. Telugu and Konkani New Testaments, and Pentateuchs. Nineteen other New Testaments, and Five one-or-more Gospels" (424). The nineteen "other New Testaments," are Lahnda, Gujarati, Bikaneri, Nepali, Bagheli, Marwari, Harauti [Haraoti], Kanouji, Kanarese [Kurnata], Dogri, Bhatneri [Bhatti], Maghadi, Malvi, Braj Bhasha, Garhwali [Gurhwali], Manipuri, Palpa, Khasi, and the, "five one-or-more Gospels," are Balochi, Mewari, Awadhi, Jaipuri, and Sindhi (426). Interestingly, though the number forty is sometimes associated with translations that William Carey personally accomplished, he deprecated such talk. Smith, *Life of William Carey* (1909), 177. Smith explains that, strictly speaking, only the Bengali, Hindi, Marathi, and Sanskrit translations of the Bible were Carey's own. Other translations, such as the Chinese translation of the Bible accomplished by Joshua Marshman, were carried out by Carey's colleagues, and much translation was also done at the hands of learned Indian *pandits*. But, since Carey was involved in the revising and editing of these translations, and in the corrections of the same before they went to press, the number of forty translations is rightly attributed to Carey in terms of, "conception and advocacy" (178).

[13] Joshua Marshman, *Divine Grace the Source of All Human Excellence* (Serampore: Mission Press, 1823), 35 (a funeral sermon for William Ward).

Introduction

famed Serampore Trio.

In the end, Ward was remembered in his day for his piety, i.e., for his Christian character, or, as we might say today, for his spirituality. This spirituality represented the whole of his person and was woven through the many roles he filled in the Serampore Mission and beyond. It was an ecumenical spirituality that took root in the Wesleyan piety of his mother and later flowered in shared communion with a Presbyterian captain aboard the *Criterion*, times of prayer with Anglican ministers in Bengal, and fellowship with Christians of many stripes in Calcutta. It was a humble spirituality that was felt more than heard; whose presence was often undetected—because things ran so smoothly when he was around—but whose absence added to the administrative weight felt by his closest colleagues. It was theologically sound and erudite but not pedantic. It was pastoral, delighting in mentoring and shepherding those in his sphere. But chiefly, Ward's spirituality was a spirituality of love for God and his fellow man.

Such a man is worth remembering. Such a man is worth knowing—if, for no other reason, than to remind ourselves that missions and churches—then and now—need warm-hearted, pastoral administrators to be healthy and effective. They are heroes too.

1
The Life of William Ward

William Ward's journey to India in 1799 aboard the *Criterion* marked a distinct, second phase of his life, precipitated by his acceptance of God's calling to serve as missionary and printer in Bengal, India. Consequently, his biography divides naturally between his life prior to departing for Serampore and his subsequent missionary career after arriving there.

Early Upbringing
William Ward was born in the town of Derby, England, October 20, 1769. He was born into a working-class family, his father, John having worked as a carpenter and builder, and his grandfather, Thomas Ward, as a farmer at Stretton, near Burton in Staffordshire.[1] Concerning the religious character of his father we know nothing, and he passes from his son's narrative by death when William was only a child. Regarding his mother, though her name is not preserved in print, Ronald Ellis has identified her as Ann Fletcher who died at Thurvaston, near Derby, on July 12, 1810, at the age of seventy-three.[2] A small amount has been preserved regarding her Christian piety and the upbringing she gave her son. According to Ward's memoirist, she traced her first "serious thoughts to a discourse by a female Quaker at the Town

---

[1] Samuel Stennett, *Memoirs of The Life of the Rev. William Ward, Late Baptist Missionary in India; Containing A Few Of His Early Poetical Productions, and A Monody to His Memory* (London: Simpkin and Marshall, 1825), 6.

[2] This information regarding Ward's mother's name was transmitted to me Peter de Vries, resident historian and volunteer librarian at the CLRC. Concerning the place and date of her death see *Monthly Circular Letters Relative to the Missions In India, Established By a Society In England, Called the "Baptist Missionary Society"* (Serampore: Mission Press, 1811), 4:132; and Ward to Rev. Fletcher, December 5, 1811 in *Baptist Magazine* (n.p., 1812), 4:443.

Hall in Derby" and was "an attendant on the preaching of the Methodists, and appears to have been a truly christian woman."[3] There is no record of the manner in which she sought to inculcate a sense of religion in her son, but both Stennett and J.C. Marshman attribute Ward's largely vice-free youth to her godly instruction.[4] Ward himself wrote,

> I was blessed with a mother who frequently took my sister and me aside to pray with us; and often have I heard her pray with such earnestness, mingling her tears with her petitions, and throwing so much of the feelings of the mother into her prayers, that, young as I was, it went to my very heart.[5]

We know that his early schooling took place in Derby at the hands of one Mr. Congreve and that he was later tutored by a Mr. Breary.[6] Beyond this, the record of Ward's youth is primarily concerned with that trade which would eventually take him to Bengal, namely, printing.

Secular Printing Career and Activism

His schooling concluded, Ward was placed under the apprenticeship of John Drewry, who was a printer and bookseller of Derby.[7] In time, he progressed to the grade of corrector of the press and was eventually rewarded with the editorship of his master's weekly paper, *The Derby Mercury*, a position he held for

---

[3] Stennett, *Memoirs*, 6.
[4] Stennett, *Memoirs*, 7; John Clark Marshman, *The Life and Times of Carey, Marshman and Ward* (1859; repr., Serampore: Council of Serampore College, 2005), 1:93.
[5] William Ward, *The Love of Christ Beareth Us Away* (London, 1820), 14.
[6] Stennett, *Memoirs*, 9.
[7] Stennett records his master's name as "Drewry" while J.C. Marshman spells the same "Drury." Stennett, *Memoirs*, 10; Marshman, *Life and Times*, 1:93; W.H. Carey, *Oriental Christian Biography* (Calcutta: Baptist Mission Press, 1850), 2:136.

Life

the next three years from 1789 to 1791.[8] As his printing career progressed, Ward moved first to Stafford, where he wrote prospectuses for another of Mr. Drewry's papers, and then to the port of Hull in Yorkshire, where he served as editor of the *Hull Advertiser and Exchange Gazette*.[9] At these newspapers, Ward gained invaluable experience in typesetting and editing—skills which would uniquely qualify him to establish and run a printing operation in Serampore that eventually grew to include eleven presses and over one hundred employees.[10] The experience he gained in writing and drafting during this period foreshadowed the role he would eventually play in drafting many key documents for the Mission.

Ward edited British newspapers at a very turbulent time in Western history. William Pitt was Prime Minister of England. William Wilberforce was campaigning for the abolition of the slave trade in England's dominions. A little over a decade before Ward began as editor of *The Derby Mercury*, the American colonies successfully revolted against British rule. In Ward's first year with the paper, the Bastille was stormed, signaling the start of the French Revolution. In Ward's last year with the paper, Thomas Paine (1737-1809) published his landmark, *Rights of Man*, in support of the French Revolution. In very sanguine

---

[8] Marshman, *The Life and Times*, 1:93; A. Christopher Smith, *The Serampore Mission Enterprise* (Bangalore, India: Centre for Contemporary Christianity, 2006), 24; A. Christopher Smith, "William Ward, Radical Reform, and Missions in the 1790s," *American Baptist Quarterly* 10, no. 3 (September 1991): 221-222; Stennett, *Memoirs*, 11.

[9] Smith, *Serampore Enterprise*, 25; Stennett, *Memoirs*, 11. It is unclear just how long Ward worked at each newspaper. Holcomb has Ward at *The Derby Mercury* for six years while J.C. Marshman assigns six years to Ward's work as editor of both *The Derby Mercury* and the *Hull Advertiser and Exchange Gazette*. H. Helen Holcomb, *Men of Might in India Missions* (New York: Fleming H. Revell, 1901), 76; Marshman, *Life and Times*, 1:95. In contrast, W.O. Simpson allots ten years to Ward's work as typesetter for Mr. Drewry's paper in Stafford *and* the two previously mentioned papers. W.O. Simpson, introduction to *A View of the History, Literature, and Religion of the Hindoos*, 5th ed. (Madras: J. Higginbotham, 1863), 2.

[10] Marshman, *Life and Times*, 1:421; 2:249; Stennett, *Memoirs*, 183.

terms, J.C. Marshman writes that Ward, "in the enthusiasm of youth," "imbibed" these revolutionary feelings of his day.[11] In all of these matters, passions ran high on both sides of the debate, and as the editor of an influential newspaper, Ward had a voice to call for change.

The Derby Mercury was a politically conservative paper, but as previously stated, Ward's personal convictions ran in a more progressive direction.[12] As a Methodist, Ward was in the same predicament as Presbyterians, Congregationalists, and Baptists. Largely because of convictions in the area of church polity and the extent to which the church should be reformed, these denominations began to separate from the Established Church in the latter part of the sixteenth century. They were united by their common Reformed faith as well as their dissent from the Anglican church, hence the moniker, "Dissenters." For over one hundred years, the public gatherings of Dissenters had been heavily regulated and at times banned outright. Because they were not willing to take communion in the Established Church, Dissenters were prohibited by the Test and Corporation Acts from holding any public office. At this time, Ward was still a Methodist, and therefore, a Dissenter. So, having long suffered the unjust suppression of their liberties, it is understandable that many Dissenters, including Ward, felt a natural sympathy for others' struggles for liberty in their day—and acted on it.

In 1790, Ward produced two unsigned pieces "On Government" that were likely spawned from his concern over constitutional matters, namely, that a proper balance be maintained between "Monarchy, Aristocracy and Democracy."[13] Through his paper, he voiced his support of William Wilberforce and Thomas Clarkson, who stood against slavery and championed the right of

---

[11] Marshman, *Life and Times*, 1:94.
[12] Smith, "William Ward, Radical Reform," 221.
[13] Smith, "William Ward, Radical Reform," 222.

Life

the press to critique the government.[14] Though he never signed his name to his printed opinions, Ward ran a real risk of incurring government charges of seditious libel.[15] It is also noteworthy that among these activist pieces, Ward also published an item in 1790 on India and on "missionary discoveries" in Africa.[16]

As a conscientious Christian, Ward was not alone in his political activism. Prominent ministers in the denomination he would soon adopt as his own grounded their activism in Scripture itself. Caleb Evans (1737-1791), who served as principal of the Bristol Academy from 1781-1791, considered the American resistance "one of the best causes in the world," and he considered such sentiment to be founded in sound exegesis of passages like Romans 13 and 1 Peter 2 which led him to believe that "it is the will of God for people to submit to government only insofar as it represented lawful authority and promoted the general good."[17] Similarly, future Particular Baptist colleague, Robert Hall, Jr., voiced similar convictions in his *Christianity Consistent with a Love of Freedom* and *An Apology for the Freedom of the Press, and for General Liberty*.[18]

In bolder steps of activism, some time in December 1791, Ward joined prominent members of the Derby Philosophical Society to form the Derby Society for Political Information (SPI), a middle-class organization whose aim was to "'arouse the People to a peaceable pursuit of Reforms in Government' so that 'full, free and frequently elected representation' would be achieved instead of the current, corrupt system."[19] On July 16, 1792, the SPI held its first public meeting on the third anniver-

---

[14] Smith, "William Ward, Radical Reform," 222-223, 229.
[15] Smith, "William Ward, Radical Reform," 222-223.
[16] Smith, "William Ward, Radical Reform," 222.
[17] James E. Bradley, *Religion, Revolution, and English Radicalism: Nonconformity in Eighteenth-Century Politics and Society* (Cambridge: Cambridge University Press, 1990), 149, 154.
[18] Smith, "William Ward, Radical Reform," 223, 229.
[19] Smith, "William Ward, Radical Reform," 225.

sary of the storming of the Bastille. Again, in anticipation of the drafting role he would later play at Serampore, Ward was tasked with drawing up an "Address declaratory of their principles, &c." which "outlined its 'policy on social problems as well as on matters of political theory.'"[20] Ward complied, but it was not immediately published, perhaps because it was uncertain which paper would be willing to carry it. Then, on Christmas day, whether by Ward's doing or that of others, Ward's "Address" landed in the nationally read, *Morning Chronicle*.[21] Soon after this, the revolution in France took an ugly turn, loyalist sentiment grew, England went to war with France, and after Easter, 1793, preliminary proceedings began to prosecute the editor of the *Morning Chronicle*, James Perry, for publishing the SPI's July 1792 "Address."[22] In terms of the development of the BMS, Smith draws attention to the fact that William Carey's famous sermon from Isaiah 54:2-3, "Expect Great Things" was also preached at this time (May 1792), a very inauspicious time for the birthing of a missionary society on foreign shores.[23]

The case came to trial on December 9, 1793, to determine whether the SPI's "Address" had been written with peaceable or sinister intentions.[24] The trial was significant as it was the first test of a recently passed bill granting protective rights to those accused by the government of seditious libel. Perry and his printer, Lambert, were defended by Thomas Erskine and were narrowly acquitted.[25] In all likelihood, this was also a narrow escape for Ward as it is possible that he could have been exposed as the

---

[20] Smith, "William Ward, Radical Reform," 227.
[21] Smith, "William Ward, Radical Reform," 226-227.
[22] Smith, "William Ward, Radical Reform," 227-229.
[23] Smith, "William Ward, Radical Reform," 226-227. To further illustrate the perilous times in which the BMS was birthed, Smith notes that Richard Phillips, who sold Carey's *Enquiry*, was imprisoned for eighteen months for distributing seditious political literature. Smith alleges Ward and Phillips had much in common (221).
[24] Smith, "William Ward, Radical Reform," 230.
[25] Smith, "William Ward, Radical Reform," 230.

Life

"Address" author and asked to give a public defense.[26] But while Perry's trial must have been sobering to Ward, he would soon be involved in his own imbroglio.

In the midst of this tumultuous time, we read of Ward's first encounters with Baptists. The details are not clear, but it seems, perhaps as early as 1791, Ward's denominational and convictional allegiance began to change from Methodism to the Baptist way, likely through contact with Particular Baptists in Derby.[27] Stennett records that Ward was a "warm and active supporter of the Baptist Church which was formed in Derby" and frequently visited "Baptist meetings in the neighborhood," but adds that "it does not appear ... that he made a public profession of his faith before his removal to Hull, which took place about the year 1794 or 1795."[28] Whether based on optimistic conjecture or inside knowledge, Simpson writes, "After much thought it appeared to him that the opinions held by the Baptists were most in accordance with the word of God."[29] Interestingly, on March 31, 1793, in a meeting that would prove a harbinger of associations to come, Ward met William Carey after the latter preached in John Rippon's Baptist chapel, just three months before his departure for India. Reflecting on this meeting, Smith wonders whether Ward was considering a "change of direction, at least within England."[30] Later, writing to Andrew Fuller from a struggling indigo factory in Mudnabatty, Bengal, Carey recalled Ward and declared, "If a serious printer could be found willing to engage in the mission, he would be a great blessing to it. ... Such a printer I knew at Derby before I left England." Smith wonders if these remarks alerted Fuller to Ward's usefulness to the mission.[31]

---

[26] Smith, "William Ward, Radical Reform," 229.
[27] Smith, "William Ward, Radical Reform," 230.
[28] Stennett, *Memoirs*, 13-14.
[29] Simpson, introduction to *A View of the History*, 2.
[30] Smith, "William Ward, Radical Reform," 229.
[31] Carey to Fuller, November 16, 1796, quoted in Smith, "William Ward, Radical

The Spirituality of William Ward

Returning to Ward's printing career, Ward traveled to London in October of 1794 to study typography. Following this, perhaps sometime in 1795, came the move to Stafford where Ward wrote prospectuses for Drewry's *Staffordshire Advertiser*.[32] Then, toward the end of 1795, Ward moved to Hull where he began what would prove a short stint as editor of the *Hull Adviser and Gazette Exchange*. For unknown reasons, but likely not because of any lack of printing ability, Ward was released after only nine months.[33]

Around this same time, Ward became involved with the Baptist church in Hull and was baptized. Stennett records that the church was meeting "in Salt-house lane, under the pastoral care of the late Mr. Beatson," who later baptized him.[34] But Marshman and Smith record that the event took place after the church relocated to George Street at the hand of Rev. Pendered in August of 1796, Smith fixing the exact date as the 28th of that month.[35] After a trip to London in October, possibly in search of new employment, Ward redeemed this period of unemployment by engaging in preaching in the villages around Hull, an experience which would prove useful in the land of his future employment.[36]

Though it seems Ward's attentions were gradually beginning to focus in a religious direction, it is clear that he still felt ample amounts of sympathy for activist causes of his day. In 1797, he no longer possessed the voice of a newspaper editor, but he gave assistance where he could, welcoming to the Particular Baptist Chapel in Derby one John Thelwall, who was a proponent of

---

Reform," 243 n48.

[32] Smith, "William Ward, Radical Reform," 231.
[33] Smith, "William Ward, Radical Reform," 232.
[34] Stennett, *Memoirs*, 14.
[35] Marshman, *Life and Times*, 1:96; Smith, "William Ward, Radical Reform," 233.
[36] Stennett, *Memoirs*, 29.

civil liberty and member of the radical reform society, the London Corresponding Society (LCS). In August of the previous year, Thelwall's lectures in Yarmouth had incited a riot from which he saved himself by brandishing his pistol.[37] This maverick behavior coupled with the fact that he was not known for holding religious convictions made him an unlikely candidate to deliver a speech in a Baptist chapel. Yet, in an early indication of his willingness to overlook differences in pursuit of a common cause, Ward, on March 20, 1797, "without the consent of the church, admitted Thelwall ... to deliver a political lecture. The result was disastrous; the windows were broken by a mob; the lecturer and his audience were expelled with violence; and great odium was brought on the character of the denomination in the town."[38] Ward well could have been prosecuted for the damage his invitation had enabled, but again, he was providentially spared.[39] The riot, however, was significant in Ward's life as it seems to mark the end his involvement in secular activism.[40]

Ministerial Calling and Preparation

In light of the debacle at the Particular Baptist Chapel in Derby, one would think English Baptists would have moved swiftly to put as much distance between themselves and Ward as possible. Instead, by the summer of 1797, his village labors attracted the attention of his church, fellow Baptists, and one Mr. Fishwick, of Newcastle-upon-Tyne, a man of large fortune, who offered to sponsor Ward in his preparation for gospel ministry.[41] Though nothing is known of Ward's feelings towards vocational ministry prior to his reception of Mr. Fishwick's attention, Stennett right-

---

[37] Smith, "William Ward, Radical Reform," 234.
[38] Marshman, *Life and Times*, 1:94; Smith, "Radical Reform," 235–236.
[39] Smith, "William Ward, Radical Reform," 236–237.
[40] Smith, "William Ward, Radical Reform," 236.
[41] Marshman, *The Life and Times*, 1:96; Smith, "Radical Reform," 237; Stennett, *Memoirs*, 30.

ly surmises that Ward was not motivated in his response by a desire for earthly gain. Indeed, a career in secular printing held forth more promise and profit.[42] In his memoir however, we do gain a glimpse of his frame of mind soon after his surrender to God's call. In a letter to a friend dated July 20, 1797, Ward writes,

> I thought I had been fixed at Hull. ... I was occupied in a situation, in which I often indulged my pen and my fancy, to the satisfaction of my employers. I was surrounded by friends. ... My mind was calm, and I had some leisure for my friend and my books. ... In the midst of these employments and pleasures, I received an invitation to go to Ewood-Hall—to leave Hull—perhaps for ever!! Conscience commands me to go.[43]

The simplicity of Ward's understanding of his calling and his childlike acceptance of it would soon be mirrored in his response to God's call to missions in India.

Ewood Hall

Ewood Hall was not the premier institution of theological learning in Baptist circles at this time. That distinction went to Bristol Baptist Academy, then headed by Particular Baptist Missionary Society founding member, John Ryland Jr. (1753-1825). Bristol, however, is in southern England, nearly 230 miles from Hull, while Ewood Hall, by contrast, was only 80 miles away. The need for a seminary in Northern England had been published by way of an associational circular letter in 1773.[44] But the bid failed,

---

[42] Stennett, *Memoirs*, 30-31.
[43] Stennett, *Memoirs*, 32-33.
[44] [John Fawcett, Jr.], *An Account of the Life, Ministry, and Writings of the late Rev. John Fawcett Who Was Minister Of The Gospel Fifty-Four Years, First At Wainsgate, And Afterwards At Hebdenbridge, In The Parish Of Halifax; Comprehending Many Particulars Relative To The Revival And Progress Of Religion In Yorkshire And Lanca-*

Life

and in place of a formal institution, a "parsonage seminary" was begun at Brearley Hall near Luddenden, under the direction of Rev. John Fawcett (1740-1817).[45] In this fashion, "a few young men, designed for ministry," would be admitted to study under Rev. Fawcett's tutelage. They would reside with him and his family at Brearley Hall.[46] Then, around Christmas, 1796, Fawcett and the school moved to Ewood Hall, "a large mansion in the neighbourhood, capable of accommodating his own family."[47] So it was, in August of 1797, Ward moved to Ewood Hall,

---

shire; And Illustrated By Copious Extracts From The Diary Of The Deceased, From His Extensive Correspondence, And Other Documents (London, 1818), 284.

[45] [Fawcett], *Account of the Life of Fawcett*, 304; "Early initiatives in theological education usually took the form of personal oversight of a student's training by a leading pastor in whose home the prospective minister came to live." Raymond Brown, *The English Baptists of the Eighteenth Century* (London: Baptist Historical Society, 1986), 126. Ward was not the only missionary to be trained in this manner. Founding Particular Baptist Missionary Society member John Sutcliff also studied at Fawcett's parsonage seminary, and in time Sutcliff managed his own where he pastored in Olney. At least thirty-three students studied there, and an astonishing third of these went on to labor overseas (126)! In fact, Serampore missionaries Daniel Brunsdon, John Chamberlain, and Richard Mardon were among the students received there. Michael A.G. Haykin, "'With light, beauty, and power': Educating English Baptists in the Long Eighteenth Century," in *Challenge and Change: English Baptist Life in the Eighteenth Century*, ed. S.L. Copson and P.J. Morden (Baptist Historical Society, 2017), 191.

[46] [Fawcett], *Account of the Life of Fawcett*, 304.

[47] [Fawcett], *Account of the Life of Fawcett*, 284. This quote continues, "And the writer of these Memoirs, who was connected with him in the education of youth," acknowledging that the anonymous writer also resided with Fawcett and his family at this time and made the move from Brearley to Ewood Hall. Interestingly, Stennett attributes this "anonymous" work "to the elegant pen of his [that is, John Fawcett Sr.'s] son, the Rev. John Fawcett." Stennett, *Memoirs*, 34. Other noteworthy students who studied under Fawcett include John Sutcliff (1752-1814), pastor of the Baptist church at Olney and founding BMS member, who worshipped with his family and was converted at Fawcett's church at Wainsgate. *An Account of the Life of Fawcett*, 162. Under Fawcett, Sutcliff received "considerable assistance in the study of English grammar, and made some progress in the classics" before being "recommended to the patronage of the Bristol Education Society." *Account of the Life of Fawcett*, 164. Other noteworthy students include Samuel Stennett, the author of Ward's memoir, who studied with Ward at Ewood Hall. Smith, "William Ward, Radical Reform," 240 n2.

near Halifax, in Yorkshire, to prepare for ministry under the instruction of Rev. Fawcett.[48]

Fawcett was a product of the Great Awakening in England, having been converted in his youth under the preaching of George Whitefield (1714–1770).[49] Ordained in 1765, he continued in gospel ministry for fifty-four years, "first at Wainsgate, and then at Hebdenbridge, in the parish of Halifax."[50] Other influences included Anglican evangelicals, William Grimshaw (1708–1763), pastor at Haworth, where Fawcett attended around the time of his conversion while still a Methodist, and Henry Venn (1725–1797), Clapham Sect founder and vicar of Huddersfield, from whose ministry many with whom Fawcett was "intimately connected ... received their first religious impressions."[51] Though ministers of the Established Church, both of these men were considered "Methodist," not because they were followers of John Wesley, but because they were "earnest in their inquiries respecting the salvation of their souls."[52] These details concerning the evangelical faith of Fawcett, Grimshaw, and Venn are salient because they represent an important part of Ward's spiritual pedigree. Hitherto, Ward had likely never been associated with someone of the stature of Fawcett, one of the most prominent English Baptists of his day. At an impressionable juncture in his life, amidst a drastic transition from secular printing career to gospel ministry, he spent a year to a year and a half receiving impressions from Rev. Fawcett.[53] So, while there is hardly a trace in extant literature of Ward giving credit to spiritual men-

---

[48] Stennett, *Memoirs*, 34.
[49] [Fawcett], *An Account of the Life of Fawcett*, 17.
[50] [Fawcett], *An Account of the Life of Fawcett*, title page.
[51] [Fawcett], *An Account of the Life of Fawcett*, 30.
[52] [Fawcett], *An Account of the Life of Fawcett*, 17.
[53] Stennett mentions that Ward spent "about a year and a half" at Ewood Hall while he includes a letter of Ward's to a friend in which Ward writes, "I think it would be a crime not to enjoy the twelve months, which Providence has given me to be happy in." Stennett, *Memoirs*, 37, 39.

Life

tors in his past, he embodied many of the same evangelical traits possessed by these men. When the Methodist-Anglican Grimshaw proclaims, "I love Christians, true Christians of all parties; I do love them, I will love them, and none shall make me do otherwise," he can be seen as a spiritual grandfather of sorts, as Ward was known for a similar warm-hearted evangelical ecumenism.[54] As Fawcett "considered it as an incumbent duty to endeavour to instil into the minds of the young the principles of piety and morality," so Ward was known to have "interested himself much in the prosperity of the family, particularly of the younger branches of it."[55] As the manner of Fawcett's instruction, "was such as to win the heart and affections," so Ward counselled the writer of his memoir, "Study—yes, study to be quiet—but above all, study to get at the affections, the consciences, and the false refuges of sinners."[56] In these matters, Ward's spirituality bears a striking resemblance to that of his teacher, Fawcett, and that of Fawcett's influences, Grimshaw and Venn.

Though he engaged in "classical studies" at Ewood Hall, Ward was not there long enough to make "very great progress in the learned languages," but it would seem that a thorough foundation was laid "which enabled him afterwards to be so useful in forwarding that great work, the translation and publishing of the Holy Scriptures into the languages of the East."[57] But academic learning was only part of his education at Ewood Hall. As he had done in the villages around Hull, so he engaged in itinerant hamlet preaching while at Ewood Hall as the writer of Fawcett's memoir records:

---

[54] [Fawcett], *An Account of the Life of Fawcett*, 23.
[55] [Fawcett], *An Account of the Life of Fawcett*, 232; Stennett, *Memoirs*, 162.
[56] [Fawcett], *An Account of the Life of Fawcett*, 232; Stennett, *Memoirs*, 121-22.
[57] Stennett, *Memoirs*, 36.

The Spirituality of William Ward

His most delightful employment was to preach in hamlets wherever he could collect a congregation; by hints of admonition and by the dispersion of short tracts, to lead the most careless, as well as inquiring souls, to a serious attention to the best things.[58]

In his own words, Ward offered the following witty description to a friend regarding one particular itinerant outing:

On Saturday I walked seventeen miles on a preaching errand, being disappointed of a horse. "The rain descended—the winds blew, and the floods came;" but 'God tempers the wind to the shorn lamb!' My feet were sore, and my stockings were wet; in other respects I fared pretty well.[59]

In time, Ward "established ... a week-day lecture in a village called Midgley" at which he would often preach "with his little Bible in hand ... with fervor and affection, the unsearchable riches of Christ to an audience crowded to the full extent of the little cottage-room, in which it was assembled."[60] While a student, he supplied the pulpit at various churches, and was even offered the pastorate of one at Gildersome, though he declined rather than abandon his studies.[61] Of his Lord's Day routine while at Gildersome, Ward records, "I am generally quite weary on the Sunday evening: I preach three times, and catechize the children, endeavouring to impress on their minds some of the plainest truths of natural and revealed religion."[62]

Though Ward had met Carey shortly before his departure for India, it does not seem that the former entered Ewood Hall with

---

[58] [Fawcett], *An Account of the Life of Fawcett*, 306.
[59] Stennett, *Memoirs*, 47.
[60] Stennett, *Memoirs*, 39–40.
[61] Stennett, *Memoirs*, 41–42.
[62] Stennett, *Memoirs*, 44–45.

Life

intentions of ministering overseas. In a letter to a friend at that time, Ward appears quite content there. "Without much concern for the future, I think it would be a crime not to enjoy the twelve months, which Providence has given me to be happy in. I find a good air and good men, good companions; I feel no want of the pipe, or wine, or any thing else ..."[63] But this began to change in Autumn of 1798 when one of the members of the newly formed Particular Baptist Missionary Society, probably Sutcliff, visited Ewood Hall to learn about printing.[64] While there, this member "held many conversations with [Ward] on the important object of that Society."[65] As mentioned previously, Carey had written Fuller from India, expressing his need of a printer, and Ward's principal, Rev. Fawcett, was "deeply interested" in the "commencement and progress" of the BMS.[66] So, Ward's memoirist surmises,

> It was probably at this period, that he recalled more forcibly to his recollection what Dr. Carey had said to him just before he departed for India in the year 1793. Having, in one of his farewell visits to his friends, met with Mr. Ward, who was then following the business of a printer, the Doctor said, "If the Lord bless us, we shall want a person of your business, to enable us to print the Scriptures; I hope you will come after us."[67]

Whether Ward entertained thoughts of this exact nature or

---

[63] Stennett, *Memoirs*, 38–39.
[64] Stennett, *Memoirs*, 49. Smith feels the visiting BMS member was probably John Sutcliff. Smith, "William Ward, Radical Reform, and Missions in the 1790s," 237. Ironically, Fawcett, though not a professional like Ward, had a keen interest in printing. Having purchased a cheap printing press "he frequently amused himself with printing short pieces of poetry, original and selected from approved writers, for the use of his pupils, and for distribution in the neighbourhood." [Fawcett], *An Account of the Life, Ministry, and Writings of the Late Rev. John Fawcett*, 282.
[65] Stennett, *Memoirs*, 49.
[66] [Fawcett], *An Account of the Life of Fawcett*, 290.
[67] Stennett, *Memoirs*, 49–50.

The Spirituality of William Ward

no, a definite change is seen in Ward's ministerial trajectory following this visit. In short order, Ward wrote to Society secretary, Andrew Fuller, to express his "readiness to engage in this great cause."[68] Fuller shared Ward's letter with the BMS committee when it met at Northampton on September 20, 1798.[69] He was then invited to preach at their next meeting on the October 16 at Kettering, following which he was accepted as a missionary of the Society.[70]

On May 7 of the following year, Ward's acceptance as a missionary of the Society was formalized, and he, along with Daniel Brunsdon, were "set apart to the work of a Christian Missionary."[71] In response to the "questions, which Mr. Fuller proposed to the missionaries respecting their motives and their religious principles," the following is a portion of Ward's reply which reveals his understanding of the constitution of the "missionary call:"

> "I have received," said he, "no new revelation on the subject; I did not expect any. Our Redeemer has said, *Go ye into all the world, and preach the gospel to every creature: and lo! I am with you always, even to the end of the world.* This command I consider as still binding; since the promise of Christ's presence reaches to the utmost corner of the earth, and to the utmost boundaries of time."[72]

---

[68] Stennett, *Memoirs*, 50.
[69] Stennett, *Memoirs*, 50.
[70] Smith, "William Ward, Radical Reform," 237.
[71] Stennett, *Memoirs*, 61.
[72] Stennett, *Memoirs*, 61–62. The first section of William Carey's *Enquiry* is entitled "An Enquiry whether the Commission given by our Lord to his Disciples be not still binding on us." William Carey, *An Enquiry into the Obligations of Christians, to Use Means for the Conversion of the Heathens: In Which the Religious State of the Different Nations of the World, the Success of Former Undertakings, and the Practicability of Further Undertakings Are Considered* (Leicester: A. Ireland, 1792), 7. Many in Carey's day argued that it was not. In his own words, "There seems also to be an opinion existing in the minds of some, that because the apostles were extraordinary officers and have no proper successors, and because many things which were right for them to do would be utterly unwarrantable for us, therefore it may not be immediately

Life

From the events of this same meeting, we gain a glimpse, not only of Ward's sense of calling, but also of the theology undergirding that call:

> The being and attributes of God, the total depravity of man, free and full salvation by the grace of God through a Mediator, the deity of Christ, the work of the Holy Spirit in regeneration, and the final salvation of all believers, are the doctrines which I believe, and consider as inclusive of all others. It is to the doctrine of the cross, that I look for success in the conversion of the heathen.[73]

In this declaration of faith, we learn much regarding Ward's nascent spirituality. First, it is clearly of the evangelical Calvinist strain, shared by the likes of Whitefield, Grimshaw, Venn, John Newton (1725-1807), William Wilberforce (1759-1833), Andrew Fuller (1754-1815), and others of his day and since. This is seen in his emphasis on man's depravity and God's free grace in sal-

---

binding on us to execute the commission, though it was so upon them. To the consideration of such persons I would offer the following observations" (8). In cogent succession, Carey argues that Christ's Great Commission was indeed still binding on Christians in his day. Carey's third observation is noteworthy as it seems the basis for Ward's rationale why the Great Commission was still binding on him in particular. It reads, "THIRDLY, If the command of Christ to teach all nations extend only to the apostles, then, doubtless, the promise of the divine presence in this work must be so limited; but his is worded in such a manner as expressly precludes such an idea. *Lo, I am with you always, to the end of the world.*" William Carey, *Enquiry*, 9.

[73] Stennett, *Memoirs*, 63. This declaration of Ward's theological convictions, given in response to Andrew Fuller's questioning, is markedly different from his "creed" expressed in a letter written a little over two years prior. At that time he opined, "If I were asked for my creed, I could soon give it: *God is love*... Were I going to establish a church, I would have such a creed as this, and I would subjoin to it an abridgment of the christian morality." Stennett, *Memoirs*, 242-243. In context, Ward had in mind God's love expressed in the sending of his Son, Jesus Christ, into the world to save sinners. This salvation was to be received by believing on Christ. As God loved us, we were to love one another. While this "creed" was written on March 16, 1797, around five months before beginning his theological education at Ewood Hall, one sees two hallmarks of his spirituality, when compared with his more developed statement given at his commissioning, namely, a warm-hearted piety that majored on faith expressing itself through love, and the doctrines of evangelical Calvinism which he held to be "inclusive of all others."

vation. The regenerating work of the Holy Spirit, not the deciding power of man, is on display. The "final salvation of all believers" is an allusion to his belief in the doctrine of the perseverance of the saints. In Ward's mind, these doctrines of grace were not a man-made theological "system" but rather a synopsis of all other biblical doctrines. Second, Ward's affirmation of his belief in the "deity of Christ" was a clear rejection of the heresy of Socinianism, which rejected the Christ's divinity.

Following his missionary commissioning, Ward had a mere seventeen days until he embarked for India with fellow missionaries, Joshua and Hannah Marshman, Daniel Brunsdon and William Grant, and their spouses. They traveled aboard the American *Criterion* which was piloted by the Presbyterian, Captain Benjamin Wickes, who would later prove a great champion of their cause. After four and a half months at sea the eager band arrived in Serampore, Lord's Day morning, October 13, 1799, and "[Joshua] Marshman immediately went on shore, and falling on his knees, blessed God for having brought them in safety across the ocean, and landed them on the soil of India."[74] Apart from one international tour toward the end of his life, Serampore would be the center of Ward's life and ministry for the rest of his days.

Serampore
Though Ward and his companions eventually disembarked at Serampore, the Danish settlement was not their intended destination. It was, however; a welcome refuge from a British government that opposed a Dissenting missionary presence in their dominion. The opposition of the British government to the Serampore missionaries will be discussed in detail later, but the reality and force of its existence is born out in the very vessels on

---

[74] Marshman, *Life and Times*, 1:111.

Life

which both Carey and Ward traveled to India. In June of 1793, unable to secure passage on an English vessel, Carey and Dr. John Thomas booked passage on the Danish ship the *Cron Princessa Maria*, piloted by Captain Christmas, a Dane of English origin.[75] In May of 1799, in similar fashion and for the same reason, Ward, Marshman, Brunsdon, Grant, and their families set sail, not on an English vessel, but this time on an American one, the *Criterion*, piloted by the evangelical Presbyterian, Captain Wickes.[76]

When faced with government opposition to the essential task of their divine calling, missionaries to the present day have wrestled with the proper response to questions regarding their identity and profession. In their case, though they had been advised by Carey to declare themselves assistants in his indigo factory, they decided instead to openly declare themselves missionaries, and to "trust to Divine Providence to protect them from the consequences of such a declaration."[77] This open acknowledgement caught the attention of both the British Government and the local newspaper. With respect to the British Government, this was the first time missionaries had landed in India without the permission of the East India Company's Court of Directors, and they gave orders that Captain Wickes should be refused entry to the Calcutta port until the missionaries were handed over to the police for subsequent deportation.[78] The coverage from the local

---

[75] Marshman, *Life and Times*, 1:60.

[76] Indeed, J.C. Marshman records, "The East India Company's spring fleet was then in the Downs preparing to sail for Calcutta; but to have sought a passage in any of their vessels would have been an act of insanity." Marshman, *Life and Times*, 1:109.

[77] Marshman, *Life and Times*, 1:111.

[78] After partition, the names of many Indian cities reverted to their pre-colonial, Indian name. For example, Bombay became Mumbai, and Madras became Chennai. Similarly, the colonial "Calcutta" became "Kolkata." Despite this change however, the British "Calcutta" is still often used, and one still finds "Calcutta" on numerous signs throughout the city. Sometimes local residents will simply refer to Kolkata as "Cal."

newspaper gained the missionaries even more notoriety. Perhaps due to an unfamiliarity with the Baptist denomination, they announced that "four Papist missionaries had arrived in a foreign vessel and proceeded to Serampore."[79] To be aligned with Roman Catholics was to be aligned with France with whom England was at war. From deportment and scandal, the new band of missionaries were rescued by the protection offered them by Colonel Bie, governor of Serampore.

In retrospect, it is providential that there was a Danish-held Serampore in which Ward and his colleagues could find refuge from the British. The Danish had purchased the Bengali town from the *nawab* of Moorshedabad in 1755.[80] Just two years later, Lord Robert Clive (1725-1774) conquered a large swath of territory which included the provinces of Bengal, Bihar, and Orissa, but the British honored Denmark's claim on Serampore.[81] Later, when nearby colonial outposts, Chinsurah (Dutch) and Chandernagore (French) were captured by the British in the war of the French Revolution, they again honored Serampore's sovereignty. So, when Ward and his band arrived, Serampore was still an independent Danish settlement in the "zenith of its prosperity."[82]

In an additional providence, Serampore's Governor General, Colonel Bie, was already favorably disposed to Protestant missions. This was due to his prior service as an official of the Danish Governor of the South Indian settlement of Tranquebar. While there, he, "had enjoyed the ministry and instructions of Schwartz."[83] The Schwartz to which J.C. Marshman refers is Christian Frederick Schwartz, who was heir to the Moravian mission that was originally begun by King Frederick IV (1671-

---

[79] Marshman, *Life and Times*, 1:115.
[80] *Nawabs* were regional rulers in the Mughal empire.
[81] Marshman, *Life and Times*, 1:112.
[82] Marshman, *Life and Times*, 1:113.
[83] Marshman, *Life and Times*, 1:114.

Life

1730), and pioneered by Moravian missionaries, Bartholomew Ziegenbalg and Henry Plütschau, the first of which had been personally recommended by renowned German pietist and University of Halle professor, August Hermann Francke (1663-1727).[84] In fact, in the early 1770s, Moravian missionaries established a mission at Serampore, only to be abandoned a year before Carey's arrival in 1793.[85] So, Helen Holcomb writes,

> Thus the work of that early Danish Tamil mission furnished the basis for the commencement of what are often known as Modern Missions in the East. To Ziegenbalg and Schwartz, Carey, Marshman and Ward owed their home at Serampore.[86]

Indeed, in their settling in Serampore, Divine Providence not only protected them, but through the sympathetic Colonel Bie, prepared the way for their coming.

Realizing the advantages of establishing their mission in the sanctuary of Serampore, it fell to Ward to convince Carey of the sensibility of this plan. So, under the protection of his new Danish passport, Ward made his way to the tiny village of Khidderpore, near Mudnabatty, in Malda District, about 520 kilometers north of Calcutta, and found Carey, "less altered than [he] expected," healthy, and still a "young man."[87] The proposal met

---

[84] Hugh Pearson, *Memoirs of the Life and Correspondence of the Reverend Christian Frederick Swartz. to Which Is Prefixed, a Sketch of the History of Christianity, in India*, 1st American ed. (New York: D. Appleton & Co., 1835), 17.

[85] Penelope Carson, *Worlds of the East India Company*, vol. 7, *The East India Company and Religion, 1698-1858* (Woodbridge, UK: Boydell Press, 2012), 27-28.

[86] Helen H. Holcomb, *Men of Might in India Missions* (New York: Fleming H. Revell, 1901), 65-66.

[87] Marshman, *Life and Times*, 1:121. The measurement of 520 kilometers from Calcutta to Mudnabatty comes courtesy of Serampore historian, Peter de Vries who notes that Carey calculated distances not over land but over river according to James Rennell's tables from his atlas of Bengal which measured the distance in miles between the major cities of Calcutta [Kolkata], Dacca [Dhaka], Moorshedabad [Murshidabad], and Patna and other towns in Bengal via "principal inland naviga-

The Spirituality of William Ward

with Carey's approbation, and on January 10, 1800, he, his four sons, and suffering wife took up residence at Serampore.[88] So, in this small, secure Danish enclave, the Particular Baptist Mission was unexpectedly established.

Life at Serampore

As Serampore was the context in which much of William Ward's spirituality was expressed, it will be worthwhile to take a brief look at what life was like in the Serampore Mission before moving on to the many roles that Ward played in it.

As one reads Ward's journal, it becomes quickly apparent that the church and the Lord's Day were of paramount importance in the Serampore Mission. From the start, the Lord's Day was especially employed for the preaching the gospel to native Bengalis and expatriates alike. Just over three months fol-

---

tions." James A. Rennell, *A Bengal Atlas: Containing Maps Of The Theatre Of War And Commerce On That Side Of Hindoostan* (n.p., 1781), 9. De Vries deduces accordingly, "Carey was 30 miles North of Maldah (George Smith, *The Life of William Carey, D. D.: Shoemaker & Missionary*, [London: John Murray, 1885], 94), or via the Tangan River, this was near Currydah (Table 50, 13), 324 miles [from Kolkata]. Khidderpore was another 12 miles from Mudnabatty. Serampore was 12 ¾ miles from Calcutta [Kolkata] (Table 122, 23), so Khidderpore was 324 minus 13 plus 12 is 323 miles. This equates to 520 kms!" Peter de Vries, e-mail message to author, January 17, 2019. De Vries notes, "This [distance] is confirmed by Carey's letter to his father [from] Mudnabatty Nov. 9, 1799:"

> Calcutta is in about 21 Degrees or about 600 Miles North of Madras; from Calcutta to the mouth of the Hooghly River where it leaves the Ganges is 244 Miles further North when we cross the Ganges and enter the Mahanmunda River up which we go 48 Miles more, and then enter the Tanguan River up which we come 32 Miles further to Mudnabatty, so that from Madras to Calcutta is 600 Miles and from Calcutta to this place 324 making the whole distance from, Madras to this place 924 Miles – Mudnabatty is in North Latitude 25' 20", and exactly the Longitude of Calcutta. (Carey to his father, November 9, 1799, MSS Regent's Park College, copy Carey Library, Serampore)

> Today, Mudnabatty is nonexistent and is not found on modern maps. Now, the location is known as "Nalagola," which is on the Tangan river in Malda District, West Bengal. The current location of nearby Khidderpore is uncertain. Peter de Vries, e-mail message to author, February 6, 2019.

[88] Marshman, *Life and Times*, 1:124.

Life

lowing Carey's arrival, a day of thanksgiving was set aside "for the establishment of the Mission, & for the divine goodness towards us," and on this day, as one of their first formal acts as a family, they constituted their church:[89]

> We each prayed & singing betwixt. Brother Fountain produced a hymn. After breakfast we again met, and after our Brethren had received us into the church we chose Brother Carey pastor & Brethren Fountain & Marshman deacons. We then gave a short abstract of our Xn. Experience to each other. In the afternoon following an address of thanks was voted to the Governor, & the Society's letter & Mr Booth's address were read. In the evening Brother Carey preached. A good day.[90]

Though the events of other days are sometimes omitted, Ward rarely neglected to record the events of the Lord's Day. This day was clearly set aside for religious exercises and the preaching of the gospel, but as the following excerpts reveal, the missionaries took little rest:

> Fernandez, John Sandys (the son of Capt. Sandys, a hopeful youth,) Rotton, Presaud & Ram Mahun & I went down to Calcutta at four this morning. I preached twice & Presaud in Bengalee [Bangla[91]] once. We had about 50 na-

---

[89] William Ward, Journal MSS, Thursday, April 24, 1800, 80.

[90] Ward, Journal MSS, Thursday, April 24, 1800, 80. Though Ward was not selected for a formal church role at this time, he was later selected and ordained as a deacon. Ward, Journal MSS, Lord's Day, July 1, 1804, 377, and Lord's Day, August 5, 1804, 381. Carey later mentioned that he would like Marshman and Ward to serve with him as joint pastors of the church in Serampore (Ward, Journal MSS, Thursday, July 19, 1804, 380, Lord's Day, July 14, 1805, 427) and on Saturday, October 5, 1805, the church affirmed Carey's desire and chose Marshman and Ward as co-pastors of the Serampore church along with Carey. Ward, Journal MSS, 440.

[91] Today, there is often much confusion between the words, Bangla and Bengali. The former refers to the language. Hence, the country east of India is Bangladesh; literally, "the land of Bangla" as Bangladesh won their independence from Urdu-speaking West Pakistan in 1971. Bengali on the other hand, refers to the people, and in Ward's day was spelled Bengalee and sometimes Bengallee. Today, Bengalis con-

31

tives of different casts (chiefly servants sent or brought by their masters) to hear. Bro. M. preached in English at home and Felix in Bengalee [Bangla]. Bro. C. was amongst the native brethren.[92]

Though this is a typical Lord's Day entry, the names of those preaching at the different stations change depending on the rotation. In addition to the Lord's Day, there were regular prayer meetings, experience meetings, accountability meetings, and question meetings as well as the occasional institution of special meetings such as a series of weekly lectures by Brother Carey on "principal doctrines of the Gospel."[93]

The Roles Ward Played

Though the primary contribution envisioned for Ward was in the area of printing, he came, in time, to fill many vital roles in the Serampore Mission and beyond. Others have recognized that Ward "served with distinction as peacemaker, personnel manager, pastoral counselor and publisher" and that he devoted himself to "the training for missionary duties, of the advanced youth in the college." In fact, Carey himself "relied on William Ward

---

stitute one of the largest unreached people groups in the world, numbering in excess of 250 million across predominantly Muslim Bangladesh, and the neighboring Indian state of West Bengal in which Calcutta (modern-day Kolkata) is situated. In the words of CLRC resident historian and archive librarian, Peter de Vries, "Today Bengali is *both* used for the language *and* the people group. Bangla is the endonym of Bengali, just as Deutsch is of German." Peter de Vries, in attachment of e-mail message to author, January 17, 2019.

[92] Ward, Journal MSS, Lord's Day, October 28, 1804, 390.

[93] Ward, Journal MSS, Lord's Day, January 17, 1802, 203. It seems there was significant overlap between what were called "experience" and "question" meetings. But, at these meetings, questions of both doctrinal and practical import were posed to those present, and a discussion of the same ensued. Some examples include, "What is the nature, content, and usefulness of Xn. watchfulness?" (Ward, Journal MSS, Thursday, August 22, 1799, 37); "Why could not God pardon sin without the death of Christ?" (Ward, Journal MSS, Lord's Day, May 25, 1806, 488); and "Why are we Dissenters?" (Ward, Journal MSS, Tuesday, August 22, 1809, 701). For a fuller discussion of the devotion of question meetings, see Appendix 1.

Life

to maintain the vital psychological middle ground in his team."[94] A more comprehensive list includes the roles of preacher, evangelist, mentor, mission administrator, missiologist, theologian, historian, draftsman, author, college professor, pastor, husband, father, counselor, peacemaker, and friend. The theology and beliefs that gave rise to Ward's spirituality, as well as specific instances of the peacemaking and harmonizing effect of his spirituality on the Trio and on the Mission as a whole will be explored later. But the effect of Ward's spirituality as manifest in these roles will provide a full-orbed foundation of his spirituality and explain why he became indispensable to the Mission and was greatly loved by all who knew him.

Itinerant preacher and pastor

Though printing was Ward's vocation, it is noteworthy how seldom it receives attention in his journal. Instead, the early portions of his journal chronicle the almost ceaseless itinerating that was carried out by missionaries and national brethren alike. The frequency of these entries reveals much concerning the prominence of itinerancy in the Mission's strategy as well as Ward's personal theology. And this theology underlies Ward's spirituality. This interconnection of theology and missiology with itinerancy is seen in the following excerpt:

> I then told them that three of us were come to this country to make known the true way of salvation. I then attempted to describe the fall, & consequent universal depravity of man. Then the free mercy of God in salvation, & the fruits of faith in Xt.'s holiness & heaven, I told them that to make this known we were come to India; that we had printed part of God's word in Bengalee [Bangla].[95]

---

[94] Smith, *Serampore Enterprise*, 24; Holcomb, *Men of Might*, 89; Smith, *Serampore Enterprise*, 81.
[95] Ward, Journal MSS, Wednesday, October 28, 1801, 184.

33

The Spirituality of William Ward

These same themes are seen in his own descriptions of his preaching. Following an outing with his regular itinerating partner, Felix Carey, Ward states that the "subjects handled" included the "depravity of man, the inefficacy of the Hindoo [Hindu] religion, the death of Xt., the day of judgment."[96] And again, after speaking with a European who feared death, Ward summarizes, "I went & talked with him, of repentance, faith in Xt. & the grace of God."[97] On another occasion, he stated, "My principle aim was to bring home their sins—to shew that God would judge them either as righteous or unrighteous, not as Hindoos [Hindus]."[98]

Demonstrated here are the grand themes of evangelical Calvinism—the sinful depravity of man, the sufficiency of Christ, and God's free, gracious, and effectual choice of sinners unto salvation. Ward's theology will be explored in more depth in chapter 2, but one more example, taken from his *Reflections on the Word of God For Every Day of the Year*, written toward the end of his life, will demonstrate these theological emphases were persistent throughout his missionary career:

> The doctrine which our Lord teaches us when he says "Without me ye can do nothing," is, not only that his death is the sole procuring cause of salvation; but that the blessings of this salvation are never applied to the heart but by his efficient agency. There can be no real prayer without a previous sense of want, and without what is called the spirit of prayer: now our Saviour bestows both these or we shall never call on his name. We are not able to repent, but Christ is exalted as a Prince and a Saviour, "to *give* repentance." Faith is his gift; and all good thoughts and good works are impossible to us but as he renews within us "a right spirit."[99]

---

[96] Ward, Journal MSS, Saturday, February 7, 1801, 139.
[97] Ward, Journal MSS, Thursday, October 22, 1801, 181.
[98] Ward, Journal MSS, Thursday, September 29, 1803, 327-328.
[99] William Ward, *Reflections On the Word of God For Every Day in the Year In Two*

Life

Ward's theological convictions concerning man's depravity and God's gracious sovereignty informed his perception of both. In the case of pagan sinners Ward strove to reach, he was moved to pity and compassion. Once, while itinerating with one of the national brethren, a discouraged Prasad remarked concerning their audience in Dinagepore, "The people of these upper parts will never be converted," to which Ward replied:

> "Never" is saying too much, but I feel towards them as much pain as I should if I were to see a person drowning & on account of the distance of the water I was unable to help him.[100]

In the case of the God to whom Ward longed to introduce the Indian masses, Ward was moved to utter dependence for any fruit of eternal significance as seen in the following record of itinerancy in Nadia District which he felt was "as unfavorable a place for the Gospel as any in Bengal:"[101]

> Every conversation that I have with the natives makes me perceive more & more at what a distance these immense multitudes of immortals are from embracing the truth as it is in Jesus. Their prejudices, habits, cast, aversion to English manners & people, & ignorance of the religion of nature & conscience, proves that God only can make them put on the profession of Xt. in sincerity. Yet still the work seems nearer than ever:—who can despair—"God's eternal thought moves on"—& miracles have been performed already.[102]

But in the midst of Ward's Godward dependence, there was

Volumes (Serampore: Mission Press, 1822), 1:174.
[100] Ward, Journal MSS, Wednesday, November 23, 1803, 348.
[101] Ward, Journal MSS, Wednesday, September 28, 1803, 326.
[102] Ward, Journal MSS, Wednesday, September 28, 1803, 327.

confidence, not despair, as seen in the following excerpt written to a friend while on a mission outing in Jessore. "We have tried our weapons and we know their strength; the doctrine of the Cross is stronger than the cast, and in this we shall be *more than conquerors*."[103] Though the increasing demands of discipleship of new believers, mentorship of younger missionary colleagues, and of responsibilities in the print shop, meant less time for itinerating, Ward rued the loss and continued throughout his life to acknowledge its importance in their mission as well as his fondness for it.[104]

---

[103] Ward to a friend, November 13, 1805, quoted in Stennett, *Memoirs*, 144.

[104] As early as 1802, Ward and his evangelism partner, Felix Carey, were beginning to spend less time in itinerancy and more time in discipleship of new believers. Ward, Journal MSS, Lord's Day, May 9, 1802, 230. Stennett, speaking of the same phenomenon around the year 1808, assigns the reason for decline in itinerancy to "the progress of the translations and the increasing number of them" and to the increasing need of oversight of more recent missionary arrivals from England and the increasing number of native preachers. Stennett, *Memoirs*, 160–161. Alongside these activities, there was an uptick in fruit among Asiatics (those of mixed European and Indian ancestry) and Europeans. Ward welcomed these "advancements" but at the same time recognized that "our success among the natives is slackened, owing, I suppose, in some measure to our not being able to itinerate." Ward to a friend, January 14, 1809, quoted in Stennett, *Memoirs*, 164. Again, in an entry on the Lord's Day, April 14, 1811, Ward expresses being uneasy that "for some time we have not been able to do no more in the itinerating line in this neighbourhood." Ward, Journal MSS, Lord's Day, April 14, 1811, 752. But in the midst of the increasing demands on his time, the fondness for itinerancy and evangelism remained. In the midst of government strictures on preaching in Calcutta, Ward remarked, "Oh! if we could get leave to itinerate ourselves, & fix stations in different parts, we should care for nothing else in the world." Ward, Journal MSS, Saturday, August 30, 1806, 505. And again, while itinerating in Dinagepore, "Perhaps in all these labours we are casting bread on the waters, which will not be seen till after many days, but I never felt myself more in the path of duty." Ward, Journal MSS, Wednesday, October 5, 1803, 332. Even in the year prior to his international tour of England, Holland, and America, Ward waxed lyrical in an 1818 letter to a friend as he described his ideal retirement: "I have been thinking of looking out for some spot for my future retirement, where I may erect a bungalow and have a Christian village, and devote my remaining days to the instruction of inquirers and the formation of young Hindoos for the ministry. It must be by the side of one of these lakes. I do not know what destiny may await me, but at present I do contemplate something of this kind, if I can but see a comfortable settlement of things at Serampore, and I see nothing now so desirable as such a mode of closing life." Marshman, *The Life and Times*, 2:161. In noting the decline in itinerancy, Serampore scholar, A. Christopher Smith finds fault with the Trio stating,

Life

In addition to serving as itinerant preacher and evangelist, Ward also served faithfully as pastor, both at the Mission Church and at the church in Calcutta which in time became Lal Bazaar Chapel.[105] In addition to these, he regularly filled the pulpit at various worship services that took place in the homes of non-Anglicans in the city at a time when Dissenters were allowed no

---

"Although the foundational *Form of Agreement* forcefully asserted that open-air evangelism was each missionary's primary duty, the troika rarely ever engaged in such work after 1805." Smith, *Serampore Enterprise*, 313. Smith is right to recognize a disparity between the principles of the *SFA* and the reality at the Mission in the area of itinerancy, but he fails to give credence to the Trio's own admissions of their inability in itinerancy when compared to the skill of the national workers. As early as 1801, Ward observed, "There has been but little new in our Bengalee [Bengali] Services lately, except that the people manifest mostly a very great contempt of the word. We can seldom raise half a score people at once. Yet at Creeshnoo's house & shop three, four & half a dozen people hear daily, & get papers." Ward, Journal MSS, Lord's Day, April 19, 1801, 151. Ward expressed doubt that Europeans would ever be used to "convert souls by preaching, in this country." Ward, Journal MSS, Monday, November 13 [15], 1802, 268. Even the pamphlets which were printed by Ward were better received at the hands of Creeshnoo than Ward himself. "At length I offered them books. Nobody would receive them. We were going, but Creeshnoo being a little behind, they eagerly took them of[f] him, so that in a little time we had scarcely one left with us." Ward, Journal MSS, Tuesday, October 13, 1801, 175. (Unless otherwise noted, brackets in citations from Ward's journal have been supplied by E. Daniel Potts in his typewritten transcription of the same.) And again, "Almost all our Members lately have been brought forward in their first impressions thro' Creeshnoo & his family." Ward, Journal MSS, Monday, May 9, 1803, 299. When these admissions of the superior usefulness of national workers over European ones is duly considered, a picture emerges of a Trio that remained convicted of the need for itinerancy and felt strong affection for the same, but who, over time, gravitated to those pursuits for which they were most gifted, whilst training Indian converts for the work of evangelism in which they were uniquely skilled.

[105] Ward was named co-pastor along with Marshman and Carey at the Serampore church on October 5, 1805. Ward, Journal MSS, October 5, 1805, 440. Carey, Marshman, and Ward later served as co-pastors at Lal Bazaar Chapel from the time of its opening on January 1, 1809 "until 16th June 1825, when the Survivors of them, the Revd. Dr. Carey and Marshman resigned the Pastorate publicly on the ordination of the Revd. W. Robinson" who served from that day until November the 11th, 1838. *Lal Bazar Baptist Church, Calcutta Letter-Book & Records With _____y, December 1876 to April 1885*, 443. In addition to the co-pastorate of the Trio, they were joined by Missionaries John Lawson and Eustace Carey from September, 1815. *PA*, 6:91-92. Also, Edward Steane Wenger, ed., *The Story of the Lall Bazar Baptist Church Calcutta Being The History Of Carey's Church From 24th April 1800 To The Present Day* (Calcutta: Edinburgh Press, 1908), 86. Both Eustace Carey and John Lawson resigned from the pastorate of Lal Bazaar Chapel in October, 1819 (145).

The Spirituality of William Ward

public place of worship.[106] It has been earlier stated that the Trio acknowledged their ineffectiveness in preaching for conversion among native Hindus and Muslims. But Ward's and others' efforts were greatly blessed among Asiatics (those of mixed Indian and Portuguese background) and British citizens, especially soldiers.[107] As a result, many traced the beginning of their serious impressions to a sermon they heard from Ward.[108] Ward's labor in his pastoral work was indefatigable, often preaching in English and Bangla three or more times on a Lord's Day, visiting prisoners in jail and the infirm in the hospital, distributing Bibles and tracts, and all in the tropical heat of a Calcutta about which he quipped, "Preaching in black clothes in this climate is a sad burden. My clothes have been three times as wet as dung today, & the very papers in my pockets have been dyed black with sweat."[109]

With regard to his spirituality, it is instructive to consider Ward's heart in these pastoral endeavors. It is on full display as he gives pastoral advice to his Ewood Hall fellow and eventual memoirist, Samuel Stennett. This excerpt displays Ward's evangelical-Calvinistic warmth and yields a glimpse of the themes in Ward's spirituality that will be discussed in chapter 4, namely, love and usefulness:

> Keep this constantly in mind. You may preach twice a week, and have a great name among certain kinds of Chris-

---

[106] Some of the hosts of these "house churches" include Mr. Rolt, Mr. Lindeman, Mr. Derozio, and Mr. Petruse, the Armenian. Ward, Journal MSS, in *passim*.

[107] Eighty-seven soldiers from various regiments were received as members by baptism at Lal Bazaar Chapel from 1810 to 1815. Wenger, *Lall Bazar*, 61.

[108] To note a few examples, one woman named Ananda, "dated the change that had taken place in her heart and conduct from a sermon which I preached at the Bengalee school one Lord's Day morning." Ward, Journal MSS, Saturday, November 2, 1805, 448. Again, one Mr. Burford became anxious over his soul after hearing Ward preach. Ward, Monday, January 27, 1806, 473.

[109] Ward, Journal MSS, Lord's Day, June 17, 1810, 729.

Life

tians for orthodoxy or oratory; but you are a minister of the gospel so far exactly, as your zeal, your gifts, your efforts and your conduct, are calculated to produce the conversion of souls. For my part, I set a very small value upon most modern doctrinal sermons and controversial writings; and I think their value will be less appreciated, when Christians *see as they are seen*. I would not discard controversy altogether; but I dislike the devil (as the Hindoos [Hindus] would say) in its belly; and I fear very few controversial writers could say, while they were writing, *not I, but Christ that liveth in me*. I would not discard doctrinal sermons; but I confess I have seen or heard few, that had either a devotional or a practical tendency; and that, in which there is neither devotion nor practice, is rather worse than nothing. ... Study—yes, study to be quiet—but above all, study to get at the affections, the consciences, and the false refuges of sinners:—study to be useful—then you will become a spiritual father. ... If you become a useful, you will first be (as the Puritans said) a painful preacher of the gospel.[110]

As will be shown, Ward did not hold himself aloof when controversy was warranted. But as seen above, neither was he fond of it. He was irenical, not polemical. He was not averse to doctrine, but he bemoaned showy dry doctrine that obfuscated heartwarming gospel truths. His gospel presentations, sermons, and devotional writings are full of doctrine of a robust evangelical Calvinist stamp. He and the rest of the missionaries considered these doctrines of sovereign grace "glorious." But as seen, above, Ward loved doctrine that was "useful" to transform men's lives and increase their love for Christ.[111]

---

[110] Ward to Stennett, May, 1803, quoted in Stennett, *Memoirs*, 118–22.
[111] *PA*, 3:198.

Printer

Though Ward felt most in the line of duty while itinerating, and, as will be shown, received the warmest approbation in connection with roles yet to be discussed, Ward spent most of his working hours in the print shop. A glimpse at the mundane nature of this work is seen in the following:

> *Wednesday, July 1, 1808 [1807]*—Translated for my book till night. After worship in the office, settled a number of accounts, &ca. and examined a proof in Orissa. After dinner attended office business & read two proofs of my books—journalized, &ca."
>
> *Wednesday, July 2, 1808 [1807]*—Translated for my book before breakfast—attended to Persian exercise—read a Bible proof; translated for my book till ten; read another of my proofs.[112]

Though mundane, the work of the press was part of the Mission's core strategy.[113] It was here at the Mission Press that Ward published tens of thousands of tracts and pamphlets, grammars, dictionaries, Hindu works, original works, and of course, numerous translations of the Bible into various Indian languages. Once published, the tracts and Scriptures became "paper missionaries" in the hands of BMS and national mission-

---

[112] Ward, Journal MSS, Wednesday, July 2, 1808, 662.

[113] In an address Ward drew up for the British public in 1819 on his voyage to England, he set forth three departments of labor which had existed since the beginning of the Serampore Mission, viz., preaching, translation, and schools. All members at different times and to varying degrees and ways, participated in the first two labors, while their labor in schools was under the care of John and Hannah Marshman. Part of the reason for Ward's return to England was to raise support for a new, fourth labor of the Mission, in the establishment of a college "intended chiefly for the instruction of native teachers and pastors in secular and Christian knowledge." Marshman, *Life and Times*, 2:197.

Life

aries alike.[114] The following entry from Ward's *Journal* shows the typical role of the press in mission outings:

> This forenoon we had about 30 people from different villages. ... They sat down in my room, & Presad talked excellently to them. Rotton said a little. We then sung; after which I talked. Before they broke up we gave each one a tract, & to three of them we gave the Scriptures, two testaments & one old testament. Others wanted the Scriptures, but we had none to give them.[115]

White foreigners and the literature in their own tongue were often the initial draws, but it was through the testimony of men like themselves—former Hindus who had renounced their caste—that new converts were made.[116] Then over time, a steady stream of enquirers began to make their way to Serampore to learn more about what they had read in the tracts and Scriptures. Those that had serious impressions were considered for baptism, and those that weren't returned to their homes.[117]

But in addition to its missiological role, the press also served as an alternating source of contention and pacification with regard to the British Government whilst providing the Mission with much needed revenue. The press was contentious because of its potential to agitate the natives against British rule. This will be discussed in greater detail in chapter 4, but East India Company officials, their professed Christian faith notwithstanding,

---

[114] J. Ryan West, "Evangelizing Bengali Muslims, 1793-1813: William Carey, William Ward, and Islam" (PhD diss., The Southern Baptist Theological Seminary, 2014), 236-37.

[115] Ward, Journal MSS, Saturday, October 22, 1803, 339.

[116] Ward, Journal MSS, Lord's Day, April 19, 1801, 151; Tuesday, October 13, 1801, 175; Monday, May 9, 1803, 299.

[117] Describing the reception of one group of enquirers, Ward writes, "Creeshnoo takes in all these people from time to time. They are entertained for a day or two at our expence talked with, & then according to their impressions they either go or come forward for baptism." Ward, Journal MSS, Friday, February 18, 1803, 282.

The Spirituality of William Ward

were wary lest imprudent dissemination of the gospel offend the religious sentiments of local Hindus and Muslims. But on the other hand, the Mission Press served to pacify the Company by catering to their printing needs. Fort William College was a frequent and lucrative customer ordering on different occasions, a hundred Mahratta dictionaries, a Sanskrit dictionary, an order for 100 copies of the Indian folk tale collection, *Hitopadesha*, and a request for the "publication of books in the Bengali language for use in the classes."[118] In some cases, translation and printing was enjoined *because* British money was offered.[119]

A separate book could be written on the voluminous publications that rolled forth from the Mission Press and the role of the press in the overall strategy of the Serampore Mission. However, in terms of the intersection of Ward's spirituality with his role as printer, its primary effect is seen in times of disagreement within the Trio over missions strategy or in tensions with the British Government in times of national uprising. Both of these will be explored in chapter 4.

By the time Ward returned from his international tour, Serampore's printing operation demanded his oversight of a foundry for the manufacture of metal types, nineteen presses, and over two hundred people who were employed at the printing office.[120] Indeed, Ward grew so busy with his responsibilities at the press that he wondered if all of the activity were indeed justified with respect to their end goal:

---

[118] Ward, Journal MSS, 81, 220, 364, and 437.

[119] This was the case with the Chinese translation and publication of the Scriptures which Joshua Marshman championed. Ward offers the following wry description of its genesis: "Bro. Carey has brought word that the College will be at the expence of providing men from Macow who know Chinese & Latin, if any one of our family will begin to learn & superintend a translation of the Scriptures into the Chinese language. Bro. Marshman, I suppose, will embrace the opportunity." Ward, Journal MSS, Saturday, February 16, 1805, 409–410.

[120] Marshman, *Life and Times*, 1:421; 2:249; Stennett, *Memoirs*, 183.

Life

> I know not how it would be if conversions among the natives were very numerous, our hands are so full with translating and other foundation work. I am encouraged to hope, that the foundation is not thus laying, to such an extent and to such a depth, without reason.[121]

According to Smith, "As the senior partners produced prodigious publications and multiplied their translation projects, they departed from a 'pilgrim' model of mission."[122] This criticism has some merit, but printer was just one of many roles that Ward played so that the impact of his spirituality was not limited solely to it.

Mentor

Ward was a mentor and father figure to many in the Serampore Mission. This included the children of fellow missionaries and junior missionary colleagues, for whom Ward, "acted *in loco parentis* as a much-appreciated 'uncle.'"[123] In addition, Ward took great interest in the spiritual and ministerial development of the Bengali evangelists and pastors with whom he labored. As the following quotes make clear, the spiritual progress of neither group was a given. But Ward's steady, intentional, and godly influence was a welcome ballast during the stormy times of youth and frequent backslidings of new converts.

Though he bore many responsibilities in the Mission, "Mr. Ward ... interested himself much in the prosperity of the family, particularly of the younger branches of it."[124] The following excerpt reveals the manner in which this interest was expressed:

> I have begun a meeting in my room, in which Felix, Wil-

---

[121] Ward to a friend, December 28, 1813 quoted in Stennett, *Memoirs*, 183-184.
[122] Smith, *Serampore Enterprise*, 195.
[123] Smith, *Serampore Enterprise*, 31.
[124] Stennett, *Memoirs*, 162.

liam, John Fernandez & I engage in prayer in Bengallee [Bengali], & bring a piece written in this language of our own composition not less than ten lines. ... We pray that we may be Missionaries; & that the heathen may be saved. We meet once a week, at 6 in the morning.[125]

He describes a similar meeting six years later: "I was at the Bengalee [Bengali] School in the morning; had John [Marshman] and Jonathan [Carey] & Francis & Jonathan Hasted in my room to talk to them, after dinner."[126] And again in 1810, on the eve of the Mission's anniversary, after spending time with the rest, he records, "I had the young people of the family separately, in my room to talk with them.—I found them all more or less affected with what I said."[127]

A similar *modus operandi* is seen in his discipleship of the native brethren. On Monday, August 17, 1801, Ward recorded, "I have Creeshnoo & Gokal's children to catechize every Monday evening."[128] Ward's investment in the spiritual development of Bengalis was still the same eight years later:

> In getting accounts of their experience I have been several times pleased lately. On a Lord's-Day evening, at some one of their houses; I generally enquire, when it falls to my lot to be at home & amongst them at these times, how things are respecting the power of the truth on their hearts; & I try to deal as close as I can with the unbaptized. These meetings I have often found very pleasant.[129]

These represent intentional efforts Ward made to mentor expat and native youngsters alike. But the same pastoral heart is

---

[125] Ward, Journal MSS, Lord's Day, May 17, 1801, 153.
[126] Ward, Journal MSS, Lord's Day, July 5, 1807, 556.
[127] Ward, Journal MSS, Lord's Day, January 7, 1810, 719.
[128] Ward, Journal MSS, Monday, August 17, 1801, 167.
[129] Ward, Journal MSS, Monday, December 4, 1809, 710.

Life

seen in more spontaneous efforts that were expended along the way. On one occasion, he enforced "the necessity of private prayer on Creeshnoo," and inquired whether he asked a blessing on his food. Creeshnoo replied that he had done so ever since receiving Christ and went on to describe the way he prayed with his family every morning and evening and instructed them on the Sabbath.[130] Later that year Ward related a conversation that proceeded from an impromptu visit from a national brother named Gokal:

> Gokal came into my room one evening & asked, whether it was right that he should always have his mind on Xt.'s death. He said by always keeping his thoughts on that, his mind got dry & exhausted. This is a very common thing amongst Hindoos [Hindus] to think that holiness consists in always thinking of one thing, or one name; & if a name, to be always repeating it. I told him that we were to act by divine things as we did by natural ones, think of all & learn all, tho' some were of prime importance. If ever he thought his mind dry or exhausted the Holy Spirit was to be his life.[131]

Ward's role as mentor was not an "official" role but one he took on himself, arising more from affection than from duty. This is seen especially in his response when those under his charge were either not progressing in the faith or had fallen into sin. Regarding the latter, the children of the other members of the Trio were most notorious. In Ward's journal entry for Friday, August 12, 1803, one reads, "Tuesday night to our great grief Wm. Carey [Jnr.] was caught by a maid-servant trying to get into the young lady's sleeping room. It was in the middle of the

---

[130] Ward, Journal MSS, Friday, February 13, 1801, 139.
[131] Ward, Journal MSS, Lord's Day, August 30, 1801, 169.

night."¹³² The "young lady" in question was "Miss Herklots, a child of 10 years old," whom young William had been trying to court contrary to "repeated advice" and "a solemn promise made to Mr. Marshman, & to the rules of the family."¹³³ Following this shameful event, Ward and Joshua Marshman,

> had a long conversation with Wm. [Carey Jnr.] in which we tried to make him sensible of the dreadful nature of falsehood, & of the scandal brought upon the cause by his attempt to get into the young ladies room in the middle of the night. He made not the least reply.¹³⁴

Similarly, on May 2, 1806, Ward records a similar scandal with more dire consequences. "This evening we held our church meeting, when Mohun & Roop were restored to fellowship, & John [Marshman] was excluded for cohabiting with an unmarried woman."¹³⁵ Potts' insertions in Ward's journal are generally helpful as they often clarify the subject under discussion by supplying the rest of a name which Ward signified with a single initial. But in this case, Potts is mistaken. CLRC historian, Peter de Vries notes that had the culprit been John Clark Marshman, he would have been a bit shy of his twelfth birthday at this time! It is more likely that the "John" in question was a so-called Portuguese man of Muslim background who "received impressions under Bro. Carey at Calcutta" and was subsequently received into the church at Serampore and baptized three years before this event.¹³⁶

---

¹³² Ward, Journal MSS, August 12, 1803, 318.
¹³³ Ward, Journal MSS, August 12, 1803, 318.
¹³⁴ Ward, Journal MSS, Thursday, August 25, 1803, 319.
¹³⁵ Ward, Journal MSS, Friday, May 2, 1806, 486.
¹³⁶ Ward, Journal MSS, Lord's Day, July 3, 1803, 311. The manner in which de Vries discovered John's true identity is fascinating. He writes, "On our mysterious (sad case of) John, I checked Wenger's notes 'Register of members admitted to the Serampore-Lall Bazar Church,' and found one 'John' [without last name] who was

Life

As John lived in Calcutta, it is unclear whether Ward personally mentored this John, but backslidings by anyone in the church would have been grievous to him. How much more the struggles of missionary children whom he had instructed in the faith:

> In the afternoon I talked to John Marshman with many tears. Jabez [Carey], Jonathan [Carey] & John are growing up to manhood fast: no signs of real grace. Many many prayers are offered up for these children. Jabez the eldest seems far from righteousness.[137]

A year later, it was the same:

> Besides preaching, I had the bigger boys of the school, one by one, up into my study after dinner, & talked with them. They hear, & promise, but their goodness is like the morning dew. Jabez [Carey], Jonathan [Carey] & John Marshman are still in the gall of bittering. The first is the most hopeless.[138]

Even more incidents are recorded in Ward's journal regarding the backslidings of their national brethren. Frequently they were found making visits to the houses of "bad women," stealing, or returning to their former faith, whether Hindu or Muslim. These events grieved Ward greatly and, but for his faith in Christ

---

baptized on 3rd July 1803, and 'exluded for immorality on 30th May 1806.' Source: Edward S. Wenger, *Missionary Biographies*, 4:261, mss. ... I checked Wenger's *Story of Lall-Bazar Baptist Church*, and he appears there as 'John' on p. xx of the Appendix. All the other John's have last names, and have separate entries: John Thomas, John Fountain, John Chamberlain, John Lewis Fernandez, and John Biss. The baptismal date solves the problem, however; Checking the *PA*, Xiii (1804), 409, [that is *PA*, 2:409 as figured in this book] Marshman's Journal entry for July 3rd 1803, I found a 'John, a Portuguese from Calcutta was also baptized.' ... So the issue can now easily be resolved." (Peter de Vries, e-mail message to author, December 27, 2018).

[137] Ward, Journal MSS, Lord's Day, December 24, 1809, 716.
[138] Ward, Journal MSS, Lord's Day, July 22, 1810, 731.

The Spirituality of William Ward

and his gospel, he would have despaired and given up.[139] Ward's investment in these new believers, his longing for their spiritual advancement, and grief when they did not, are all evidence of his heart for the sanctification and progress in the faith of junior missionaries and national converts alike.

Ward was more encouraged with the development of Carey's oldest surviving son, Felix. Once, Ward noted that he had spent the entire night in religious exercises.[140] He was Ward's partner in itinerancy when he was a mere 15 years of age.[141] A month later, Ward wrote in a letter that "God, I hope, has blessed my labours to the conversion of Mr. Carey's too [sic] eldest sons."[142] Ward not only mentored Felix in the faith but also in the printing office, and in the period between John Fountain's and Daniel Brunsdon's deaths, he encouraged himself with the thought, "If I die, Felix Carey will be able to print."[143] When it came to Felix's ordination at the age of 21, it was Ward who gave him his charge, recording that he was "a good deal affected, & I wished to feel thankful."[144] Felix would go on to nobly represent the Serampore Mission in pioneering work in Burma. Ward hoped a press could be set up there as well and was confident Felix could do the job, asserting that "he knows well how to conduct, as he labored diligently many years in the printing-office at Serampore."[145]

Before leaving Ward's role in mentoring, there is one more manifestation of his spirituality that is worth considering: the catechism of children. On Saturday, June 6, 1801, Ward read to his brethren a catechism he had written for the children of con-

---

[139] Ward, Journal MSS, Monday, November 1, 1802, 265.
[140] Ward, Journal MSS, Monday, October 20, 1800, 108.
[141] Ward, Journal MSS, Thursday, October 28, 1800, 109.
[142] Stennett, *Memoirs*, 104.
[143] Ward, Journal MSS, Saturday, March 14, 1801, 145; Ward to a friend, March 24, 1801, quoted in Stennett, *Memoirs*, 94.
[144] Ward, Journal MSS, Lord's Day, August 23, 1807, 575.
[145] *Circular Letters*, 6:11.

Life

verted natives, which he hoped to translate with Felix's help.[146] This they did and in his catechism of Bengali children, he invested in them much as he had in the missionary children and native brethren. "We do this in turn on a Lord's day afternoon, & go over the sermon, requiring from them the text, & what they remember of it."[147] A Bengali version of Isaac Watts' children's catechism was also used, of which some of the younger catechumens were able to repeat by heart, 160 lines.[148] With the adult national believers, there is a note after a baptism, "These people are under daily instruction," and two years later Ward records, "We have begun to go thro' the Testament daily with our native brethren. Each one reads a verse & tries to give the meaning, & one of us helps them out."[149]

In time, this bore fruit as one convert, Komol, began a catechetical school himself, using the same work.[150] As was the content of Ward's preaching, so "Creeshnoo's chief topic in his daily conversations with the natives [was] the love & death of Xt. & the fruits of faith."[151] Similarly, as the Serampore family met regularly for prayer, so Ward records a prayer meeting begun by the natives.[152] Ward was a mentor and pastor by heart and nature. He invested in others from the overflow of his own spirituality. The fruit of that investment is seen in these junior missionaries and native brethren above who cherished the same gracious doctrines, preached the same gospel, and observed the same practices they had observed in Ward.

---

[146] Ward, Journal MSS, Saturday, June 6, 1801, 157; Lord's Day, July 12, 1801, 164.
[147] Ward, Journal MSS, Lord's Day, March 28, 1802, 221.
[148] Ward, Journal MSS, Monday, June 28, 1802, 240.
[149] Ward, Journal MSS, Tuesday, June 1, 1802, 235; Lord's Day, April 15, 1804, 370.
[150] Ward, Journal MSS, Friday, May 22, 1802, 229.
[151] Ward, Journal MSS, Friday, June 12, 1801, 158.
[152] Ward, Journal MSS, Thursday, January 12, 1802, 203.

The Spirituality of William Ward

Author/draftsman

Ward's years as editor of the *Derby Mercury*, and *Hull Advertiser* rendered him uniquely qualified both to draft works on behalf of the Trio and Mission and to author works of his own. Ward's works found their impulse within, while much of what he drafted devolved on him, sometimes ruefully, from Carey or Marshman. In 1805, there is record that the Mission Press had completed a small volume (which is lost) called *Happy Deaths*, being a compilation from evangelical magazines of the time, containing "accounts of the happy deaths of young people." Ward continues wryly, "I hope it may be useful here, & perhaps in England. Bro. Carey, Marshman & I have signed a Recommendatory Address prefixed. This address, & the drudgery of compilation, fell on me."[153] In 1801, at Anglican chaplain Claudius Buchanan's recommendation and Carey's request, Ward drew up a proposal for a chapel in Calcutta, whose funds and preachers would be supplied by different dissenting denominations.[154] In December of 1809, on the tenth anniversary of the Mission's establishment in Serampore, Ward drew up "a general review of the progress which had been made during this period ... at the request of his brethren."[155] Then, in 1816, in the midst of wranglings with the BMS over ownership of Serampore Mission property, after long and anxious deliberation, it was Ward who drew up a "comfortable settlement" which was submitted to his colleagues and then sent, in a private letter, to a friend on the BMS committee in

---

[153] Ward, Journal MSS, Thursday, September 12, 1805, 436.

[154] Ward, Journal MSS, Friday, September, 4, 1801, 169. This chapel would go on to become Lal Bazaar Chapel which today is called Carey Baptist Church. Lal Bazaar Chapel became a Baptist church within a decade of its founding. But by that time, another church, Union Chapel, was established for paedo-baptists and was supplied by missionaries of the London Missionary Society (LMS). Today, this church is part of the Church of North India. Marshman, *Life and Times*, 2:130–131. For more detail on the histories of these places of worship.

[155] Marshman, *Life and Times*, 1:421.

Life

England.[156] Thus, the Mission often turned to Ward again and again when it came time to pen their thoughts.

Regarding Ward's works, a thorough treatment is beyond the scope of this book. More will be said in chapter 2 regarding the two sources which most abundantly reveal Ward's spirituality, namely, his journal and *Reflections on the Word of God For Every Day of the Year*. But some attention will now be given to the *Serampore Form of Agreement*, as it is one of his most enduring missiological contributions and offers much insight into his spirituality.[157]

The forerunner of the *SFA*, was a "set of rules" that the Mission adopted "for the government of the family."[158] In general terms it stipulated that

> all are equal, all preach & pray in turn, one superintends the family for a month & then another; Bro. C. is treasurer & has the regulation of the Medicine Chest; Brother Fountain is his librarian. The Saturday evening is devoted to the adjusting of differences, & pledging ourselves to love each other.[159]

These rules appear to have been sufficient during the Mission's infancy, but with the arrival of five new missionaries by the end of 1804, there was a need to formalize Mission guidelines

---

[156] Marshman, *Life and Times*, 2:137. Though this letter was sent privately until the time a more mature plan could be sent to the Society, it was submitted publicly at the annual meeting of the Society in October, 1816. The misunderstanding that ensued has become known as the Serampore Controversy, and was still not completely resolved when the latest surviving member of the Trio, Joshua Marshman, died in 1837.

[157] That the *SFA* was drafted by Ward is "explicitly stated by John Clark Marshman (*Carey, Marshman and Ward*, 1859, Vol. I., p. 229) and is confirmed by internal evidence and questions of style." [Ernest Payne?], "The Serampore Form of Agreement," *Baptist Quarterly* 12, no. 5 (1947): 125.

[158] Ward, Journal MSS, Saturday, January 18, 1800, 66.

[159] Ward, Journal MSS, Saturday, January 18, 1800, 66.

for posterity.[160] So, Ward wrote in his journal on Saturday, October 5, 1805,

> At our evening council I delivered to each Bren. a copy of a "Form of Agreement respecting the Principles upon which we think it our duty to act in instructing the Heathen." I wished much that we should leave to our successors something like this, & therefore drew it up, read it to the Brethren, & to-night gave to each a copy for their corrections & additions.[161]

The following day, the Mission marked the thirteenth anniversary of the Baptist Missionary Society with prayer, multiple preachings, baptisms, and the reorganization of the church at Serampore by installing missionaries Mardon, Biss, Moore, and Rowe and two Indian converts, Krishna Pal and Krishna Prasad as deacons and Marshman and Ward as co-pastors with Carey.[162] The agreement itself is found in Volume 3 of the *PA*, pages 198-211.

The agreement is divided into a preamble, ten articles, and an epilogue, and states the principles which would govern the Mission. Article I declares the absolute necessity of setting an "infinite value upon immortal souls;"[163] Article II, the importance of gaining knowledge of cultural and religious "snares and delusions" in which the Indian heathen were held;[164] Article III, the need to abstain from "those things which would increase their

---

[160] John Chamberlain (1777-1821) arrived in Serampore in 1802, while John Biss (1776-1807), William Moore (1776-1844), Joshua Rowe (1781-1823), and Richard Mardon (1775-1812) arrived in 1804.

[161] Ward, Journal MSS, Saturday, October 5, 1805, 440. In this citation and in Marshman's *Life and Times*, the *SFA*'s writing is attributed to Ward. Marshman, *Life and Times*, 1:229.

[162] [Ernest Payne?], "The Serampore Form of Agreement," *Baptist Quarterly* 12, no. 5 (1947): 126.

[163] *PA*, 3:199.

[164] *PA*, 3:200.

Life

prejudices against the gospel," and to humbly pursue the example of the Apostle Paul who became all things to all men that some might be saved;[165] Article IV, the urgency of taking advantage of every opportunity to communicate the gospel to the natives;[166] Article V, the expediency of making "the great subject of our preaching, Christ the crucified;"[167] Article VI, the necessity of kind and equitable treatment of the natives that they might have "entire confidence in us;"[168] Article VII, the importance of discipling native converts in "the great principles of the gospel;"[169] Article VIII, the duty of building up their native brothers and sisters that the gospel might, by their hands, be permanently established in India;[170] Article IX, the need to translate and distribute the "sacred scriptures in the languages of Hindoostan [Hindustan]," and to found native "free schools" which they considered important for, "future conquests of the gospel;"[171] Article X, the fitness of prayer in their labor, which they held to lie "at the root of all personal godliness;"[172] and the epilogue, the imperative of denying themselves for the sake of the gospel of Christ and its progress among the Indian peoples, with special reference to common ownership of property within the Mission.[173]

But the conviction underlying all ten principles is stated in the Agreement's preamble:

> We are firmly persuaded that Paul might plant and Apollos water in vain in any part of the world, did not God give the

---

[165] *PA*, 3:200.
[166] *PA*, 3:201.
[167] *PA*, 3:201.
[168] *PA*, 3:202.
[169] *PA*, 3:203.
[170] *PA*, 3:205-208.
[171] *PA*, 3:208-109.
[172] *PA*, 3:210.
[173] *PA*, 3:210-11.

increase. We are sure, that only those who are ordained to eternal life will believe, and that God alone can add to the church such as shall be saved. Nevertheless we cannot but observe with admiration, that Paul, the great champion for the glorious doctrines of free and sovereign grace, was the most conspicuous for his personal zeal in the work of persuading men to be reconciled to God. In this respect he is a noble example for our imitation.[174]

In the words of Holy Scripture, they saw in Paul a theologian *and* missionary *par excellence*. Therefore, on the one hand, they declared their belief in and dependence on the power of a sovereign God to save his elect. But on the other hand, they acknowledged their duty to be zealous in proclaiming the good tidings of the gospel that God's elect might hear the gospel and be saved. These convictions both spurred Ward and the other missionaries to action and anchored their hopes when tempted to despair.

Regarding the *SFA*'s significance, the *Baptist Quarterly* maintains,

It has rightly come to be regarded as one of the foundation documents for a study of the missionary strategy of the early nineteenth century. It has, however, more than an historic interest. It remains a moving and challenging statement of the main principles which must underlie the Christian mission in any age and any land.[175]

And though Christopher Smith has written much in criticism of the *SFA*, he still acknowledges it to be a, "milestone."[176]

---

[174] *PA*, 3:198.

[175] [Payne?], "The Serampore Form of Agreement," 125.

[176] Smith, *Serampore Enterprise*, 39. Smith's critique of the *SFA* is found in appendix 3 of *The Serampore Mission Enterprise*, 297-318. In short, he faults the Serampore Mission in general and the Trio in particular for not adhering to the "great principles" of the *SFA*. Specifically, he alleges nonadherence to the principles of Mission economy (common property, from the *SFA*, Epilogue), itinerancy, the

Life

Husband and father

Sadly, the wives and families of the Serampore Mission are rarely mentioned in Ward's journal or in the seminal account of the Serampore Mission, J.C. Marshman's *Life and Times of Carey, Marshman, and Ward*. But from information he recorded here and there in his journal and from personal letters preserved by his memoirist, Stennett, it is apparent that he loved both his wife and children and cared greatly for their spiritual state.

Ward came to the mission field single but on May 10, 1802 wed Mary Tidd, widow of deceased missionary colleague John Fountain.[177] Ever the draftsman and proposer, Ward records that "the marriage covenant & ceremony were of my choosing," while it was performed by Carey in the presence of friends, expat and Bengali.[178] Amidst Ward's modest description of the mar-

---

principles for which are found in articles I and V of the *SFA*. He finds further fault with the Serampore Mission for failing to apprise the Society in England of revisions in missionary strategy following the 1805 Agreement. Though this is not the place to respond in full to Smith's critique, two general responses will be given. First, Smith does a superb job of chronicling changes in Mission strategy through the years, and he is right to note that the *SFA* was not consistently followed *as strategy*. He also does well to note the difference between the "prescriptive and descriptive" principles set forth in the *SFA* contrasted with the explicit strategy set forth in the *Plan for Taking All Asia* that was drafted by Joshua Marshman in 1806 (see 305n14). But in the critique that follows, Smith seems to forget his own distinction, holding the Trio liable for not following a *strategy* in line with the *SFA*. On the contrary, this author would argue that despite changes in strategy, Ward continued to be animated by these great principles.

[177] John Fountain was the third missionary sent out by the BMS (after Carey and John Thomas), arriving in India toward the close of 1796. He came to Bengal on an East India Company ship rated as a servant and subsequently obtained permission from George Udny (evangelical indigo planter who later succeeded Charles Grant as Commercial Resident at Malda) and Rev. David Brown (1763-1812; Anglican chaplain at Ft. William) to journey toward Udny's indigo plantation in Mudnabatty where he joined Carey. Passionate and indiscreet in the expression of his political convictions, he was rebuked numerous times by Andrew Fuller who had already advised noninterference in political matters. He died on August 20, 1800 before his first wedding anniversary while Mary was pregnant with their first child. Marshman, *Life And Times*, 1:75-77; Smith, "William Ward, Radical Reform," 239; Ward, Journal MSS, Monday, August 18, 1800, 94 and Friday, August 29, 1800, 95; Stennett, *Memoirs*, 108-109; Smith, *Serampore Enterprise*, 31.

[178] Ward, Journal MSS, Monday, May 10, 1802, 230.

riage ceremony is a summary of Carey's address which explains much concerning the scant presence in his journal of details concerning his wife and marriage:

> Then Bro. C. made a very appropriate address to the married couple on the duties of husband & wife, & made a very pleasant allusion to our family situation, in which all personal interests were swallowed up in the interest of the whole.[179]

The "family situation" to which Carey alludes is not the situation of the new family created by the wedding but rather the common-property situation of the Serampore Family. All possessions were held in common, excepting a small personal allowance for each member. But it was a general principle that interests of the Mission were put above personal and familial interests. To some degree, it would seem even Ward's marriage to a deceased colleague's widow was an outworking of this principle. Perhaps there is a hint of an arranged marriage for the sake of the family in Ward's comment that "this marriage had been intended for some time, but circumstances hindered."[180]

But from a brief comment following his marriage, it seems William and Mary Ward were happy together. Ward writes, "We are very happy in our family, enjoying uninterrupted harmony & love; our temporal wants are all supplied."[181] And from a couple of comments during Mrs. Ward's illnesses, it is evident Ward cared greatly for her. In March of 1805, Ward "sat for two or three hours near in a violent state of distraction" when he feared his wife would miscarry their child.[182] On another occasion, he writes, "I took down Mrs. Ward to Dr. Hare, respecting

---

[179] Ward, Journal MSS, Monday, May 10, 1802, 231.
[180] Ward, Journal MSS, Monday, May 10, 1802, 230.
[181] Ward, Journal MSS, Monday, November 13 [15], 1802, 268.
[182] Ward, Journal MSS, Friday, March 22, 1805, 413.

Life

a pain in her side. He ... removed a mountain of fears from me, by declaring that the pain in her side was not an affection [infection] of the liver; but is only arose from cold."[183] He also had regard for her need of rest and renewal as seen in the frequent recording of Mrs. Ward's "annual trip" to Calcutta.[184] And in a comment perhaps demeaning to a wife's domestic duties, he nonetheless displays a keen desire for the spiritual development of all the wives of the mission. On the occasion of Hannah Marshman's beginning of experience meetings for native sisters, he records his approbation adding, "I cannot bear that our sisters should be mere house-wives."[185]

Ward was father to five children, including Mary's son by her late husband, John Fountain, who died shortly before the boy's birth.[186] In addition to this adopted son, Ward and Mary had four daughters, two of which died young, while the other two survived to adulthood.[187] His love for his children and his concern for their spiritual state is evident in the following correspondence to a friend on March 26, 1812, following both the devastating fire that destroyed most of the printing office and the death of their second daughter, Mary:

> Notwithstanding this loss by the fire so great, I felt much more for the loss of my dear child, than for this; she was a

---

[183] Ward, Journal MSS, Saturday, February 11, 1809, 687.
[184] Ward, Journal MSS, 529, 616-17, 682, 702, 744.
[185] Ward, Journal MSS, Tuesday, May 25 [26], 1807, 550.
[186] Stennett, *Memoirs*, 108-09; Smith, *Serampore Enterprise*, 31.
[187] Stennett, *Memoirs*, 112; Smith, *Serampore Enterprise*, 31. William and Mary's first daughter was Hannah, born around August 1803. Stennett, *Memoirs*, 135. Their second, Mary, was born in 1806 and died of a sore throat in 1812, the same year as numerous other Mission family deaths and the devastating fire that consumed many Scripture translations and other manuscripts. Ward, Journal MSS, Wednesday, September 14, 1808, 673; Stennett, *Memoirs*, 172, 175-76, 178; *Circular Letters*, 6:3. Another daughter was born in 1808, but whether Ann or Amelia is unclear. But Ann is mentioned in a letter to a friend "about the beginning of the year 1813." Stennett, *Memoirs*, 179. And in a letter from 1814, mention is made of Amelia losing sight in one eye due to a neglected cold. Stennett, *Memoirs*, 187-88.

charming child, and had entwined herself round my heart so much, that I seem never to have seen affliction till this child was taken from me. I had never calculated on the death of any of my family; but had always been thinking of being taken from them. ... I have now two daughters left, and Mrs. Ward's son by Mr. Fountain. ... I have many comforts left, and am very happy in my family; but I much wish to see the work of grace begun in the hearts of my children, before I go hence.[188]

Friend and counselor
But, perhaps of all the roles Ward played, he was most renowned as a friend and counselor. This is no coincidence, for as the following poem illustrates, Ward highly esteemed friendship:

Hail Friendship! Queen of earthly joys,
Without thee, diadems are toys
And vain is nature's store,
With thee I would for ever rest,
Made by thy smile supremely blest;
Nor ask the world for more.[189]

Consequently, he had many friends and was counted a dear friend by many. Regarding his situation in Calcutta, he could say,

I have many friends in this country, whose affection is one of the great consolations in my life. When I go to Calcutta, I could spend a whole week in going from house to house, and in every house I find my friends all eager to make me a guest.[190]

---

[188] Stennett, *Memoirs*, 176-77.
[189] From "Ode To Friendship," written by Ward in Hull, July 10, 1797. Stennett, *Memoirs*, 282-283.
[190] Ward to a friend, January 11, 1810, quoted in Stennett, *Memoirs*, 166-167.

Life

Many looked to him for spiritual counsel.[191] And his own colleagues looked to him for counsel in missionary matters.[192] So much was this the case that Joshua Marshman, upon Ward's death, confessed, "I feel the loss of Mr. Ward as a counsellor beyond everything. I never did anything, I never published a page, without consulting him."[193]

Of course, there is nothing of a uniquely Christian spiritual stamp in the fact that someone highly esteems friendship or even in someone's being a good friend (though we would certainly hope that, in varying degrees, these characteristics would indeed mark Christians). But it was friendship of a Christian stamp that Ward prized in particular. For, it is only that friendship which exists between Christians on earth that will endure for all eternity. So, assuring a friend, presumably in England, that he would not forget him, he wrote concerning friendship:

> Oh! that we may be forming for that rational, sublime and eternal friendship, which befits the presence of God above. Why are friends severed? Why are friendships mixed with so many painful circumstances? If we are to die like the beasts, who can answer these questions? But if the light,

---

[191] In addition to those mentioned previously who received their first serious impressions from sermons Ward preached, one, Mr. Barlow wrote to Ward expressing concern for his soul and his desire to meet to discuss the same. Ward, Journal MSS, Tuesday, June 23, 1807, 554. Another, one Foster, whom Ward visited in the jail, when read his death sentence, exclaimed, "O that I could see Mr. Ward now!" Ward, Journal MSS, Friday, December 8, 1809, 711.

[192] After going through a split with fellow BMS colleague, John Chamberlain, the Trio was trying to decide where William Robinson (1784-1853) should be redeployed. Robinson had desired to remain in Serampore but seems to have been at least partially convinced by Carey to "choose a situation on the borders of Bengal where he might learn a new language & translate." Ward's sweetened the counsel, proposing that he settle "on the skirts of Bootan, though in the Company's territory," and Robinson's fears "seemed so much removed," that "he asked me to propose it to Brn. Carey & Marshman." Smith, *Serampore Enterprise*, 104-105; Ward, Journal MSS, Monday, December 5, 1808, 679.

[193] From an excerpt of a letter from Joshua Marshman. Marshman, *Life and Times*, 2:280-281.

which exhibits life and immortality, be the true light, and no delusive meteor, then we have an answer to these momentous enquiries—the house of friendship and of love is above.[194]

International Tour and Death
Like many who serve in India today, Ward suffered from ailments of the stomach throughout his missionary career. So, J.C. Marshman writes regarding his health in 1818, "Mr. Ward's incessant labours had now begun seriously to affect his health. ... and his medical advisers insisted on a voyage to England."[195] Reluctantly Ward agreed and shortly embarked on a convalescent journey to England. However, unable to put aside his routine assiduity, the trip doubled as an international tour which also included stops in the Netherlands and America. On board the ship to England, Ward wrote his year-long family devotional *Reflections on the Word of God for Every Day of the Year* and on the journey back to Serampore, his *Farewell Letters*, in which he reflected on his experience in India and sounded a clarion call for world evanglization.[196] Though the trip proved mildly beneficial for the regaining of his health, it was very beneficial for another aim, namely, the raising of funds for the new College the Trio had recently started in Serampore.[197] In England and Scotland, Ward raised $15,000 and in America, another $10,000, while securing the professorly services of Mr. John Mack, who would prove vital to the administration of the College after Ward's passing.[198]

In 1821, Ward returned from his convalescent international

---

[194] Ward to a friend, March 16, 1803, quoted in Stennett, *Memoirs*, 114–115.
[195] Marshman, *Life and Times*, 2:187–188.
[196] Smith, *Serampore Enterprise*, 45n23. For more information regarding Ward's writing of *Reflections* during his voyage to England.
[197] Smith, *Serampore Enterprise*, 45.
[198] Holcomb, *Men of Might*, 88–89; Marshman, *Life and Times*, 2:219–221.

Life

tour and resumed duties at the Mission and the College.[199] At that time, there were numerous mission stations that were dependent on the mother Mission, translations were still rolling off the presses, and a new and very expensive College had been founded for the Christian education of "the children of native Christians" and the secular education of "other youths, Hindoo [Hindu] or Mahomedan."[200] In all of these, the Trio was heavily dependent on Ward's administrative and visionary skills. But not a year and a half after returning from America, while going about his normal duties, he had a sudden and severe bout with cholera and died on March 7, 1823.

The loss to the Mission was incalculable. Ward had been the face of the Mission while Carey plodded away at translations and Marshman tended to their educational endeavors. Thus, Ward's death

> was an event from which their mission never really recovered. Thereafter, it was too much to expect much creative thought to flow from the pens of his survivors. This was most unfortunate because it meant that the Trio were unable to reach anything like their missiological potential. Ward had become the only one of them who appeared able to make much of a contribution to mission theology or theory, but it was all nipped in the bud.[201]

In a funeral sermon preached at Union Chapel, Calcutta, his long-time colleague Joshua Marshman lamented, "Our beloved brother was so endeared to us in every capacity, that had our feelings been consulted, we should never have suffered him to

---

[199] Ward was head of the theological department at Serampore College. Smith, *Serampore Enterprise*, 46.

[200] Marshman, *Life and Times*, 2:173.

[201] Smith, *Serampore Enterprise*, 223 n129.

enter into rest but with ourselves."[202]

Because of the unexpected nature of Ward's death, the surviving members of the Trio may well have felt (as Smith asserts above) that much had been "nipped in the bud." But in retrospect, it is rather a marvel of Providence that, though numerous colleagues, wives, and children perished along the way, Carey, Marshman, and Ward were permitted by God to labor together in Bengal for little over twenty-three years and accomplish as much as they did.

---

[202] Stennett, *Memoirs*, 230–231.

2
The Essence of Ward's Spirituality

In the previous chapter, many examples of Ward's warmhearted piety were shown in connection with various roles he played within the Serampore Mission. It was also asserted that undergirding his piety was a robust evangelical Calvinism. This chapter will explore both the source and nature of this evangelical Calvinism and the overarching themes of Ward's spirituality as manifest in his theological writings as well as that written about his piety by others.

Historical Theological Context

The warmhearted, ecumenical, evangelical Calvinism of Ward's day did not develop in a vacuum. Nor did it arise overnight. Many forces were at work both within and without the Particular Baptist denomination that Ward called his own. And regarding the expression of evangelical Calvinism among Particular Baptists, it was, to some degree, a reaction against theological trends that preceded it. To the examination of the historical and theological context of evangelical Calvinism we now turn.

The Rise of Evangelicalism

Historically, the word "evangelical" has often been used to describe churches of various denominations arising out of the Reformation in the sixteenth and seventeenth centuries. Its connection with the Reformation can be found as far back as 1531 when Sir Thomas More, "referred to advocates of the Reformation as "Evaungelicalles."[1] But by the eighteenth century, it's connotation was simply, "of the gospel" in a non-partisan sense.[2] Initially, evangelicalism focused on, sin, justification, and forgiveness of sins through the atoning death of Christ on the cross, and the new birth; or in the words of the late Puritan minister, Matthew Henry, "ruin, redemption, and regeneration."[3] In that day, though the Bible was clearly central to evangelical belief, its authority was taken for granted rather than explicitly stated. But with the dawn of Protestant liberalism, evangelicals began to self-declare their belief in and adherence to the authority of Scripture. Though evangelicalism has been identified by slightly different emphases through the years, David Bebbington has identified "four qualities that have been special marks of Evangelical religion: *conversionism*, the belief that lives need to be changed; *activism*, the expression of the gospel in effort; *biblicism*, a particular regard for the Bible; and what may be called *crucicentrism*, a stress on the sacrifice of Christ on the cross."[4]

But it was the Great Awakening of the 1730s and 40s, propelled by the preaching of Welsh preacher, Howel Harris, and English preachers, George Whitefield and John Wesley that catalyzed evangelicalism into a movement.[5] These men and others were used by God to instigate an evangelical revival that swept, Wales, England, and Scotland. Simultaneously but at first, independently, a similar awakening occurred in the American colony of Massachusetts, under the preaching of Jonathan Edwards (1703–1758).[6] These preachers preached to the heart and called for a heartfelt, personal response. As their Puritan forefathers

---

[1] David Bebbington, *Evangelicalism in Modern Britain: A History from the 1730s to the 1980s* (Grand Rapids: Baker Book House, 1992), 1.
[2] Bebbington, *Evangelicalism in Modern Britain*, 1.
[3] Bebbington, *Evangelicalism in Modern Britain*, 3.
[4] Bebbington, *Evangelicalism in Modern Britain*, 2–3.
[5] Bebbington, *Evangelicalism in Modern Britain*, 20.
[6] Bebbington, *Evangelicalism in Modern Britain*, 20.

before them, they believed that men must first understand the word, be affected in the heart, and moved to obedience in the will. Ties to the Established Church were weakened as preaching moved from the church to the fields and the parish boundaries were extended to the world.[7] Dissent was at a low ebb prior to the revival, but began to grow significantly because of it.[8]

"In *The Complete Duty of Man* (1763), Henry Venn, vicar of Huddersfield, defines saving faith as, 'a dependence upon Christ for righteousness and strength, as having paid to the justice of God full satisfaction for his broken law, and obtained acceptance for all believers in his name, to the reward of eternal life.'"[9] This work is significant both because of its stature in the evangelicalism of that day, as well as the fact that Henry Venn, along with Rev. Grimshaw, were Ward's spiritual grandfathers as it were, having greatly influenced his teacher and mentor, Rev. John Fawcett.[10]

Such preaching, though it did not intend to weaken attachment to the Established Church, often achieved it all the same. This was due to the fact that while Arminian-leaning followers of John Wesley were organized into Methodist societies, initially within the auspices of the Anglican Church, Calvinistic followers of Whitefield were not, and they often gravitated to Independent churches of one type or another. As John Fawcett's son re-

---

[7] John Wesley, *The Journal of John Wesley*, Monday, June 11, 1739 (Chicago: Moody Press, n.d.), 74.

[8] Bebbington, *Evangelicalism in Modern Britain*, 21.

[9] Henry Venn, *The Complete Duty of Man; Or A System of Doctrinal & Practical Christianity; To Which Are Added, Forms of Prayer And Offices Of Devotion For the Various Circumstances In Life* (New Brunswick, NJ: J. Simpson and Co., 1811), 3, as found in Bebbington, *Evangelicalism in Modern Britain*, 21-22.

[10] [John Fawcett Jr.], *An Account of the Life, Ministry, and Writings of the late Rev. John Fawcett Who Was Minister Of The Gospel Fifty-Four Years, First At Wainsgate, And Afterwards At Hebdenbridge, In The Parish Of Halifax; Comprehending Many Particulars Relative To The Revival And Progress Of Religion In Yorkshire And Lancashire; And Illustrated By Copious Extracts From The Diary Of The Deceased, From His Extensive Correspondence, And Other Documents* (London, 1818), 30.

marked in his father's memoir, "Many who received their first religious impressions under his sermons were as 'sheep without a shepherd;' and while they retained the greatest veneration for him, they were led by necessity, as well as by conscience and duty, to connect themselves with the dissenters of different denominations, among whom the same truths were preached."[11] "Men converted through the Calvinistic Methodists soon swelled the ranks of Dissent." Baptists and Independents alike profited.[12] "Robert Robinson and John Fawcett, two of the most influential Baptist ministers of the later eighteenth century, were both converted under Whitefield."[13] Evangelicals tended to hail from the middle class, being neither from the "poorest and outcast," nor the "prosperous and successful" classes.[14] This generalization of evangelical socio-economic status was true of Ward, though Carey would have been on the poorer end of this spectrum.[15]

As for the coupling "Evangelical Calvinist," the latter adjective has been used to distinguish evangelicals holding Reformed views from those holding Arminian views. The most notable proponent of the latter view were the Wesleyan Methodists, led by the Wesley brothers, John and Charles. Wesley rejected the Calvinistic belief of God's predestining of sinners unto salvation and the doctrine of perseverance of the saints for he felt these removed motivation to live holy lives.[16] General Baptists of for-

---

[11] [Fawcett], *An Account of the Life of Fawcett*, 33.

[12] Bebbington, *Evangelicalism in Modern Britain*, 32.

[13] Bebbington, *Evangelicalism in Modern Britain*, 33.

[14] Bebbington, *Evangelicalism in Modern Britain*, 25.

[15] Decades after his brief secular career, Carey, while dining with the Governor-General at the cantonment at Barrackpore, opposite the Hoogly River from Serampore, "one of the guests, a general officer, making inquiry of one of the aides-de-camp, whether Dr. Carey had not once been a shoemaker, on which he stepped forward and exclaimed, 'No, sir! only a cobbler.'" John Clark Marshman, *The Life and Times of Carey, Marshman, and Ward* (1859; repr., Serampore: Council of Serampore College, 2005), 1:8.

[16] Bebbington, *Evangelicalism in Modern Britain*, 27-28.

Ward's Spirituality

mer Wesleyan, Dan Taylor's New Connexion held similar Arminian views. On the other hand, Particular Baptist missionaries Ward, Carey, Marshman, and BMS Committee members, Ryland, Sutcliff, and Fuller were part of the broad camp of Evangelical Calvinists, including others of similar conviction from the Established Church as well as fellow Nonconformists such as Presbyterians and Congregationalists or Independents. In Wales, especially, there were even Methodist Calvinists—Methodist in their discipline and organization, and Calvinist in their theology.[17] Thus Particular Baptists, along with these Dissenting denominations, were descended from the Reformation through their English Puritan forefathers.

Consequently, the Evangelical Revival produced a surprising unity between Churchmen and Dissenters. Though at odds with each other regarding the proper relationship of church and state, the use of the Book of Common Prayer, and the extent of reform needed within the church, they were bound together by a similar understanding of the gospel and a common personal appeal for heartfelt faith in Christ for salvation. One touching example of the ecumenical unity that followed in the wake of the Great Awakening is recorded in the December, 1841 issue of the London Missionary Society's, *The Evangelical Magazine and Missionary Chronicle*. The denominations of each minister are added to elucidate this unity:

> During the ministry of Mr Drake [Independent], some delightful scenes were witnessed. Mr. Newton [Anglican], who was then the vicar of Olney, frequently heard Mr. Drake at the Tuesday evening lecture. When that lecture was occasionally preached by the late Rev. William Bull [Independent], of Newport, (the intimate friend of Cowper, the poet,) it was the custom of Mr. Newton to invite

---

[17] Bebbington, *Evangelicalism in Modern Britain*, 30.

The Spirituality of William Ward

Mr. Bull to his table, and afterwards to accompany him to the Independent chapel. When the late excellent John Sutcliffe, [*sic*] (one of the Secretaries of the Baptist mission,) was ordained pastor of the Baptist church at Olney, Mr. Newton was present the whole day.[18]

Descended from English Puritans George Whitefield, Henry Venn, and John Fawcett, Ward was an heir of Evangelical Calvinism.

The Hurdle of High Calvinism

Thus far, only the warm-hearted, ecumenical brand of Calvinism has been discussed. But among many English Particular Baptists of the mid-1700s, a different form of Calvinism known as Hyper Calvinism predominated. In the London area, John Gill (1697–1771), Benjamin Wallin (1711–1782), and John Brine (1703–1765) were noteworthy proponents:[19]

> It was a system of theology, or a system of the doctrines of God, man and grace, which was framed to exalt the honour and glory of God and did so at the expense of minimizing the moral and spiritual responsibility of sinners to God. It placed excessive emphasis on the immanent acts of God . . . . In practice, this meant that "Christ and Him crucified", the central message of the apostles, was obscured. It also made no distinction between the secret and the revealed will of God, and tried to deduce the duty of men from what it taught concerning the secret, eternal decrees of God. This led to the notion that grace must only be offered to those for whom it was intended. ... So Hyper-Calvinism led its adherents to hold that evangelism was not necessary.[20]

---

[18] *The Evangelical Magazine and Missionary Chronicle* (London: Thomas Ward and Co., 1841), 19:662.

[19] [Fawcett], *An Account of the Life of Fawcett*, 94.

[20] Peter Toon, *The Emergence of Hyper Calvinism in English Nonconformity 1689-*

Ward's Spirituality

In this doctrinal environment, J.C. Marshman records a rebuke purportedly given by John Ryland Sr. (1723-1792) to a young, zealous William Carey at a ministers meeting in Northampton: "Young man, sit down. When God pleases to convert the heathen, he will do it without your aid or mine."[21] There is some question as to whether such harsh words were actually delivered by Ryland to Carey, but it is certainly true that Carey's ambitions to take the gospel to the nations were regarded by many in that day as presumptuous and fantastic.[22] It is also true that Calvinism has often been maligned because of the doctrinal excesses of Hyper Calvinism. This is regrettable as Calvinists of the seventeenth century did not endorse this particular doctrine. Regarding the necessity of publishing of the gospel, John Owen (1616-1683), considered by many as the greatest Puritan theologian, argued that

> to complete this communion on the part of Christ, it is required, (1.) That there be added to what he hath done, *the gospel tenders* of that complete righteousness and acceptation with God, which ariseth from his perfect obedience and sufferings. Now, they are twofold. [1.] *Declaratory*, in the conditional promises of the gospel ... (and) [2.]. ... that whosoever receives it, shall be so accepted. But Christ knows the condition and state of his in this world. This will not do; if he do not effectually invest them with it, all is lost. Therefore, (2.) He sends them his Holy Spirit to quicken them; John vi. 63. To cause them that are, "dead

---

1765 (London: The Olive Tree, 1967), 144-145 as found in Tom J. Nettles, *By His Grace And For His Glory; A Historical, Theological and Practical Study of the Doctrines of Grace in Baptist Life*, Revised (Cape Coral, FL: Founders Press, 2006), 424.

[21] John Ryland Sr. delivered this rebuke at a minister's meeting of the Northamptonshire Association around 1788 in which William Carey had proposed that they discuss, "The duty of Christians to attempt the spread of the Gospel among heathen nations." Marshman, *Life and Times*, 1:10.

[22] For a fuller account of the events surrounding Ryland Sr. and Carey's interaction on this matter see Michael A.G. Haykin, *One Heart and One Soul: John Sutcliffe of Olney, His Friends and His Times* (Durham, UK: Evangelical Press, 1994), 193-197.

The Spirituality of William Ward

to hear his voice."[23]

Thus, in Owen's words, we see many biblical doctrines that were obscured in the Hyper Calvinism of Ward's day. First, in addition to Christ's work of atonement for God's people, a declaration of the Good News is necessary if sinners are to hear and believe and be saved. Second, the indiscriminate publication of the gospel to sinners is based, not on the secret will of God in election, but rather, on the revealed "conditional promises of the gospel." From this understanding of the gospel, the Christian is not to dither concerning the identity of the elect, but should rather preach the gospel to all, for "whosoever receives it, shall be so accepted." Did Owen then conclude that the salvation of those hearing the gospel depended on them? No indeed. The same teachings of Scripture that led him to believe the gospel must be published for sinners to have communion with Christ, also convinced Owen that belief was impossible for deaf sinners unless the Holy Spirit quickened them that the dead might hear His voice. Owen's convictions are thoroughly biblical. Coincidentally, they are Calvinistic. In the end, Hyper Calvinism erred by forming doctrine based on extrapolations from human reason instead of Scripture. A biblical Calvinism was to be recovered by the likes of Jonathan Edwards, Robert Hall Sr. (1728-1791), and Andrew Fuller.

---

[23] John Owen, *The Works of John Owen, D.D.*, ed. Thomas Russell, vol. 10 (London: 1826), 214-215. Such open invitations include Mark 16:15: "He that believeth shall be saved," and Matthew 11:28: "Come unto me, and I will give you rest," and Romans 10:4: "Christ is the end of the law for righteousness to every one that believeth." J. I. Packer acknowledges John Owen's widely regarded preeminence among Puritan theologians in J.I. Packer, *A Quest For Godliness; The Puritan Vision Of The Christian Life* (Wheaton, IL: Crossway, 1990), 81.

Ward's Spirituality

Help from Jonathan Edwards

Chronologically, the first help over the hurdle of Hyper Calvinism came courtesy of Jonathan Edwards' *Freedom of the Will*. This treatise was intended not as a help to Particular Baptists, but rather as a refutation of what he considered the erroneous notion of freedom that was asserted by many Arminians and Deists of his day.[24] They maintained that in order for the will to be free it had to act free of any cause other than itself as if "the will were an agent independent of the person in whom it resided."[25] Edwards responded that this notion of freedom was nonsense. Instead he argued that the "will" was "simply a term for a person's power of choosing."[26] In Edwards' own words, "The Will itself is not an Agent that has a will: the power of choosing, itself, has not a power of choosing."[27] In Edwards' view, it was more sensible to speak of "free will" as the freedom to do what one wants to do.[28]

Of course, there are many things we are not free to do even when we desire to do so. In this sense, our wills are constrained by lack of opportunity or ability or both. In fleshing out the nature of freedom and constraint with regard to our wills, Edwards made a distinction between moral and natural ability and consequently between moral inability and natural inability. As for natural inability, Edwards maintained, "We are said to be naturally unable to do a thing, when we cannot do it if we will ... or because of some impeding defect or obstacle that is extrinsic to the

---

[24] George M. Marsden, *Jonathan Edwards, A Life* (New Haven, CT: Yale University Press, 2003), 440.
[25] George M. Marsden, *A Life*, 440.
[26] Marsden, *A Life*, 440.
[27] Jonathan Edwards, *A Careful And Strict Inquiry Into The Modern Prevailing Notions Of That Freedom of the Will, Which Is Supposed To Be Essential To Moral Agency, Virtue And Vice, Reward And Punishment, Praise And Blame*, in *The Works of President Edwards, In Four Volumes With Valuable Additions And A Copious General Index, And A Complete Index Of Scripture Texts* (New York: Robert Carter and Brothers, 1881), Pt. 1, Sect. 5, 2:18.
[28] Marsden, *A Life*, 440.

will."[29] So, as for man's ability to do good, he is not unable to do good in the natural sense. Unlike animals, he possesses the rational faculties to make good, moral choices. But, due to his fallen nature, man is *unwilling* to do good. In the end, the result is the same as being naturally unable to do it, with the distinction that inability stems not from lack of *ability* but from lack of *inclination* or *desire*.[30] (cf. Ps. 14:1-3; Rom. 3:10-12)

Help from Robert Hall Sr.
The distinction between natural and moral inability was a great boon to the likes of Robert Hall Sr. and Andrew Fuller as it offered a *reasonable* answer to the duty-faith dilemma. For Hyper Calvinists, man's duty arose from what he had or had not the ability to do in his unfallen state. On the one hand, man, in his unfallen state had the ability to keep God's law. Therefore, he was still obligated to keep it in his fallen state, and therefore, culpable before God for sin. However, from this line of reasoning they concluded that man was not duty bound to believe the gospel as saving faith had not lain within man's powers in his fallen state.[31] Of course, common sense tells us that man in his unfallen state had no *need* to believe the gospel. But, bound by the reasonableness of their position, Hyper Calvinists eschewed exhortations to sinners to believe the gospel, for it would be wrong to ask men to do what they were unable to do. Instead, the sinner first required a "warrant" from the divine Word that God was a Redeemer for them in Christ. So, both sinner and preacher required

---

[29] Jonathan Edwards, *Freedom of the Will*, in *The Works of President Edwards*, Pt. 1, Sect. 4, 2:15.

[30] Jonathan Edwards, *Freedom of the Will*, in *The Works of President Edwards*, Pt. 1, Sect. 4, 2:15-216.

[31] John Brine held that "with respect to special faith in Christ, it seems to me that the powers of man in his perfected state were not fitted and disposed to that act." John Brine, *A Refutation of Arminian Principles* (London, 1743), 5 as found in Nettles, *By His Grace And For His Glory; A Historical, Theological and Practical Study of the Doctrines of Grace in Baptist Life*, 428.

Ward's Spirituality

special knowledge of such a warrant before either preaching or attempting repentance and faith.[32]

In the midst of this confusion, Robert Hall Sr., in 1779, preached a sermon before the Northamptonshire Baptist Association which was published in 1781 under the title, *Help to Zion's Travelers: Being An Attempt To Remove Various Stumbling Blocks Out Of The Way, Relating To Doctrinal, Experimental And Practical Religion*.[33] In Part 2, Hall addresses the "experimental difficulty" posed by the requirement that sinners demonstrate a "warrant to apply to Christ." It was held that a sinner could figure he had obtained a warrant to believe when he "beholds by faith the Redeemer as dying for his transgressions, or at least [has] hope that his sins are forgiven him."[34] But Hall shows the fault of this reasoning:

> But is it not strange that a person cannot be sorry for a fault till he hopes he shall not be punished; nor sincerely beg for a favor till he enjoys it? How shall a person while he is in a state of impenitency, know that Christ died for him in particular? There is nothing in Scripture to encourage an impenitent sinner to believe that he is in a safe condition.[35]

Instead, Hall asserts that Scripture teaches the reverse,

---

[32] Tom J. Nettles, *The Baptists: Key People Involved in Forming a Baptist Identity* (Fearn, Scotland: Christian Focus Publications, 2005), 289.

[33] Robert Hall Sr. was pastor of the Baptist church in Arnsby, Leicestershire from 1753 throughout the remainder of his ministry. His church was one of the founding churches of the Northamptonshire Association, and Hall exercised considerable influence in it. See Nathan A. Finn, "Robert Hall's Contributions to Evangelical Renewal in the Northamptonshire Baptist Association," *Midwestern Journal of Theology* 6, no. 1 (Fall 2007): 24.

[34] Robert Sr. Hall, *Help to Zion's Travelers: Being An Attempt To Remove Various Stumbling Blocks Out Of The Way, Relating To Doctrinal, Experimental And Practical Religion*, 3rd ed. (1824; repr., Philadelphia: American Baptist Publication Society, 1851), 119.

[35] Hall, *Help to Zion's Travelers*, 120.

namely, that *through* repentance and faith one comes to know that he is finally safe from God's righteous judgment.[36] In fact, it is

> repentance, therefore, [that] implies the primary actings of faith, and is the immediate effect of grace in the soul; but the first actings of faith are not a believing the person is pardoned. Nothing can be more false than that an impenitent person has a revealed right to pardon; if he ought to believe he is pardoned before he repents, then he ought to believe a lie.[37]

In Part 3 dealing with "Practical Difficulties" Hall addresses the stumbling block associated with the duty-faith quandary of Hyper Calvinism. He does so by applying Edwards' distinction between natural and moral inability. "For the relief of such," Hall writes, "I propose to their calm and candid consideration a distinction between natural and moral inability, which seems necessary to be well understood in order to obtain consistent views of Divine revelation, relating to the requirements of God's righteous law and the nature of his precious gospel."[38] In explicating this distinction, Hall maintained, "Duty is measured by natural ability. ... His commands are not grievous in their own nature, whatever they be to our corrupt minds. They are agreeable, and suited to the natural *powers* of men, however contrary and disgustful to their natural *inclinations*."[39] In such a state, we see both man's obligation to believe on Christ by virtue of his natural ability and our desperate need for "omnipotent grace to deliver them from a state evidently helpless, and deplorable,"

---

[36] Hall, *Help to Zion's Travelers*, 121.
[37] Hall, *Help to Zion's Travelers*, 122.
[38] Hall, *Help to Zion's Travelers*, 219-220.
[39] Hall, *Help to Zion's Travelers*, 225-226.

Ward's Spirituality

arising from our moral inability.[40] In conclusion, Hall writes that "by observing this distinction, Scriptural exhortations to repentance and faith, appear quite consistent, which could never be defended if criminality arose from natural, and not moral inability."[41] Knowledge of this distinction also offers great encouragement to "seeking souls" dithering over whether they have a warrant to believe, "for as none *can* come unto him but such whom the Father draws, therefore spiritual desires after Jesus, and delight in religion, are *evidences* of a gracious change, holy dispensations, or a new heart."[42]

Help to Zion's Travelers helped one encumbered traveler in particular, i.e. William Carey. In his preface to the second edition, John Ryland Jr. records that Carey had been wavering between Arminianism, Calvinism, and even Antinomianism, but found truth in the Reformed understanding through Hall's winsome presentation.[43] In his own words regarding Hall's *Help*, Carey stated,

> I found all that arranged and illustrated which I had been so long picking up by scraps. I do not remember ever to have read any book with such raptures as I did that. If it was poison as some then said, it was so sweet to me that I drank it greedily to the bottom of the cup. And I rejoice to say, that those doctrines are the choice of my heart to this day.[44]

So great was the influence of this work in Carey's life that Ryland conceded the whole of Carey's body of divinity to it.[45]

---

[40] Hall, *Help to Zion's Travelers*, 226.
[41] Hall, *Help to Zion's Travelers*, 243.
[42] Hall, *Help to Zion's Travelers*, 244.
[43] Hall, *Help to Zion's Travelers*, 10.
[44] Nettles, *The Baptists*, 283.
[45] Hall, *Help to Zion's Travelers*, 10. Also see George Smith, *The Life of William Carey, D. D.: Shoemaker and Missionary* (London: John Murray, 1885), 16-17.

Help from Andrew Fuller

What Robert Hall Sr. began in *Help To Zion's Travelers*, Fuller further explained in detail in his 1785 thesis, *The Gospel Worthy of All Acceptation*.[46] In particular, Fuller set out to solve the duty-faith dilemma, or as some put it, to answer the "modern question" i.e. "whether it be the duty of all men to whom the gospel is published, to repent and believe in Christ?"[47] Exposing the missions-killing implications of the hyper-Calvinistic answer for the modern question, Fuller writes that if faith is not required of all men who hear the gospel, then to seek to inculcate that faith, namely, to preach the gospel, "would be unwarrantable and cruel to our fellow sinners, as it subjects them to an additional charge of abundance of guilt."[48] In Section Two of his work, Fuller establishes that "whatever God commands, exhorts, or invites us to comply with, is the duty of those to whom such language is addressed."[49] So, if there is indeed no duty for sinners for repentance and faith, one would expect to find no commands or exhortations to that effect in Scripture. But Fuller, like Hall before him, shows from text after text that such commands and exhortations to sinners abound in both Testaments. Conversely, Fuller shows from Scripture that when sinners do not respond to the gospel call to repent and believe they are found guilty of heinous sin and threatened with "the most awful punishments."[50]

---

[46] Raymond Brown, *The English Baptists of the Eighteenth Century* (London: Baptist Historical Society, 1986), 116.

[47] Nettles, *The Baptists*, 248.

[48] Andrew Fuller, *The Gospel of Christ Worthy of All Acceptation, Or The Duty Of Sinners To Believe In Jesus Christ, With Corrections And Additions; To Which Is Added An Appendix, On The Necessity Of A Holy Disposition In Order To Believing In Christ* (1801), Pt. 1, in *The Complete Works Of The Rev. Andrew Fuller: With A Memoir Of His Life, By Andrew Gunton Fuller* (Third London Edition; Reprint, Harrisonburg, VA: Sprinkle Publications, 1988), 2:332-333.

[49] Andrew Fuller, *The Gospel Worthy*, Pt. 2, Sect. 1, in *The Works of Andrew Fuller*, 2:343.

[50] Andrew Fuller, *The Gospel Worthy*, Pt. 2, Sects. 4, 5, in *The Works of Andrew Fuller*, 2:354-355, 358.

Ward's Spirituality

Here, he draws on Edwards work concerning natural and moral inability when he writes,

> No man is reproved for not doing that which is naturally impossible: but sinners are reproved for not believing, and given to understand that it is solely owing to their criminal ignorance, pride, dishonesty of heart, and aversion from God.[51]

Fuller acknowledges that some hyper-Calvinists find fault with his conclusions on the basis that "a general invitation to sinners to return to God, and be saved through Christ ... [is] inconsistent with an election of some and a consequent rejection of others,"[52] but answers that

> a minister is not to make inquiry after, nor to trouble himself about, those secrets of the eternal mind of God, viz., Whom he purposeth to save, and whom he hath sent Christ to die for in particular; it is enough for them to search his revealed will, and thence take their directions, from whence they have their commissions.[53]

So as ministers of the gospel cannot know whom in particular God has elected for salvation, Fuller believed they were compelled to preach the gospel to all sinners indiscriminately. In the concluding arguments of his treatise, Fuller argues,

> The work of the Christian ministry, it has been said, is to preach the gospel, or to hold up the free grace of God through Jesus Christ, as the only way of a sinner's salvation. ... If the foregoing principles be just, it is the duty of

---

[51] Andrew Fuller, *The Gospel Worthy*, Pt. 2, Sect. 4, in *The Works of Andrew Fuller*, 2:355.
[52] Andrew Fuller, *The Gospel Worthy*, Pt. 3, in *The Works of Andrew Fuller*, 2:371.
[53] Andrew Fuller, *The Gospel Worthy*, Pt. 3, in *The Works of Andrew Fuller*, 2:373.

ministers not only to exhort their carnal auditors to believe in Jesus Christ for the salvation of their souls; but *it is at our peril to exhort them to any thing short of it, or which does not involve or imply it.*[54]

Help from William Carey

John Ryland Sr.'s less than encouraging response to Carey's proposal that the Northamptonshire ministers discuss the subject of "the duty of Christians to attempt the spread of the Gospel among heathen nations" has already been stated.[55] Carey was in agreement with Ryland concerning God's sovereignty in election. But Carey was convicted that God had also ordained means for the reaching of his elect. So, at the encouragement of ministers in the Northamptonshire Association, Carey wrote and published in 1792 his case for the same in a treatise entitled, *An Enquiry Into The Obligations Of Christians, To Use Means For The Conversion Of The Heathens: In Which The Religious State Of The Different Nations Of The World, The Success Of Former Undertakings, And the Practicability Of Further Undertakings Are Considered.*[56]

Speaking anachronistically, Carey's *Enquiry* was an *Operation World* and *Perspectives* course combined.[57] In it, Carey implores, "It becomes us not only to express our desires of that event [the coming of God's kingdom] by words, but to use every lawful method to spread the knowledge of his name."[58] To those who

---

[54] Andrew Fuller, *The Gospel Worthy*, Pt. 3 (Concluding Reflections), in *The Works of Andrew Fuller*, 2:386-387.

[55] Marshman, *Life and Times*, 1:10.

[56] *PA*, 1:2.

[57] Patrick Johnstone's prayer guide for the nations, *Operation World* and *Perspectives on the World Christian Movement* course, developed by Ralph Winter, have been the means for many in modern times of sensing and accepting God's call into missions. To know more about *Operation World* visit www.operationworld.org and for more information on *Perspectives*, visit www.perspectives.org.

[58] William Carey, *An Enquiry into the Obligations of Christians, to Use Means for the Conversion of the Heathens: In Which the Religious State of the Different Nations of*

Ward's Spirituality

objected that the command to "make disciples of all nations" applied only to the "Apostles, or those under the immediate inspiration of the Holy Ghost," Carey answered that in order to be consistent, baptism—a conviction and ordinance at the core of Baptist identity—should be restricted to the same as well.[59]

He also answered the objections of some ministers who, on the basis of postmillennial convictions, argued that "the time is not yet come that the heathen should be converted."[60] But if from this conviction, some would argue against the preaching of the gospel to the heathen, Carey answers first that such an argument must either be based on an assumption that the secret counsels of God are the rule of our duty, or that none of the heathen will be converted until God pours out his Spirit in the last days. But Carey asserts that if the first assumption be valid, even prayer for the heathen would be precluded. And the second assumption is shown to be invalid by the success of the gospel among the heathen that was already being seen in Carey's day.[61]

Following the publication of Carey's *Enquiry*, Carey preached his now famous sermon from Isaiah 54:2-3 containing the oft quoted motto, "Expect great things from God. Attempt great things for God." After this and more imploring, the Particular Baptist Missionary Society was finally formed on October 2, 1792.[62] A little less than a year later, this society sent its first missionaries, William Carey and surgeon, Dr. John Thomas to Ben-

---

the World, the Success of Former Undertakings, and the Practicability of Further Undertakings Are Considered (Leicester: A. Ireland, 1792), 3.

[59] Carey, *Enquiry*, 8-9.

[60] Carey, *Enquiry*, 12. Postmillennialism was the standard position of many divines in Carey's day. It was also known as the "latter day glory." When combined with hyper Calvinism, the result was a conviction that missionary efforts would be futile until certain prophecies were fulfilled, and a special outpouring of the Holy Spirit had occurred at Christ's second coming. So a human missionary effort that ran ahead of the signs of the dawn of such latter day glory would not only be vain, but presumptuous.

[61] Carey, *Enquiry*, 12.

[62] Marshman, *Life and Times*, 1:15.

gal. And in 1799, with a slightly larger company, Ward himself would follow; heir of a Reformed, ecumenical evangelicalism and pioneer on a missionary path that had been cleared by many in his own denomination and beyond.

The Spirituality of William Ward

William Ward was highly esteemed for his spirituality in his own day. He is less known today for his piety only because he is, in general, little known. So, after giving a brief summary of Ward's career, W.O. Simpson, in his "Introduction" to a fifth edition of Ward's opus on Hindus, could still exclaim some forty years after the missionary's death, "The power which fixed his future course lay ... in that inner life of piety."[63] Again, Simpson acknowledges that while Ward was not renown for his genius, he was remembered for his "spiritual mind" and "amiable disposition," and as such, was a model missionary.[64]

Spirituality defined

In the above reminiscences of Ward by Simpson, he refers both to his "piety" and to his "spiritual mind." This is illustrative of the similarity that continues to exist between what was more frequently known as "piety" in former days, and "spirituality" today. "The word 'spirituality' comes from a Latin term, *spiritualitas*, which, in turn, is derived from the word *spiritus*, the Latin word for 'spirit.'"[65] So, "True spirituality is intimately bound up with the Holy Spirit and his work."[66] As such, Christian or Biblical Spirituality has in view the same as the Apostle Paul envisioned when he wrote, "But I say, walk by the Spirit, and you

---

[63] W.O. Simpson, introduction to *A View of the History, Literature, and Religion of the Hindoos*, 5th ed. (Madras: J. Higginbotham, 1863), 2.
[64] Simpson, introduction to *A View of the History*, 6.
[65] Michael A.G. Haykin, *The God Who Draws Near: An Introduction to Biblical Spirituality* (Darlington, England: Evangelical Press, 2007), xviii-xix.
[66] Haykin, *The God Who Draws Near*, xix.

Ward's Spirituality

will not gratify the desires of the flesh" (Gal 5:16). It is the ongoing and consummate effect of the Holy Spirit's work in the life of a Christian. As this work of the Spirit is observed by others, it is a life of devotion to God. So, though the term "spirituality" is more in vogue today than the classical term "piety," both are used interchangeably in this work with reference to William Ward's religious devotion.

It is noteworthy to consider Ward's own thoughts on spirituality, though he often uses different terms to describe it. "True Christians," he notes, are measured by the psalmist in their latter end in the results of a life of faith.[67] Similarly,

> a spiritual man has impressed on his spirit a lively sense of the evil of transgression, and the blessedness of those who are accepted in the Lord Jesus Christ. His heart is warmed by the love of Christ, and is an abode for the Holy Spirit, as the spirit of peace. All the graces of the Spirit have more or less found a place in his mind; so that his frame of mind and conversation during the day are spiritual, and his affections are set on things above: the element in which he lives, and moves, and has his being, is religion: "he dwells in God:" and he has in consequence a vigorous soul and a tranquil conscience.[68]

As Christian Spirituality is an effect of the work of the Holy Spirit, we may also say that the Holy Spirit is the *source* of the Christian's spirituality. Historically, Christians have sought to encounter God the Spirit in two ways. The first way is through the unmediated influence of the Spirit, often via ascetic or ecstatic means. Examples of this way include many Roman Catholic mystics such as John of the Cross (1542-1591), Teresa of Avi-

---

[67] William Ward, *Reflections On the Word of God For Every Day in the Year In Two Volumes* (Serampore: Mission Press, 1822), 2:85.
[68] Ward, *Reflections*, 2:289.

la (1515–1582), Bonaventure (1221–1274), Thomas Merton (1915–1968), and even Quaker founder, George Fox (1624–1691), who regarded as authoritative the "inner light" of the Holy Spirit. Advocates of such an approach may acknowledge God's objective revelation in Holy Scripture, but primary attention is often given to experiencing God, his Spirit, and his Christ subjectively.

The other way Christians have sought to connect with God is through the Spirit-mediated revelation of Holy Scripture. In this understanding of spirituality, people are more or less *spiritual* to the degree that their lives adhere to the teachings of Scripture. Ward expressed the same sentiment regarding what he called "real religion." "For a more correct idea of real religion can hardly be formed by us, than that it is a deep and lasting impression of the immeasurable importance of the truths of the Gospel, and fervency of spirit in seeking to be brought permanently under their influence."[69] In Ward's understanding, spirituality or "real religion" was a matter of "seeking to be brought permanently under" the influences of the truths of the gospel. The spirituality he esteemed could be measured objectively by the degree to which one's life adhered to Scripture. And in this sense, it will be shown that William Ward was a very spiritual man.

Sources
Ward's spirituality is revealed in his most personal works: his Journal, his letters, his daily devotional, *Reflections on the Word of God For Every Day in the Year*, a few published sermons, and the *Serampore Form of Agreement*, which he drafted on behalf of the Serampore Mission. The Journal, though chiefly written as an account of the larger Serampore Mission for the Baptist Mis-

---

[69] Ward, *Reflections*, 2:138.

Ward's Spirituality

sionary Society, gives unedited glimpses of his spirituality from his arrival in India in 1799 to the close of the Journal in 1811. Written in 1822, a year before Ward's death, *Reflections* reveals that a consistent Word-driven spirituality was also present in his latter days. Drafted by Ward in 1805, the *SFA*, though representing the beliefs and resolutions of the entire Mission, is useful in corroborating spiritual themes that are seen in other of Ward's writings.[70] Of Ward's letters, those written to friends, as compiled by Samuel Stennett in his *Memoir* will primarily be considered.

On the one hand, these sources demonstrate Evangelical Calvinistic doctrine. This has been demonstrated generally in chapter 1 in connection with the various roles Ward played at Serampore. But in these sources, there is much specific evidence of the doctrines of grace that Ward held dear. On the other hand, these sources reveal certain themes in Ward's spirituality that are more prominent than others.

Ward's doctrine

The Calvinistic nature of Ward's doctrine is easily recognized when one compares it to that summary of John Calvin's (1509-1564) doctrine commonly known as the 'five points' of Calvinism i.e. total depravity, unconditional election, limited atonement, irresistible grace, and perseverance of the saints (TULIP).[71] These doctrines are often alternately described as

---

[70] That the *SFA* was drafted by Ward is "explicitly stated by John Clark Marshman (*Carey, Marshman and Ward*, [1859], 1:229) and is confirmed by internal evidence and questions of style." [Ernest Payne?], "The Serampore Form of Agreement," *Baptist Quarterly* 12, no. 5 (1947): 125.

[71] J.I. Packer helpfully notes that the "'five points of Calvinism,' so called, are simply the Calvinistic answer to a five-point manifesto (the Remonstrance) put out by certain 'Belgic semi-Pelagians' in the early seventeenth century. The theology which it contained (known to history as Arminianism) stemmed from two philosophical principles: first, that divine sovereignty is not compatible with human freedom, nor therefore with human responsibility; second, that ability limits obligation." From

The Spirituality of William Ward

Reformed doctrines or simply, the "doctrines of grace." In the sources mentioned above there is ample evidence that Ward held to these doctrines in general. Often, the mention of one doctrine leads to another, indicating the interconnectedness of the doctrines of grace in his understanding. There is also a fair amount of evidence that he held to each individually as well, though the amount of theological precision with which he held to each doctrine in particular, varies. Following is evidence of Ward's belief in these doctrines.

Total depravity

In a letter to a friend in 1811, Ward writes regarding human depravity:

> You know something of the dreadful depravity of the heart—your groans under a body of sin and death—your fears lest this depravity should be absolutely unpardonable—all these things teach you, that, if you are saved, it must be infinite grace and merit united—nothing less, you are sure, is sufficient to reach your case. These are often the feelings of your old friend.[72]

Commenting on Jesus' words in Matthew 15:19 regarding the evil thoughts that originate in the heart before being expressed

---

this philosophical position, the Remonstrants insisted that Scripture must be interpreted accordingly and summarized their hermeneutical position in five points. "The Synod of Dort was convened in 1618 to pronounce on this theology, and the 'five points of Calvinism' represent its counter-affirmations." The above quotes as well as a concise and lucid summary of both sets of 'five points' and their import is found in J.I. Packer's, *A Quest For Godliness; The Puritan Vision of the Christian Life* (Wheaton, IL: Crossway, 1990), 127-134. Though, as Packer acknowledges, "Calvinism is much broader than the 'five points'" (129), they provide an easily recognizable reference point in evaluating Ward's own theology which, as was shown in chap. 2, is descended from the Reformers through the English Puritans.

[72] Samuel Stennett, *Memoirs of The Life of the Rev. William Ward, Late Baptist Missionary in India; Containing A Few Of His Early Poetical Productions, And A Monody to His Memory* (London: Simpkin and Marshall, 1825), 169.

Ward's Spirituality

with the mouth, Ward expounds, "And thus our Lord taught that human nature was so totally depraved and corrupted by sin, that nothing short of a new birth could qualify a person for the kingdom of heaven, or capacitate him to see it."[73] Commenting on the nature of our depravity Ward maintains that it lies both in

> an inveterate proneness to evil, and an unconquerable aversion to good. From hence arises a spiritual incapacity which amounts to an entire prostration of spiritual strength, and the absence of every principle of goodness or energy by which the culprit might rise from his ruin.[74]

Similarly, commenting on Psalm 51, Ward explains, "The doctrine taught by the Psalmist agrees herewith, that the heart is unclean and set on impure objects; yea, is so impure and abominable that it must be created anew, a work of which God, the Creator of all things, is alone capable."[75]

Clearly, Ward affirmed the doctrine of total depravity. With regard to his spirituality, as will be shown later, Ward's belief in this doctrine made him both a very humble man and a very prayerful man. With regard to his doctrine, his conviction regarding man's depravity necessitated and strengthened his convictions on other doctrines. For example, since the source of man's problem was a depraved nature and an unclean heart, man's heart must be created anew. God alone had power to do this and did so through the act of regeneration in the Person of the Holy Spirit. He describes this supernatural process as follows:

> He opens the eyes of the understanding, and shines into

---

[73] Ward, *Reflections*, 1:101.
[74] Ward, *Reflections*, 1:101.
[75] Ward, *Reflections*, 2:130.

the heart, and conveys the light of the knowledge of the glory of God in the face of Jesus Christ. He subdues the stubborn will, and makes the obstinate sinner willing in the day of his power. He purifies the affections, and sheds abroad in the heart a Saviour's love, taking away the idols, and restoring to the blessed God his sovereignty in the soul. Finally, the conscience is purged from its subjection to error, and restored to its sensibility, so that it now becomes the friend of God, and asserts his claim to reign over the whole man. And thus the glorious Redeemer creates all things new, and begins that good work which he will never abandon till he has restored the soul to its original perfection, and given it back to God to be his eternal abode through the Spirit.[76]

In this explication of the doctrine of regeneration, it is again evident that Ward saw a connection between the various doctrines of grace. Not only did man's depravity necessitate regeneration by the Holy Spirit, but man's obstinate nature also necessitated grace to make him sensible and bring him into a state of friendship with God such that he would never fall away but be kept by him unto glory. In this way, Ward understood the doctrine of total depravity to be linked to the doctrines of irresistible grace and perseverance of the saints. To the former of these we now turn.

Irresistible grace

Irresistible grace refers to the certainty with which God's saving work in his elect will be accomplished. Man is dead in his trespasses and sins (Eph. 2:1). Dead men are capable of nothing. But God, through the power of the gospel of Christ, breathes life into dry bones and makes them live (Ezek. 37:3). Additional evidence for Ward's belief in this doctrine is seen in the following:

---

[76] Ward, *Reflections*, 1:102.

Ward's Spirituality

> Here then, in the fullest manner, our Lord teaches us that christians are called by the grace of God, and that this calling is effectual in their conversion. ... From hence we see, that religion is something more than the existence of Christian notions in the mind: a light shines into the heart, which is never put out; an anxiety is imparted to the conscience which nothing but hope in Christ can pacify; an impulse is given to the will, which nothing can successfully resist; and desires are imparted to the mind, which nothing but the living water which Christ has promised can quench.[77]

And again, in volume two of his daily devotional, speaking of God's love for His own in Christ, Ward writes:

> How astonishing does this love appear when we consider the difficulties obstructing the gracious intentions of the Almighty towards these objects of his pity: he had to sacrifice his Son before their sins could be removed: he had to conquer a rooted enmity existing in their hearts, and a criminal preference of other objects. But God commendeth his love towards us, in that when we were enemies Christ died for us, when we were afar off, he drew us to himself; when we were unholy, he put upon us the garment of salvation; when we were unwilling, he made us willing in the day of his power; when we were destitute of strength, he worked in us to will and to do of his good pleasure; when we were in the hands of merciless enemies, he rescued us; when diseased, he healed us; when on the very brink of ruin, he sought and found us. O what wonderful, matchless grace is this![78]

Ward believed not only that only God alone could save the sinner, but that he *would* save those called by his grace by over-

---

[77] Ward, *Reflections*, 1:103.
[78] Ward, *Reflections*, 2:70.

coming sinful resistance and inclining their hearts favorably toward his Son, so that they would freely and willingly believe on him for salvation.

Perseverance of the Saints

Ward not only believed that the "Glorious Redeemer creates all things new," but that he also would "never abandon" that work until "he has restored the soul to its original perfection."[79] God would enable his adopted children to persevere in the faith until their dying day or the second coming of his Son, whichever came first. Ward's belief in this doctrine is seen in the following excerpt concerning John 10:22–29: "All real christians are kept by the power of God from the possibility of falling into such sin and unbelief as to involve them in misery after death. They are 'kept through faith unto salvation.' This doctrine was fully taught by our Lord."[80] Then Ward anticipates the objection some might raise over such a doctrine:

> But may I then give up all Christian watchfulness, and live indifferent to the correctness of my conduct? If the believer cannot perish, may not I venture on paths full of danger? No: let me remember, that I am no longer entitled to the character of one of Christ's flock but while I follow the good Shepherd, and hear his voice; that the means by which I am to be kept are inseparably connected with the security of my person, and my final happiness. ... He who does not as heartily love these exhortations, as the absolute assurances of safety and perseverance, may be very certain, that he does not hold this blessed truth in righteousness.[81]

---

[79] Ward, *Reflections*, 1:102.
[80] Ward, *Reflections*, 1:109.
[81] Ward, *Reflections*, 1:110.

Ward's Spirituality

For Ward, grace reigned supreme. Grace called. Grace overcame willful resistance to Christ and his gospel. God's grace kept his own to the end. And grace was given to Christians along the way in the form of means, that, willfully availing of them, they might come to faith and be kept in the same. What did Ward mean by "means"? They included, "friends, books, providential events, but specially the influences of the Holy Spirit, by which, according to our Lord's words, the mind is drawn to Christ; and by which influences alone the outward means are made effectual."[82] Means also included, "his word, his Spirit, his ordinances, and his humbling providences." Ward maintained both that God prepares men's hearts for salvation through these means and that he was to be, "sought in the use of these means ... that they also may be prepared for his service and for his eternal kingdom."[83] By availing of these means, and by heeding God's promises and warnings, Ward believed God assured the perseverance of his saints who showed themselves to be such "in substantial acts of persevering obedience."[84]

Unconditional election

Unconditional election is that biblical doctrine that God chose a people in Christ "before the foundation of the world" (Eph. 1:4), not because of any foreseen goodness in those chosen, but solely because of his grace (Rom. 9:11, 16). God's grace in the predestination of his elect was the first link in the "golden chain" of Romans 8:30 which states, "And those whom he predestined he also called, and those whom he called he also justified, and those whom he justified he also glorified."[85] It was also

---

[82] Ward, *Reflections*, 1:103.
[83] Ward, *Reflections*, 2:156.
[84] Ward, *Reflections*, 2:158.
[85] The name "golden chain" was coined by Puritan divine, William Perkins (1558-1602) in his work, *A Golden Chaine Or The Description Of Theologie containing the order of the causes of Saluation and Damnation, according to God's word. A view*

The Spirituality of William Ward

fundamental for Ward and his fellow missionaries in the Mission principles they set forth in 1805:

> We are firmly persuaded that Paul might plant and Apollos water in vain in any part of the world, did not God give the increase. We are sure, that only those who are ordained to eternal life will believe, and that God alone can add to the church such as shall be saved.[86]

Commenting on John 10:30, Ward acknowledges, "The divine foreknowledge all admit; but some persons seem unwilling that God should foreappoint?"[87] Speaking from Luke 4:14–30, Ward asserts this is so because "this doctrine, that God has a right to dispense his favours as he will, is very galling to human pride."[88] Nevertheless, Ward maintains this doctrine is taught in both of these passages, with regard to salvation, conformation to the image of God's Son, and even extending "to the meanest circumstances of life," i.e. the numbering of the hairs on our head.[89]

For Ward's High Calvinist ancestors, this belief stymied the proclamation of the gospel. But for those of Ward's and Fuller's generation, it highlighted the need to tirelessly use means God had provided that his elect might be gathered in. Hence, the above preamble continues, insisting on the use of means that they might realize what God had foreordained:

> Nevertheless we cannot but observe with admiration, that Paul, the great champion for the glorious doctrines of free and sovereign grace, was the most conspicuous for his personal zeal in the work of persuading men to be reconciled

---

whereof is to be seen in the Table annexed (Cambridge, 1660).

[86] *SFA*, Preamble in *PA*, 3:198.
[87] Ward, *Reflections*, 1:100.
[88] Ward, *Reflections*, 1:115.
[89] Ward, *Reflections*, 1:100.

to God. In this respect he is a noble example for our imitation.⁹⁰

In this respect, the Apostle Paul is both the greatest theologian and the greatest missionary. He clearly taught the doctrine of God's gracious election. But he also exemplified the doctrine of means, arduously reasoning with unbelievers in order that he might persuade them that the tenets of the gospel were true. Man pits the doctrine of election against his notion of free will. Scripture does not. Therefore, for Ward and the Serampore missionaries, the doctrine of election was not an impediment to their mission but a boon.

Limited atonement

While there are five points of Calvinism, some are comfortable expressing adherence to only four or sometimes just three of the points. In these instances, the first "point" to be jettisoned is usually limited atonement because of the "negative cast" that it carries as if those who affirm it delight in "confining the limits of divine mercy."⁹¹ And to give grace where it is due, those who jettison this point may do so because they genuinely believe Scripture does not teach it.

But for many who hold to all five points however, this position is untenable, for the "five points" are not arbitrary but rather represent an interconnected understanding of Scripture's teaching regarding God sovereignty in man's salvation.⁹² As renowned Baptist pastor, Charles Spurgeon (1834–1892), quipped,

> The stones of the great doctrines so fit into each other, that the more pressure there is applied to remove them the

---

⁹⁰ *SFA*, Preamble in *PA*, 3:198.
⁹¹ Packer, *A Quest for Godliness*, 129.
⁹² Packer, *A Quest for Godliness*, 129.

more strenuously do they adhere. And you may mark, that you cannot receive one of these doctrines without believing all. Hold for instance that man is utterly depraved, and you draw the inference then that certainly if God has such a creature to deal with salvation must come from God alone, and if from him, the offended one, to an offending creature, then he has a right to give or withhold his mercy as he wills; you are thus forced upon election, and when you have gotten that you have all: the others must follow. Some by putting the strain upon their judgments may manage to hold two or three points and not the rest, but sound logic I take it requires a man to hold the whole or reject the whole; the doctrines stand like soldiers in a square, presenting on every side a line of defence which it is hazardous to attack, but easy to maintain.[93]

This discussion is introduced because, his Particular Baptist affiliation notwithstanding, it is unclear whether Ward held to the Calvinistic tenet of limited atonement. In fact, from the following excerpts, it would seem he did not, for in passages dealing with the subject of Christ's death on the cross, Ward speaks generally in terms of atonement instead of particularly with regard to redemption.

For example, Article V of the *SFA* sets forth their aim in preaching, namely, to "make the great subject of our preaching, Christ the crucified," but when he speaks of the doctrine which serves as the "grand mean of conversion," he refers merely to "the doctrine of Christ's expiatory death and all-sufficient merits."[94] According to Ward, this aim was consistent with that of the Moravians who made "the atonement of Christ their continued theme" and attributed their success to "the preaching of the

---

[93] C.H. Spurgeon, "Exposition of the Doctrines of Grace," in *The New Park Street And The Metropolitan Tabernacle Pulpit; Containing Sermons Preached And Revised By The Reverend C.H. Spurgeon, During The Year 1861* (London, 1862), 7:303-304.

[94] *SFA*, art. V, in *PA*, 3:202.

Ward's Spirituality

death of our Saviour."[95]

Similarly, if Ward had strong convictions regarding the particular object of Christ's redemption, one would expect to find it in a section of his *Farewell Letters* entitled, "Certainty Of The Triumphs Of The Gospel," but again it is conspicuously absent. Referring to the certain dominion of Christ's kingdom, Ward writes,

> Further, it is not only desirable, but a full provision has been made for this universal conquest. According to the everlasting covenant, the Father says to Christ, "Ask of me, and I shall give thee the heathen for thine inheritance, and the uttermost parts of the earth for thy possession." Christ, by his death, made provision, that the gospel should ultimately bless the whole earth: "he is the propitiation for our sins, (for those already called), and not for ours only, but for the sins of the whole world." — The influences of the Holy Spirit are such, that three thousand, or a world, may be brought under their saving effects in a very short period.[96]

Later, in arguing the necessity of the eventual triumph of Christ's kingdom, Ward cites as one reason the impossibility that Christ would not receive the promised reward of his sufferings. Having formulated his argument thusly, the stage is set for a plain explication of the particular object of Christ's purchase:

> If such an extension of the kingdom of Christ were not accomplished, it appears to us that the reward promised to Christ, for his sufferings unto death, would not be given him: "He shall see of the travail of his soul, and shall be satisfied." *Now, it is true, we may not exactly know what*

---

[95] *SFA*, art. V, in *PA*, 3:202.
[96] William Ward, *Farewell Letters to A Few Friends In Britain and America On Returning to Bengal In 1821* (New York: E. Bliss and E. White, 1821), 181.

would, on this subject, satisfy the Redeemer. We do know, that his heart is made of tenderness, that he is "full of grace." There is, however, one passage which seems to be an express intimation of what Christ would consider as a full reward: "I, if I be lifted up, will draw all men unto me" (italics mine).[97]

It appears that Ward equivocates. He seems to be unsure of the extent of Christ's atonement, or, perhaps, mindful of his ecumenical readership, unwilling to state it. A similar ambivalence is seen in his comments on Hebrews 13.

On the one hand, Ward acknowledges that "the divine methods of grace in redemption" have been "revealed to us under the idea of a covenant between the Father, the Son, and the Holy Spirit," which seems to imply belief in the blood redemption of a particular people.[98] But then, as Ward unfolds the roles of the Persons of the Godhead in this covenant, the scope of the Son's death is stated in terms of the world and not God's elect: "Hence the Father is said to have pitied the world, and have sent his Son. The Son is represented as coming from the Father to die for the world. While the Holy Spirit is spoken of as 'the promise of the Father,'" given upon Christ's ascension to the Father.[99] Then, referencing John 6:37; 17:2, 10, Ward's language is tinged with particularity as he acknowledges,

> Believers are said to have been given to Christ. ... In these divine arrangements every part of the plan of redemption, and its full accomplishment, are secured, so that not a single subject of it, nor a single individual included in it, can be lost. "It is ordered in all things and sure."[100]

---

[97] Ward, *Farewell Letters*, 182–183.
[98] Ward, *Reflections*, 1:42.
[99] Ward, *Reflections*, 1:42–43.
[100] Ward, *Reflections*, 1:43.

Ward's Spirituality

What are we to make of this? How are we to understand Ward's position regarding the doctrine of limited atonement/particular redemption? First, it must be acknowledged that Ward is correct to note that Jesus died for the world. Scripture speaks in this manner on numerous occasions. It must also be acknowledged that Ward is right to speak of the bottomless love and tender compassion of our Lord in his death on the cross.

But this is not all Scripture says regarding Christ's redemption. On the one hand, as mentioned earlier, many passages speak explicitly to Christ's particular purchase.[101] And on the other hand, Scripture's use of words like "all" and "world" are often equivocal and qualified, mitigating against an unequivocal and unqualified universal application of the merits of Christ's death.[102] In addition, when Scripture speaks of Jesus' atonement

---

[101] See Exodus 15:16; Acts 20:28; Ephesians 5:25; Hebrews 9:11-12; Revelation 5:9.

[102] There is, perhaps, no better discussion of the doctrine of particular redemption and the objections to it (which stem from the occurrence of words like "all," "all men," "all nations," "the world," and "the whole world") than John Owen, *The Death of Death in the Death of Christ* (1684; 1852; repr., Edinburgh: Banner of Truth, 2007), esp. 186-187, 190-191. Owen argues convincingly that these expressions are "used by the Holy Ghost only to evidence the removal of all personal and national distinctions," and the "enlarging the kingdom of Christ beyond the bounds of Jewry and Salem, abolishing all old restrictions, and opening a way for the elect amongst all people" (187). Belief in Christ's death for his church should not, however, restrict the proclamation of the gospel an iota or limit it to one people over another, for "the purpose and decree of God is not the rule of our duty; neither is the performance of our duty in doing what we are commanded any declaration of what is God's purpose to do, or his decree that it should be done. Especially is this to be seen and considered in the duty of the ministers of the gospel, in the dispensing of the word, in exhortations, invitations, precepts, and threatenings, committed unto them; all which are perpetual declaratives of our duty, and do manifest the approbation of the thing exhorted and invited to, with the truth of the connection between one thing and another, but not of the counsel and purpose of God, in respect of individual persons, in the ministry of the word. A minister is not to make inquiry after, nor to trouble himself about, those secrets of the eternal mind of God, namely,—whom he purposeth to save, and whom he hath sent Christ to die for in particular. It is enough for them to search his revealed will, and thence take their *directions*, from whence they have their *commissions*. Wherefore, there is no sequel between the universal precepts from the word concerning the *things*, unto God's purpose in himself concerning *persons*. They command and invite all to repent and believe; but they know not in

in particular terms, it is not bereft of Christ's love and compassion. On the contrary, the purchase of his bride, the church, is held forth to husbands as the supreme example of the kind and depth of love they should show their wives (Eph. 5:25-30).

It seems, to some degree, Ward understood the import of the doctrine of particular redemption and drew encouragement from it in his missionary endeavor. This is seen in the words he drafted in the Preamble of the *SFA*: "We are sure, that only those who are ordained to eternal life will believe."[103] Presumably, these "ordained to eternal life" were the same in Ward's mind as those for whom Christ made atonement with his blood. In addition, considering the wider doctrinal context of Ward's day, it is likely that Ward, like Fuller, adhered to the atonement maxim "sufficient for all, but effectual only to the elect."[104] In terms of the worth and power of Christ's atonement, Fuller and many contemporaries—and likely Ward included—saw no "limit." They understood Christ's atonement to be such that an infinite number of sinners could be saved if they would only believe. But their understanding of Scripture's teaching on man's depravity ruled out any possibility that man *would* believe on Christ without God's election according to grace and regeneration by His Spirit.

In summary, though Ward does not speak with theological precision when handling atonement-related texts, it is clear from

---

particular on whom God will bestow repentance unto salvation, nor in whom he will effect the work of faith with power" (187-188).

[103] *SFA*, Preamble in *PA*, 3:198.

[104] This maxim comes from Andrew Fuller's *The Abuse of Reviews* in *The Works of Andrew Fuller*, 3:748. Fuller elaborates on this maxim in the second edition of *The Gospel Worthy of All Acceptation* (1801). Michael Haykin summarizes Fullers position: "Christ's death, in other words, was sufficient for all humanity, but particular in the sense that God the Father intended to extend its benefits only to the elect." Michael A.G. Haykin, "Particular Redemption in the Writings of Andrew Fuller (1754-1815)," in *Studies in Baptist History and Thought*, vol. 1, *The Gospel in the World: International Baptist Studies*, ed. David Bebbington (Carlisle, Cumbria/Waynesboro, GA: Paternoster Press, 2002), 107-28.

Ward's Spirituality

the evidence above that Ward prized the doctrines of grace as a whole and stood solidly in the mainstream of Evangelical Calvinism in his day. They were vital in his mind, leading him to remark,

> The more we know of mankind, and the more we know of ourselves, the more shall we see of the importance of the doctrines of grace; that there is an imperious necessity that these doctrines should be faithfully and fearlessly preached and as thoroughly and heartily received, seeing the very life of religion within us, the very life of the churches, and the success of the ministry, depend upon it.[105]

Ward's convictions on these doctrines provided the underpinning for his spirituality, which manifests itself most clearly in the following central themes.

Central Themes in Ward's Spirituality

In his recent work on the spirituality of American missionary to Burma, Adoniram Judson (1788–1850), Evan Burns argues that "the center of Adoniram Judson's spirituality was a heavenly-minded, self-denying submission to the sovereign will of God, motivated by an affectionate desire to please Christ through obedience to his final command revealed in Scripture."[106] Woven together, these strands produced a spirituality that enabled Judson to endure tremendous suffering and persevere in an arduous but productive missionary career. Ward was a contemporary of Judson, arriving in Bengal thirteen years before Judson and his first wife, Anne Hasseltine (1789–1826).[107] They were both

---

[105] Ward, *Reflections*, 2:66.

[106] Evan Burns, *Monographs in Baptist History*, vol. 4, *A Supreme Desire to Please Him; The Spirituality of Adoniram Judson* (Eugene, OR: Pickwick Publications, 2016), 12-13.

[107] The Judsons initially arrived in Calcutta, where they were both baptized by Ward before continuing on to Rangoon, Burma, in July, 1813.

evangelical Calvinists. Both were Baptists. Both labored among unreached peoples in South Asia. But the predominant themes of their spiritualities are very different. Burns acknowledges that the ascetic nature of Judson's spirituality "went beyond the classic categories of evangelical piety."[108] Judson's self-discipline was severe; his outlook, austere. But Ward's spirituality, by contrast was marked by a warmth and affability that endeared him to all who knew him. An examination of his own writings as well as those who knew him best reveal four, often overlapping, key strands of spirituality that combine to form a beautiful tapestry of godliness. These key strands are Ward's love, humility, prayer, and usefulness.

Love

Of all of Ward's spiritual traits, love reigned supreme. As his former Ewood Hall fellow surveyed Ward's letters, he concluded that

> a spirit of *Christian love* ... breathed through all his writings, and marked all his conversation and demeanour. ... He was *gentle* and unassuming; though firm in his sentiments, and holding no truth with a loose hand, he was never dogmatical. ... His disposition was naturally *kind*. ... *The love of Christ was the predominant affection in his heart*, and the glory of God in the good of immortal souls, the great aim of all his actions (italics mine).[109]

Similarly, Joshua Marshman, his friend and colleague for over twenty years, after speaking of Ward's blameless character, asserts, "The fear of God and the *love of Christ*, constantly ruling

---

[108] Burns, *The Spirituality of Adoniram Judson*, 13.

[109] Samuel Stennett, *Memoirs of The Life of the Rev. William Ward, Late Baptist Missionary in India; Containing A Few Of His Early Poetical Productions, And A Monody to His Memory* (London: Simpkin and Marshall, 1825), 247–248.

Ward's Spirituality

within, preserved him from the most distant approach to any thing of open sin or folly" (italics mine).[110]

Concerning the love of God, Ward himself ranked it above other doctrines, and counted it the centerpiece of his personal creed:

> The doctrines of the love of God, the atonement, the resurrection and kingdom of Jesus, are, I trust, more and more precious to me. My views of them are more consoling—my faith in them more solid—and my peace and joy more regular. Yet I can part with the dogmas of enthusiasts—with the creeds of bigots, with the utmost ease. If I were asked for my creed, I could soon give it: *God is love . ... If God so loved us, we ought also to love one another . ...* Were I going to establish a church, I would have such a creed as this.[111]

Similarly, speaking of love and humility, Ward counted them "those christian virtues which most adorn the gospel of the Lord Jesus Christ"[112] and recognized that "the first law of Christ is love."[113]

From the above citations, it is clear that core doctrines of the faith were important and dear to Ward. Yet, to Ward, the warm love of God in Christ, was to be desired over the "dogmas of enthusiasts." As the following reveals, Christlike love was also to be desired above respectability in the pulpit:

> There is a going through the outward duties of the Christian ministry with *respectability*; but ... carrying a warm and fervent spirit into the pulpit ... [though it has] little out-

---

[110] Joshua Marshman, *Divine Grace the Source of All Human Excellence* (Serampore, 1823), 47.
[111] Stennett, *Memoir*, 242-243.
[112] Ward, *Reflections*, 1:132.
[113] Stennett, *Memoir*, 243.

ward show ... [is] infinitely more important to the conversion of souls, than the best sermon that ever occupied a week's study.[114]

In addition, God expected not only outward obedience from the Christian but "affections of the soul."[115] Conversely, waning affections for God were evidence that a person was falling away from God.[116] But, in the Christian filled with the love of Christ, obedience would naturally follow. Commenting on the love shown by the immoral woman who was forgiven because she loved much (Luke 7), Ward prays, "Oh! that our obedience may be animated by a fervent love to Christ, both for his infinite excellency, and for the 'great love wherewith he loved us, even when we were dead in sins.'"[117]

It is clear not only that Ward regarded the love of Christ and fellow man as supreme among Christian virtues, but also that others saw this virtue embodied in his life. God had graciously loved him in Christ, and he felt compelled to love others accordingly. This love was manifest in a host of Godly traits such as kindness, gentleness, peacemaking, and friendship that accompanied his love. Joshua Marshman commented on these in his funeral sermon for his longtime friend. "That mildness and gentleness of temper which insensibly endeared him to all with whom he had intercourse, had its origin in the happy temperament of mind he possessed by nature, although it was improved and refined by the power of divine grace."[118] Continuing to describe his transported friend, Marshman remembers that Ward was "formed by nature for kindness and friendship. ... [and] that this happy temper, heightened by that love of Christ and that

---

[114] Stennett, *Memoir*, 121.
[115] Ward, *Reflections*, 2:222.
[116] Ward, *Reflections*, 2:22, 43.
[117] Ward, *Reflections*, 1:122.
[118] Joshua Marshman, *Divine Grace*, 35.

Ward's Spirituality

tender pity to the souls of men, which ever glowed in his bosom."[119]

Corroborating Marshman's testimony, Ward's memoirist relates, "His ministry appears to have been generally acceptable, and his amiable manners procured him many friends wherever he went."[120] It has been asserted in the previous chapter that Ward was highly valued at the Mission and beyond for his friendship. The following chapter will look specifically at the friendship within the Trio. But, it bears noting that his worth as a friend flowed from his love for his friends, which found its source in the love with which he had been loved by God in Christ.

This Divine love spurred within Ward both a passion for the lost, concern for struggling new believers, and a warm ecumenism for those of the "right stamp." Regarding Ward's love for the lost, it has already been mentioned how Ward likened his compassion for the lost Indian masses to his feelings as if he were to see "a person drowning & on account of the distance of the water ... [be] unable to help him."[121]

Ward's love for new believers is seen in the *SFA*'s recognition that "another important part of our work is to build up, and to watch over, the souls that may be gathered. ... We must be willing to spend some time with them daily, if possible, in this work. We must have much patience with them, though they may grow very slowly in divine knowledge."[122] This principle put in writing that which Ward was already putting into practice as seen from a journal entry some three years before the drafting of the *SFA*. One convert named Petumber Jr. had left with his father, it was thought, to return no more. At this Ward laments, "We are ready to despond at this falling away," then he goes on to list ten other

---

[119] Joshua Marshman, *Divine Grace*, 35.
[120] Stennett, *Memoirs*, 165.
[121] William Ward, Journal MSS, Wednesday, November 23, 1803, 348.
[122] *SFA*, art. VII, in *PA*, 3:203.

The Spirituality of William Ward

converts who have also departed their fellowship in recent days, another convert who died, and a widow who "gives us little hopes." Yet he concludes, "These are very discouraging circumstances, added to the utter contempt of the gospel expressed by the people of Serampore. Yet we do not despair."[123]

Ward's ecumenism will be dealt with in depth in the following chapter, but a few pieces of evidence will be helpful to show that his ecumenism was primarily motivated by his love for those of other denominations which were of similar evangelical heart. His memoirist noted that Ward had "learned, that the bond of christian union is the love of Christ, and where he found this, he recognized the Saviour's image, nor could he withhold his affection."[124] Correspondingly, Ward prayed, "Grant, O Lord, that I may aim more and more to love thine image wherever I see it: to own it there, and feel from my very heart something of that affection which I owe to every atom of the body of Christ."[125] This love lay behind his views on open communion. In this case, Ward argues the compulsion of brotherly love stridently:

> How you can love Christians in a proper manner, and be shy with them, and avoid their communion, merely because their opinions are not all like yours, and because they demand the right of thinking for themselves, as you do, is a perfect mystery to me. I think the shutting out from communion such a man as Doddridge, or Baxter, because he was a pædobaptist, arises from the same spirit as that, which burnt men alive.[126]

---

[123] Ward, Journal MSS, Monday, November 1, 1802, 265.
[124] Stennett, *Memoirs*, 241.
[125] Ward, *Reflections*, 1:163.
[126] Ward to [Fuller?], March 3, 1810, quoted in Stennett, *Memoirs*, 244. Philip Doddridge (1702-1751) was an Independent minister of Castle Hill Church in Northampton, England. He wielded a wide influence in England and beyond through his work as preacher, pastor, author, and tutor at his dissenting academy. Geoffrey F. Nuttall, "Doddridge, Philip," in *The Blackwell Dictionary of Evangelical Biography 1730-1830*, vol. 1, ed. Donald M. Lewis (Oxford: Blackwell Publishers, 1995). Richard

Ward's Spirituality

One final, yet prominent effect of Ward's love was the obligation and urgency it created for making peace with those around him. The following two chapters will highlight the impact of Ward's peacemaking efforts, both within and without the Serampore Trio. Addressed below is evidence that demonstrates the importance of Ward's peacemaking efforts as they relate to his overall spirituality.

It is often said that a person's true character is most truly revealed not on a public stage, but rather in the midst of mundane and routine life events and in unguarded moments when no one is looking. Therefore, it is noteworthy that some of the first mentions of this aspect of Ward's spirituality occur not on the mission field of India, but on board the ship, *Criterion*, that bore him there:

> I have proposed & my Brethren have agreed to a meeting every Saturday evening, to enquire into and to rectify any difference which may have arisen. This meeting is to be confined to the Brethren, & then we hope to pledge ourselves to love each other forever.[127]

The reason for restricting conference to the "brethren" is made explicit in Ward's entry on August 24 of the same year: "We have not had our Brethrens Conference for two or three Saturday nights: the wind is too cold to send our sisters on deck, & we don't like to tell each other of our faults before the women." [128] Later, following the missionaries' settlement in

---

Baxter (1615–1691) was initially a minister of the Established church at Kidderminster who was later ejected for his unwillingness to conform to the 1662 Act of Uniformity. Baxter was and is renowned for his writings including *The Reformed Pastor* and *The Saints' Everlasting Rest*. N.H. Keeble, "Baxter, Richard (1615-1691)," in *Oxford Dictionary of National Biography*, ed. H.C.G. Matthew and Brian Harrison, vol. 4 (Oxford: Oxford University Press, 2004).

[127] Ward, Journal MSS, Saturday, July 6, 1799, 25.
[128] Ward, Journal MSS, Saturday, August 24, 1799, 38.

The Spirituality of William Ward

Serampore, we learn from Ward's Journal that in addition to adopting "a set of rules for the government of the family," they also continued the practice established upon the *Criterion* by devoting Saturday evenings "to the adjusting of differences, & pledging ourselves to love each other."[129]

That peacemaking lay at the core of Ward's makeup is also evident in the distress Ward felt when peace was lacking as well as in his attempts to make peace between embittered colleagues. While still aboard the *Criterion*, Ward writes that "a small difference betwixt Sisters M. [Hannah Marshman (1767-1847)] & G. [Ann Grant (?-1806)] increased a little melancholy which I had; but God made it up; a fine wind sprang up in the evening; & we had a most precious prayer-meeting."[130] Similarly, after settling in Serampore, Ward records, "This has been an awful week to us as a family on account of a quarrel betwixt [Brunsdon and Fountain]."[131] In early 1802, mention is made of a meeting held to reconcile two native brothers, Creeshnoo and Gokul, though we read of further conflict between these brothers a day later.[132] At two later dates, we read of Ward's sorrow over conflict among native believers and of efforts to help them reconcile,[133] and a few years later, there is a brief record of Ward, in a church meeting, seconding Old Petumber's efforts to "heal some differences."[134]

In 1815, following the death of BMS Secretary, Andrew Fuller, a bitter conflict ensued between the BMS and the

---

[129] Ward, Journal MSS, Saturday, January 18, 1800, 66. The "set of rules for the government of the family" was an early forerunner of sorts for the later and more developed *SFA*. The full quote relating to these rules is given and discussed on page 37 of this work.

[130] Ward, Journal MSS, Monday, September 2, 1799, 40.

[131] Ward, Journal MSS, Friday, May 16, 1800, 84.

[132] Ward, Journal MSS, Lord's Day, January 31, 1802, 207 and Monday, February 1, 1802, 207.

[133] Ward, Journal MSS, Wednesday, May 19, 1802, 232 and Friday, May 21, 1802, 232.

[134] Ward, Journal MSS, Friday, March 29, 1805, 413-414.

Ward's Spirituality

Serampore Mission. This would come to be known as the Serampore Controversy and was to rage until the death in 1837 of the last surviving member of the Trio, Joshua Marshman.[135] But early in this controversy, the Mission again turned to Ward to make peace and sent him as an emissary to the home office in England.[136] And on that very journey, just as he had twenty years earlier, Ward was making peace. A fellow passenger on that journey took note, and one year after Ward's death, informed the writer of his memoir:

> As I made a passage with Mr. Ward on board ship, from India to England, and consequently had an opportunity of knowing something of his habits, I feel much pleasure in giving you all the information I possess, respecting your departed, worthy friend. During the whole of the voyage he sustained the character of a peacemaker, and his whole mind seemed to be absorbed in doing good to his fellow creatures. When any misunderstanding took place between persons on board, he seemed uneasy, until the wounds were healed, which his kind instruction and gentle rebukes contributed, in no small measure, to effect.[137]

Humility

In addition to love, another prominent theme in Ward's spirituality is his humility. Comparing the two, Stennett remarked,

---

[135] Marshman, *Life and Times*, 2:516–518.

[136] Of this trip to England, Marshman writes, "It was hoped that the visit to England would serve the double purpose of restoring health and healing the breach with the society by personal and friendly intercourse." Marshman, *Life and Times*, 2:188. Recording a slightly different purpose for the trip, Serampore scholar, A. Christopher Smith writes, "The purpose of his visit between Spring 1819 and May 1821 was twofold: to help him recuperate physically, and to raise funds for the extremely costly college that he and his partners had founded recently in Serampore," adding thereafter, "In both of these objectives, he was successful." Smith, *Serampore Enterprise*, 45.

[137] Letter from an unknown passenger to Stennett, July 1824, quoted in Stennett, *Memoirs*, 192-193.

His humility was no less remarkable than his kindness; as we have already seen, he had an intimate knowledge and a deep feeling of his natural depravity and wretchedness, and not all the good, which he was made the happy instrument in effecting, could tempt him to forget that he was still an earthen vessel.[138]

Recognizing the same, Joshua Marshman, tasked with preaching the funeral sermon for his deceased friend and recollecting Ward's "abhorrence of every thing tending to exalt self," selected as his text, 1 Corinthians 15:10: "By the grace of God I am what I am," as it was "characteristic of his deep humility and self abasement amidst those labors for the cause of God."[139] In both of these remembrances, it is noteworthy not only that both men saw in Ward a prominent manifestation of humility, but that they observed it in connection with his own self-abasement arising from his belief in his own depravity. Joshua Marshman explained that Ward's "deep and abiding sense of the evil of sin ... appeared not only in his holy solicitude to avoid sin in every form, and his deep humiliation under a sense of indwelling sin, but in his tender compassion for the souls of men."[140] Ward himself prioritized humility stating, "If the Christian character can be said to be laid in any one particular virtue, that virtue is humility."[141]

These testimonies bear witness of the prominence of humility in Ward's spirituality. They also bear witness to the way Ward's humility was intertwined with his beliefs and other aspects of his spirituality. Ward's belief in the doctrines of God's grace and man's depravity gave rise to his humility. And in turn, that humility overflowed in expressions of love and compassion towards

---

[138] Stennett, *Memoirs*, 249.
[139] Joshua Marshman, *Divine Grace*, 6.
[140] Joshua Marshman, *Divine Grace*, 41.
[141] Ward, *Reflections*, 2:194.

Ward's Spirituality

his fellow man. In his meditation on Job 42, Ward expounds the humbling effect produced by the doctrines of God's holiness, the cross of Christ, and man's depravity:

> Views of infinite power and majesty may well humble us who are worms formed from the dust, and whose life is even as the vapour. ... Meditation on the Divine goodness contrasted with our own unworthiness and ingratitude may, under a Divine blessing, serve to humble us, and lay us low in self-abasement. ... If we would cultivate proper thoughts of ourselves, we must go to Calvary. ... Reflection on the omniscience of God are calculated to make us loathe ourselves. ... Mere knowledge puffeth up, but where meditations and reflections on these subjects are sanctified, we shall surely feel as Job did: we shall abhor ourselves.[142]

Such doctrine-induced humility had an effect on the way they felt they should relate to their native brethren. In article III of the *SFA*, which emphasizes the need to "abstain from those things which would increase their prejudices against the gospel," the examples of Paul and the Moravians are enjoined, with the summary statement that "he who is too proud to stoop to others, in order to draw them to him, though he may know that they are in many respects inferior to himself, is ill qualified to become a missionary."[143] And again, in Article VI, describing the kind of relationship the missionaries hoped to have with their native brethren, Ward writes, "We ought to be easy of access, to condescend to them as much as possible, and on all occasions to treat them as our equals. ... All force, and everything haughty, reserved and forbidding, it becomes us ever to shun with the

---

[142] Ward, *Reflections*, 2:105–106.
[143] *SFA*, art. III, in *PA*, 3:201.

greatest care."[144]

Ward's humility affected the way he viewed himself. On more than one occasion, he marks his birthday with a sober evaluation of his deep sin, lack of fruit, uselessness, and the patience and grace of God.[145] Similarly, when writing in his daily devotional of the need for the increase of some godly quality, he often laments the lack of the same in his own life and beseeches God that it might be granted him. When speaking of the Parable of the Soils (Matt. 13:1-9, 18-23), Ward applies it to himself in a closing prayer that he will not be among those who fall away in time of temptation or persecution, but rather be among those who bear fruit a hundred-fold.[146] In his comments on Jesus' washing of the disciples' feet, he prays for his own humility.[147] On other occasions, Ward prays for his own sanctification,[148] deliverance from pride,[149] and perseverance.[150]

Such humility on one occasion prompted Ward personally to finish digging the grave of a native brother, Balukram, in order to set an example for the native brethren who demurred to dig a grave lest they be ostracized by the people.[151] On another occasion, Ward's humility is seen in his command to Fuller, "Don't print this," with regard to some statements he made regarding the edge he had in proofing Bible translations due to his proficiency in the local languages.[152] In another humorous example, Ward had entered a "controversy" with a captain over the receipt of some expected goods. It turned out that the captain

---

[144] *SFA*, art. VI, in *PA*, 3:202-203.
[145] Ward, Journal MSS, Wednesday, October 20, 1802, 262 and Thursday, October 20, 1803, 337.
[146] Ward, *Reflections*, 1:76-77.
[147] Ward, *Reflections*, 1:132-133, 135-136, 285.
[148] Ward, *Reflections*, 1:107, 173.
[149] Ward, *Reflections*, 1:115.
[150] Ward, *Reflections*, 1:78, 92.
[151] Ward, Journal MSS, Lord's Day, June 14, 1807, 552.
[152] Ward, Journal MSS, Tuesday, December 16, 1806, 529-530.

Ward's Spirituality

could not release them as their friends in England had neither paid the freight nor included an invoice! Ward "immediately apologised," but chided Fuller: "No Invoice. Surely you could not have neglected to send one."[153]

Such humor is proof that Ward's humility was not morose. Marshman knew as much, emphasizing that Ward's "own experience, while always partaking of deep humility, was in general happy." Because of his desire for God's glory and to "promote the best interests of his fellow-men," it was "impossible for him to be either gloomy or melancholy."[154] While knowledge of God's goodness and his unworthiness laid him low, faith in Christ raised him high and filled him with confidence:

> We see then, that this is the confidence of faith; faith in a sacrifice of the Divine appointment, and through the Eternal Spirit offered up without spot to God; faith in a perfect righteousness; faith in the Divine mercy coming in a way consistent with the demands of justice; faith in the promises, and in the unchanging nature of the Promiser. ... But wherever this unlimited confidence prevails, it will be united with a tender conscience, and prevailing humility.[155]

Such dependence and confidence combined powerfully in another salient aspect of his spirituality, namely, prayer.

Prayer

While the Preamble to the *SFA* emphasizes the missionaries' dependence on God as he alone could "add to the church such as shall be saved,"[156] the final article reveals their conviction in

---

[153] Ward, Journal MSS, Thursday, July 28, 1803, 316.
[154] Joshua Marshman, *Divine Grace*, 54.
[155] Ward, *Reflections*, 2:83.
[156] *SFA*, Preamble in *PA*, 3:198.

the centrality of prayer as the means by which this dependence on God was expressed:

> That which, as a means, is to fit us for the discharge of these laborious and unutterably important labours, is the being instant in prayer, and the cultivation of personal religion. Let us ever have in remembrance the examples of those who have been most eminent in the work of God. Let us often look at Brainerd in the woods of America, pouring out his very soul before God for the perishing heathen, without whose salvation nothing could make him happy. Prayer, secret, fervent, believing prayer, lies at the root of all personal godliness. A competent knowledge of the languages current where a missionary lives, a mild and winning temper, and a heart given up to God in closet religion, these, these are the attainments which, more than all knowledge or all other gifts, will fit us to become the instruments of God in the great work of human redemption. Let us then ever be united in prayer at stated seasons, whatever distance may separate us, and let each one of us lay it upon his heart that we will seek to be fervent in spirit, wrestling with God, till he famish these idols, and cause the heathen to experience the blessedness that is in Christ.[157]

Similarly, in his daily devotional, *Reflections*, Ward writes,

> There is no religion where there is no prayer. The total neglect of prayer must be allied to atheism and the greatest impiety. Prayer is the highest privilege, and the most necessary duty of life: the last words men utter in this world are those of supplication. Even Paine could not help calling on the name of Jesus Christ in the hour of extremity.[158]

---

[157] *SFA*, art. X, in *PA*, 3:210.
[158] Ward, *Reflections*, 2:284.

Ward's Spirituality

One could ask for no better proof of the central importance that prayer held in Ward's spirituality than we find in the above quotes. Yet, there are many more examples which demonstrate the same. These examples fall into two categories; theology and practice.

Ward's theology of prayer is revealed in what he considered to be "real" or "true" prayer. Ward spoke of prayer in such terms because he realized it was possible to pray amiss.[159] When commenting on John 16:23, he was so bold as to quip,

> What is called the gift of prayer is too often no more than the gift of prating. No wonder, therefore, we have not the blessings mentioned in our petitions, for we really ask not. ... The reason why there is so little of the appearance of answers to prayer is, that so small a part of that which is called prayer is really such.[160]

So what did Ward consider "real prayer"? Ward elucidates:

> But much is not prayer which is called by that name: the heart is necessary; and not that only, for many a person in an hour of extremity calls upon God from his heart, but there are no correct desires in his petitions. The parable of the publican brings before us a man in the attitude of *real prayer*: he acknowledges his sin; he seeks Divine mercy; and he goes for it to the throne of grace: "God be merciful to me a sinner" (italics mine).[161]

First, "real prayer" flows from a sense of one's sin which is acknowledged to God even as petitions are expressed. Second,

---

[159] At one experience meeting while on board the *Criterion*, the missionaries discussed the question, "What is it to ask amiss in prayer?" Ward, Journal MSS, Thursday, September 19, 1799, 43.

[160] Ward, *Reflections*, 1:160-161.

[161] Ward, *Reflections*, 2:283.

this contrition is coupled with a keen sense of one's spiritual poverty:

> There can be no real prayer without a previous sense of want, and without what is called the spirit of prayer: now our Saviour bestows both these or we should never call on his name. We are not able to repent, but Christ is exalted as a Prince and a Saviour, "to *give* repentance." Faith is his gift; and all good thoughts and good works are impossible to us but as he renews within us "a right spirit."[162]

Ward knew that even where sin is recognized, it would be presumptive to think that one could repent of that sin and trust again in Christ in one's own strength. Repentance and belief are prerequisites for prayer, but "real prayer" takes place only when these flow from "correct desires;" in this case a recognition of one's own spiritual poverty. Speaking again of this spiritual lack Ward writes,

> To be found in this exercise is our constant duty, for, 1. We are always in want. A christian can never say respecting Divine supplies, "I have much goods laid up for many years." His heavenly Father keeps him always dependent, as the only state suited to his imperfect character.[163]

In summary, "real prayer" rises from a biblical understanding of God and oneself. It "follows true conversion" and "proceeds from the exciting influences of the Spirit of God."[164] In missions in particular "real prayer" is a "believing dependence" which looks to God to work the peculiar work of salvation in lost men's souls which he alone is qualified and able to do.[165] It looks

---

[162] Ward, *Reflections*, 1:174.
[163] Ward, *Reflections*, 1:181.
[164] Ward, *Reflections*, 1:273.
[165] Ward, *Farewell Letters*, 108.

Ward's Spirituality

within and sees insufficiency yet looks to God and finds an everlasting supply. It appropriates Christ's gifts of repentance and faith in response to God.

In addition, as seen in the following citations, "real prayer" operates according to God's will as held out to saints in the promises of his Word. "But what is *real prayer?* The desires of the mind, when excited to seek the good contained in the promise, form *real prayer.*"[166] Those praying on the basis of God's promises could pray with confidence, for God would surely keep his promises. Commenting on the Lord's Prayer, Ward elucidates,

> It is this kingdom for the coming of which we are taught to pray. And by our being directed to pray for its coming, we know that it must come, for the Almighty never makes that the subject of prayer which he does not mean to grant. That he is able thus to set it up, we have the most ample evidence. Nor are we to suppose that he will permit Satan to rob him of his glory. No; Satan himself shall be one of the greatest contributors to the divine glory, although he meant it not so.[167]

What did such strong convictions look like in practice? Ward's theology of prayer is seen in records of his personal devotion as well as in his participation in corporate prayer, both within and outside the Mission. Though the following account does not detail his biblical intake, it would seem that he aspired to study Scripture in its original languages and that toward that goal, he labored assiduously:

> I hope to begin to spend my time more regularly. Get up at six & get my Greek exercise before breakfast; translate Lat-

---

[166] Ward, *Reflections*, 1:181.
[167] Ward, *Reflections*, 1:151.

in, copy translations &c before dinner; after dinner read something pleasing; write my Journal & go to bed at ten o'clock.—I long to reduce my studies something more to rule.[168]

Ward also left behind a record of missionaries, writers, and devotional books which he esteemed. There is frequent mention of his love for and debt to the Moravians.[169] On the Lord's Day, August 18, 1799, we read, "In the afternoon I went & read part of John Bunyan's *Grace [A]bounding* to the sailors, catechized the boys, & prayed with them all."[170] On the Lord's Day, August 25, referencing Carey's trials, Ward is reminded of and quotes a line from a Philip Doddridge poem.[171] Other times he quotes lines from the poems and hymns of Isaac Watts (1674-1748).[172] On the Lord's Day, September 8, Ward "read of *Pilgrim's Progress* to the sailors."[173] The following month, shortly after arriving at Serampore, Ward notes, "This afternoon I took my umbrella & Watt's *Dissertations on the Trinity*, & went [for] a walk."[174] On another Lord's Day, Ward records, "Have been much blessed lately in reading Baxter's *Saint's Rest*."[175] To an

---

[168] Ward, Journal MSS, Saturday, June 8, 1799, 10-11.

[169] Ward, Journal MSS, Friday, June 21, 1799, 18; Monday, July 1, 1799, 22; Friday, August 9, 1799, 33.

[170] Ward, Journal MSS, Lord's Day, August 18, 1799, 36. John Bunyan (1628-1688) was a nonconformist pastor at the separatist church at Bedford, England. He spent many years in jail for his unwillingness to conform to English laws requiring conformity with the Established Church. While in jail, he wrote many works including his spiritual autobiography, *Grace Abounding to the Chief of Sinners* (ca. 1666) and the immensely popular, *The Pilgrim's Progress* (1678). Richard L. Greaves, "Bunyan, John (*bap.* 1628, d. 1688)," in *Oxford Dictionary of National Biography*, ed. H.C.G. Matthew and Brian Harrison, vol. 8 (Oxford: Oxford University Press, 2004).

[171] Ward, Journal MSS, Lord's Day, August 25, 1799, 38.

[172] Stennett, *Memoir*, 47.

[173] Ward, Journal, MSS, Lord's Day, September 8, 1799, 41. *Pilgrim's Progress* was written by John Bunyan.

[174] Ward, Journal MSS, Saturday, October 26, 1799, 53-54.

[175] Ward, Journal MSS, Lord's Day, July 13, 1800, 91. *The Saint's Everlasting Rest* by Richard Baxter (1615-1691).

Ward's Spirituality

enquirer whom Ward was counseling, he sent Thomas Boston's (1676-1732) *Human Nature In Its Fourfold State*.[176] Then, the *Friend of India* recorded in its obituary of Ward that, shortly before his death, while returning to Serampore in a boat with his wife, he read to her "a number of extracts from Brainerd."[177] These records of Ward's devotional preferences are noteworthy because they reveal that which he considered spiritually nourishing for the sustenance of his missionary endeavors as well as what he felt would benefit those around him (i.e. sailors, children, enquirers, and family members). They are yet more evidence that Ward drew from the Evangelical Calvinistic stream that flowed from the English Puritans, through the Evangelical Awakening of the 1740s, to his own day; a stream which included Presbyterians (Richard Baxter and David Brainerd), Congregationalists (Isaac Watts and Philip Doddridge), Moravians, and Baptists (John Bunyan).

Regarding Ward's attitude toward secret prayer, we read, "I feel the want of retirement now very much. I find that secret prayer is the staff of life to me, & without it I feel a void into which evil tempers, cares, &c. creep in."[178] One Lord's Day, we read that Ward spent in fasting and prayer "on account of the state of my own soul, the state of our church, & with a view to my expected journey, as well as to the ordinance of the Lord's-

---

[176] Ward, Journal MSS, Monday, November 28, 1808, 678. Thomas Boston was a minister in the Church of Scotland (Presbyterian) at Ettrick who was involved in the Marrow controversy (1717-1723) and wrote the widely read *Human Nature in its Fourfold State* in 1720 and 1729. P.G. Ryken, "Boston, Thomas (1676-1732)," in *Oxford Dictionary of National Biography*, ed. H.C.G. Matthew and Brian Harrison, vol. 6 (Oxford: Oxford University Press, 2004).

[177] Stennett, *Memoir*, 208. David Brainerd (1718-1747) was a missionary to the Delaware Indians in New Jersey. After Brainerd's death, his diary was edited and published in 1749 by Jonathan Edwards as *An Account of the Life of the Late Reverend Mr. David Brainerd*. James P. Walsh, "Brainerd, David," in *American National Biography*, ed. John A. Garraty and Mark C. Carnes, vol. 3 (Oxford: Oxford University Press, 1999). Brainerd's diary was an inspiration and encouragement to the Serampore missionaries.

[178] Ward, Journal MSS, Saturday, October 26, 1799, 53.

supper."[179] In another entry, after noting his doubt that Europeans would ever be useful in "converting souls by preaching in this country," he concluded that "God can do all things," and then, reaching as it were for the only means ordained for moving God to do so, Ward exclaimed, "Oh! now for one great effort of prayer—by every praying soul on earth, that this kingdom for the Hindoos [Hindus] may be taken by force.[180]

And pray the Mission did. Onboard the *Criterion*, it was the missionaries practice to gather on Mondays at 11 o'clock for prayer.[181] Then, as the Mission grew in Serampore, the entire family gathered monthly, again on Mondays for prayer.[182] There was special prayer called in periods of crisis such as the Persian Pamphlet Controversy.[183] There was Lord's Day morning prayer at Lal Bazaar Chapel in Calcutta.[184] There was a Monday evening prayer meeting in Calcutta.[185] Beyond Mission prayer meetings, there were also the periodic ecumenical prayer meetings at Rev. David Brown's (1763-1812) pagoda where Carey, Marshman, Ward, and other Serampore brethren often gathered with Anglicans Rev. Brown, Rev. Claudius Buchanan (1766-1815), and others to "pray for the success of the Gospel in India," and

---

[179] Ward, Journal MSS, Lord's Day, October 3, 1802, 259. The entries just prior to this one show that his colleague Marshman's evangelistic efforts had recently been ill received by locals after which he had been burned in effigy, and the previous evening young Petumber had been suspended from the Serampore church for beating his wife and was angry instead of repentant.

[180] Ward, Journal MSS, Monday, November 13 [15], 1802, 268. (It seems Potts inserted "15" in brackets in order to correct the day-date conflict in this entry. November 13, 1802 was a Saturday while Monday would have been November 15. Therefore, assuming Ward was correct in the identification of the day of the week and incorrect in his recording of the date, Potts makes this amendment.)

[181] Ward, Journal MSS, Monday, November 9, 16, 1799, 41-42.

[182] For example, see Ward, Journal MSS, Monday, January 4, 1802, 201; Monday, July 5, 1802, 242; Monday, February 3, 1806, 474.

[183] Ward, Journal MSS, Saturday, September 12, 1807, 591; Saturday, September 19, 1807, 594. The Persian Pamphlet Controversy is discussed at length in chapter 4.

[184] Ward, Journal MSS, Lord's Day, February 12, 1809, 688.

[185] Ward, Journal MSS, Monday, March 6, 1809, 690.

Ward's Spirituality

afterwards, often dined together in Rev. Brown's home.[186] In addition to these regular prayer meetings, Ward met occasionally with the younger missionaries in his room for prayer,[187] and strove to impress the importance of secret and family prayer on the nationals he mentored.[188]

The purpose and subject of these prayer meetings is not always stated. But seen against the backdrop of Ward's convictions and theology on prayer, they argue effectively that Ward personally, and the Mission family as a whole, practiced what they preached in the *SFA*. As Ward and his fellow missionaries believed that "God alone can add to the church such as shall be saved,"[189] they were also convicted that "that which, as a means, is to fit us for the discharge of these laborious and unutterably important labours, is the being instant in prayer."[190]

Given such conviction in the necessity and power of prayer, it is fitting that Ward's last gathering with the Serampore family was at the weekly prayer meeting the morning before his death. His memoirist notes that this meeting, established by Ward and his colleagues had continued virtually without interruption for twenty-two years.[191] Believing dependence, namely prayer, was a hallmark of Ward's spirituality throughout his missionary career.

---

[186] Ward, Journal MSS, Tuesday, June 2, 1807, 551. Before being in Rev. Brown's possession, this pagoda was a Hindu temple. On the banks of the Hooghly River, the pagoda still stands and is known now as Henry Martyn's Pagoda. For other examples of this ecumenical pagoda prayer meeting, see Ward, Journal MSS, Tuesday, July 8, 1806, 495; Lord's Day, December 7, 1806, 528; Lord's Day, January 4, 1807, 533; and Tuesday, January 20, 1807, 534.

[187] Ward, Journal MSS, Lord's Day, May 17, 1801, 153.

[188] Ward, Journal MSS, Friday, February 13, 1801, 139. In this entry, Ward writes, "I was enforcing the necessity of private prayer on Creeshnoo. He complained of the want of a secret place; but he said he went out into the fields & found much comfort. I asked him respecting asking a blessing on his food. He says he always since he received the love of Xt. attended to this; & he prays with his family morning & evening. He spends the sabbath in hearing & instructing his family."

[189] *SFA*, Preamble in *PA*, 3:198.

[190] *SFA*, art. X in *PA*, 3:210.

[191] Stennett, *Memoir*, 210. Interestingly, Ward, mentions a twenty year-long running prayer meeting that met on Tuesday mornings. Ward, *Farewell Letters*, 135.

The Spirituality of William Ward

What are we to make of such an emphasis on prayer? Would the time not have been better spent doing something more *useful*? On the contrary, Ward writes, "It has been remarked, that men the most eminently *useful* have been most eminent for the spirit of prayer. The Reformers and Puritans were bright examples of this" (italics mine).[192] For Ward, prayer was useful because it was getting things done God's way. In fact, in the whole of his spirituality, if something wasn't useful, Ward had little use for it.

Usefulness

Sometimes this strand of Ward's spirituality is expressed in the word "useful" or "usefulness," and at other times, by the synonyms "practical," "experimental," and "profitable," but the idea is the same. Ward had no interest in virtue or doctrine in an abstract sense. But Ward esteemed *applied* virtue and doctrine greatly.

For this reason, usefulness is not prominent in Ward's spirituality in the same way love, humility, and prayer are. Instead, as seen above with prayer, Ward considered usefulness a necessary complement to other virtues. Where "useful" and eminent men were found, a spirit of prayer was found as well. Ward's longtime colleague, Joshua Marshman found the same to be true of the spiritual trait of love. In a sermon at his friend's funeral, Joshua Marshman declined to comment on whether Ward had exhibited sufficient amounts of love to give assurance of his spiritual state. But regarding the necessity of the presence of love in Ward's life, Marshman confidently asserted that "of this we are certain, that on the degree of love he bears to the Redeemer as the Almighty Saviour of men, will be suspended all his usefulness to his fellow-men as a Christian."[193] Ward might be remembered for many good things, but he could never be considered a "faithful

---

[192] Ward, *Reflections*, 1:93.
[193] Joshua Marshman, *Divine Grace*, 42.

Ward's Spirituality

and able minister of the New Testament" without love.[194] So important was the experiential nature of the gospel ministry that Marshman exclaimed,

> To approach the heart either of the saint or the sinner, he must with the Apostle John be able to say, "that which we have seen, and handled, and felt of the word of life, declare we unto you," ... Such was the grace given to our deceased brother, as appeared from the whole tenor of his conversation, and from almost every page he published of a religious nature.[195]

It wasn't enough merely to proclaim the word of life. The bearer of such news must have "seen" and "handled" it. So, when Marshman considered his deceased friend's ministry, he was confident that Ward, by God's grace, had done just that. Ward did not proclaim a cold gospel, but rather one that welcomed others into fellowship with himself, and through that, into fellowship with the Father and Christ, his Son. As seen in the following passage, Ward considered experimental faith the high ground between two dangerous ditches:

> Remember, my dear brother, there is a happy medium betwixt the torrid zone of Antinomianism, and the frigid zone of Socinianism. There is a connecting of doctrine, experience and precept together; let us hold these fast together; they are twins that must never be separated; if any one of them be cast away, the other two will pine and die.[196]

---

[194] Joshua Marshman, *Divine Grace*, 43.
[195] Joshua Marshman, *Divine Grace*, 43.
[196] Ward to an unknown correspondent, n.d., quoted in Stennett, *Memoir*, 241. Antinomianism is an ancient error which misconstrues grace as licentiousness. Playing devil's advocate to proponents of this ilk, the Apostle Paul asks, "What shall we say then? Are we to continue in sin that grace may abound? By no means! How can we who died to sin still live in it" (Rom. 6:1-2)? In Ward's mind, this was one ditch on the road to salvation (i.e. all doctrine [of grace] and no practice). But on the other

Stennett goes on to comment that Ward was "zealously and experimentally attached to the great doctrines of grace."[197] Similarly, Ward holds godliness to be "useful" in that it "is the devotion of the heart and life to religion."[198] Ward extolled "experimental religion" in the life of Samuel Pearce,[199] but mitigated his praise of Mr. Parson's mostly evangelical sermon because it was, "too florid."[200] Instead of such intricacy and abstruseness in the pulpit, Ward advised Stennett to

> study to be quiet—but above all, study to get at the affections, the consciences, and the false refuges of sinners:—study to be useful—then you will become a spiritual father, when, to borrow the strong language of the apostle, *you labour in birth again, till Christ is formed in the hearts of men, the hope of Glory*. If you become a useful [preacher], you will first be (as the Puritans said) a painful preacher of the gospel.[201]

Ward cherished doctrinal sermons. But though a sermon be rich in doctrine, if it had "neither devotion nor practice," Ward considered it to be "rather worse than nothing."[202] Ultimately, for Ward, a man was shown to be a useful gospel minister as far

---

side of the road was the ditch of Socinianism, based on the teaching of Faustus Socinus (1539-1604), which was antitrinitarian, denying the divinity of Christ, and which eventually gave rise to Unitarianism. Wayne Grudem, *Systematic Theology; An Introduction To Biblical Doctrine* (Grand Rapids: Zondervan, 2000), 581 n19. Modern Unitarianism, eschewing both creeds and Scripture, operates according to the dictates of reason and conscience, which can be trusted as human nature is considered essentially good. So, Unitarianism, in Ward's mind represented the opposite extreme (i.e. experience alone mattered, but without any biblically informed doctrinal parameters). *The Oxford Dictionary of the Christian Church*, ed. F.L. Cross and E.A. Livingstone (Oxford: Oxford University Press, 2009), s.v. "Unitarianism."

[197] Stennett, *Memoir*, 241.
[198] Ward, *Reflections*, 2:91.
[199] Stennett, *Memoir*, 58-59.
[200] Ward, Journal MSS, Lord's Day, October 19, 1806, 518.
[201] Stennett, *Memoir*, 121-122.
[202] Stennett, *Memoir*, 119-120.

Ward's Spirituality

as his "zeal ... gifts ... efforts, and ... conduct, [were] calculated to produce the conversion of souls."[203] Without usefulness, other spiritual traits were incomplete.

Conclusion

At the time of his death, Ward was working on a "treatise on the character of the Christian missionary, drawn from the life of St. Paul."[204] It has been asserted that the Apostle Paul is both the greatest theologian and the greatest missionary in the history of Christianity. Ward was astute theologically, standing solidly in the Evangelical Calvinistic stream of his day. As shown, his theological convictions formed the underpinning for his spirituality, of which love, humility, prayerfulness, and usefulness were most prominent. But Paul had a missionary heart that manifest itself in very practical ways. Ward noted that the Apostle Paul "was not a cold-blooded, official man, delivering a message with stoical indifference, but he was, in his work, like a man in the midst of a perishing crew after a wreck."[205] Theology and missiology. Doctrine and practice. Spirituality is where all of these coalesce in a single life. Some of a more precise theological persuasion might get nervous upon encountering Ward's warm-hearted, yet ill-defined "creed of love."[206] Others of a broader, liberal mind would likely cringe at the abundance of specifically Calvinistic language that permeates Ward's writings. When considered as a whole however, Ward's spirituality resembles that of the subject of his final treatise. Like the Apostle Paul, Ward was both theological and missiological; concerned for doctrine, but moved by a warm-hearted love for the lost.

---

[203] Stennett, *Memoir*, 119.
[204] Marshman, *Life and Times*, 2:250; Smith, *Serampore Enterprise*, 42.
[205] Stennett, *Memoir*, 251-52.
[206] See page 99 of this work.

3

"When brothers dwell in unity": Ward's Spirituality in Relationships

To what degree and extent did Ward's spirituality promote peace within the Serampore Trio and preserve the Mission as a whole? Thus far we have examined the background to Ward's spirituality in terms of his familial and religious upbringing, the missionary roles in which Ward's spirituality was manifest, the theological heritage and framework from which his spirituality springs, and most recently those aspects of Ward's spirituality which emerge as most prominent when key primary sources are considered. This chapter examines Ward's spirituality in the context of relationships, including both those closest to Ward within the sphere of the Serampore Trio, as well as those within the broader evangelical community in Serampore and Calcutta. In both cases, it is evident that Ward's spirituality had a calming, harmonizing effect which promoted peace.

Amongst the Trio

Though frequent mention has been made of the Trio of Carey, Marshman, and Ward, there were many other missionaries that labored alongside them that comprised the greater Serampore Mission. These were sent out from the BMS and arrived in India in different waves as it were. William Carey (1761-1834) and John Thomas (1757-1801), who had earlier served as surgeon on a ship of the East India Company,[1] arrived in 1793. In 1796, John Fountain (1767-1800) arrived, though he was not a great help to

---

[1] Penelope Carson, *Worlds of The East India Company*, vol. 7, *The East India Company and Religion, 1698-1858* (Woodbridge, UK: The Boydell Press, 2012), 31.

the cause.[2] In 1799, piloted by the pious Captain Wickes aboard the American *Criterion*, the next BMS instalment arrived consisting of Daniel Brunsdon (1777-1801) and William Grant (1774-1799) and their wives, Joshua and Hannah Marshman (1768-1837 and 1767-1847), Miss Mary Tidd, and William Ward, at that time, a bachelor.[3] Within two years of the latter group's arrival, Grant, Fountain, Brunsdon, and Thomas were dead, leaving only William Carey, William Ward, the Marshmans, and Mary Tidd Fountain—the widow of John Fountain, who would soon become Ward's wife. These early missionaries represent a first wave of pioneering missionaries who were largely responsible for establishing and building up the Mission at Serampore.

Leading a second wave, John Chamberlain (1777-1821) and his wife arrived in 1803, followed by William Moore (1776-1844), Joshua Rowe (1781-1823), John Biss (1776-1807), John Mardon (1776-1812) and their wives in 1805, and James Chater (1806-1829) and William Robinson (1754-1853) in 1806. A third wave of missionaries including William Johns, John Lawson (d. 1825), Eustace Carey (1791-1855), William Yates (1792-1845), William H. Pearce, James Penney (1816-1839), and William Adam (1796-1881) and their wives, were sent out between 1812 and 1818. Though at times rocky, the Trio had a cordial relationship with missionaries of the second wave who had mixed success in their missionary labors. These at least tried to cooperate with the Mission's strategy of establishing outstations beyond Serampore that locals might be converted and trained and propagate the gospel of Christ throughout India and beyond. The third wave of

---

[2] John Clark Marshman, *The Life and Times of Carey, Marshman And Ward* (1859; repr., Serampore: Council of Serampore College, 2005), 1:75.

[3] At the time of this voyage, Mary Tidd was the fiancée of John Fountain who had already arrived in Bengal. After the missionaries arrived in Serampore, John and Mary were married, but Mary was widowed before they reached their first anniversary. William Ward married Fountain's widow in May 1802.

Spirituality in Relationships

missionary recruits, however; had outright conflict with the Trio and eventually seceded from the Serampore Mission.[4]

Though Carey preceded Marshman and Ward in India by six years and was therefore far ahead of his colleagues in language ability, their joint labor and shared struggle in establishing the Mission forged an intimate friendship and an inseparable bond between them that would not exist with their younger colleagues that were to follow. Though differing significantly in personality and gifting, Carey, Marshman, and Ward enjoyed a peculiar unity in a missions partnership that endured for an extraordinary twenty-three years. And in times of rare disagreement, it was often the irenic Ward who showed a way forward.

Trio's Personalities Contrasted

Though Carey, Marshman, and Ward enjoyed a peculiar unity, their personalities were anything but similar. And though friends, they did not hesitate to candidly describe each other's faults and idiosyncrasies. It quickly becomes apparent that Marshman had the most colorful personality of the three. Interestingly, described by Ward, Marshman's quirks are often amusing.

Early in their voyage to India, Ward writes, "Had some sweet chat with dr Capt. Wickes; & afterwards some of an unpleasant nature with Bro. M. tho' I was not implicated so that it was morning before I retired to rest."[5] Around the same time, Ward recollects Marshman's evening "contest with a Deist" and an-

---

[4] Years of arrival in India for most of the missionaries mentioned here can be easily found by consulting the table of contents in volumes one and two of J.C. Marshman's *The Life and Times of Carey, Marshman, and Ward*. A thought-provoking discussion of the differences between the Trio and following classes of BMS recruits and their increasingly strained relationships can be found in chapter 4, "The Older and Younger Generations of Missionaries in Pre-Victorian Serampore," in A. Christopher Smith, *The Serampore Missionary Enterprise* (Bangalore: Centre for Contemporary Christianity, 2006), 83-123.

[5] William Ward, Journal MSS, Thursday, July 4, 1799, 24.

The Spirituality of William Ward

other passenger named, King, concluding wryly, "I suppose they were both conquered."[6] Marshman was loquacious in prayer and notorious for failing to return books he had borrowed.[7] In his zeal, Marshman was willing to debate a subject few men would dare, namely, a woman's choice of her wardrobe!

> Marshman came down [to Calcutta] to try to prevail upon Sister Biss to give up her white clothes & the children's & receive an equivalent for them, instead of taking them to England, where people will wonder to see a Missionary's wife so fine. Bro. Marshman's a good hand in getting thro' a disagreeable job, though I fancy Sister Biss is none so fond of his arguments against her thin clothes.[8]

Sometimes, Marshman's polemics got him into hot water, but Carey and Ward, though acknowledging Marshman's foibles, highly valued their impetuous friend and were quick to rise to his defense. Following hostilities that had flared up between junior missionaries and Marshman—hostilities which Marshman's son notes were *not* directed towards Ward—Carey writes to Andrew Fuller:

> I do not know that the junior brethren have any settled prejudice against him, yet a suspicion against him is, I must confess, soon excited. I believe his natural make is the occasion of it. He is a man whose whole heart is in the

---

[6] Ward, Journal MSS, Lord's Day, June 30, 1799, 22.

[7] Of Marshman's participation in a Brethren's Conference, Ward notes, "Brother M. was too long in prayer." Ward, Journal MSS, Saturday, August 31, 1799, 40. So much did Marshman's book borrowing habits vex one lender that he informed Marshman, "And now with respect to the books which you have recollected so well to return, you have made me tell more lies than any good Scotchman ever did on the same subject, by not sending them as I expected." After listing numerous specific titles that were overdue and others that had been damaged while in Marshman's possession, he exclaims, "You have cracked your credit with the whole circle of book-lenders." Marshman, *Life and Times*, 1:435-436.

[8] Ward, Journal MSS, Lord's Day, December 28, 1806, 532.

Spirituality in Relationships

mission, and who may be considered as the soul and life of it. He is ardent, nay sanguine, exceedingly tenacious of any idea which strikes him as right or important. His labours are excessive, his body scarcely susceptible of fatigue, his religious feelings strong, his jealousy for God great; his regard for the feelings of others very little when the cause of God is in question. His memory is uncommonly retentive; his reading has been and still is extensive and general; in short, his activity reproaches the indolence of some, his acquirements reproach their ignorance, and his unaccommodating mind frequently excites sentiments of resentment and dislike. He has also, perhaps, the foible of dragging himself and his children more into public observation than is desirable. These things, I suppose, lie at the bottom of all the dislike which our younger brethren have felt for him. For my own part I consider him as a man whose value in the mission can scarcely be sufficiently appreciated, and his death would be a serious loss to the undertaking.[9]

In a difficult time between the deaths of two fellow missionaries, Ward also wrote of the Mission's dependence on Marshman and Carey:

The loss of brother Brunsdon will be severely felt. Upon the life of brother Marshman depends, in some measure, half our support, by the school. Upon the life of brother Carey depends the translation, and more than I can describe. I am happy in thinking, that if I die, Felix Carey will be able to print. But, I assure you, it cannot be conceived how necessary we seem to each other. Our love to one another grows exceedingly, and every new death makes us cling the closer.[10]

---

[9] Marshman, *Life and Times*, 1:463–464. The letter containing this quote appears to be addressed to Andrew Fuller and is included in with other material from 1811 in Marshman's work.

[10] Ward to a friend, March 24, 1801, quoted in Samuel Stennett, *Memoirs of The Life of the Rev. William Ward, Late Baptist Missionary in India; Containing A Few Of*

Transitioning to the senior member of the Trio, Carey offers an interesting insight regarding his own personality compared to that of Marshman's:

> Marshman ... is all eagerness for the work [of making Christ known]. Often I have seen him when we have been walking together, eye a group of persons, exactly as a hawk looks on his prey, and go up to them with a resolution to try the utmost strength of gospel reasons upon them. Often have I known him engage with such ardour in a dispute with men of lax conduct or deistical sentiments, and labour the point with them for hours together without fatigue, nay more eager for the contest when he left off than when he begun as has filled me with shame. In point of zeal he is a Luther and I am Erasmus.[11]

Like Erasmus, Carey spent much time with manuscripts, laboring long hours translating the Holy Scriptures into the vernacular languages of the subcontinent. This was essential to the Mission's strategy for propagating the gospel in India. And according to Ward, Carey was well suited for that particular task though not as well suited for others:

> Brother Carey is half his time at Calcutta, and his soul is in translation. He is cut out exactly for sitting doggedly to such an immense work. But he is not cut out for an itiner-

---

His Early Poetical Productions, And A Monody to His Memory (London: Simpkin and Marshall, 1825), 93-94.

[11] Carey to John Ryland, May 24, 1810, letter no. 33 in the College Street Baptist Church's (Northampton) collection of BMS manuscripts, quoted in Smith, *Serampore Enterprise*, 37. John Clark Marshman also reprints a larger portion of this letter in *Life and Times*, 1:433. Desiderius Erasmus (1467?-1536) was a Dutch humanist who is most remembered for his edition of the Greek New Testament with accompanying Latin translation and annotations which was first published in 1516. The second edition, published in 1519, served as the basis for Luther's German translation of the Bible. James McConica, "Erasmus, Desiderius," in *The Oxford Encyclopedia of the Reformation*, ed. Hans J. Hillerbrand, vol. 2 (Oxford: Oxford University Press, 1996).

Spirituality in Relationships

ant, for talking to enquirers, for watching over and regulating 100 little things belonging to a Mission Settlement where there are 20 or 30 native brethren, who must be advised with, admonished, watched tenderly and encouraged in a holy walk. Brother Carey can pursue one thing with the greatest steadiness, industry and patience. ... But he is not cut out for embracing a multiplicity of objects, and regulating a machine which has many important parts and combinations. In many important instances his advice has done much for the mission, for he is possessed of great prudence. But he is not cut out for seizing on opportunities, pursuing advantages, and pushing on a work with zeal.[12]

But Carey's singular focus on translation efforts meant that he was often not available at the Mission. Later in the same letter, there is a tinge of bitterness in Ward's voice as he laments this reality:

Plans for extending the Mission, for seizing upon some present advantage and carrying it to good account, &, & [sic] scarcely ever originate with Brother Carey, who goes on like a child pursuing his darling object the Translation of the Scriptures.[13]

Regarding Ward's personality, much has already been said, but the following excerpt is worthwhile to demonstrate his worth in the eyes of his colleagues. After comparing Marshman and himself to Luther and Erasmus, Carey writes of Ward,

Brother Ward has such a facility of addressing spiritual things to the heart, and his thoughts run so naturally in

---

[12] Ward to Fuller, October 7, 1805, pp. 3ff., BMS reel no. 44, box IN 17, quoted in Smith, *Serampore Enterprise*, 34.

[13] Ward to Fuller, October 7, 1805, p. 4 quoted in Smith, *Serampore Enterprise*, 304.

that channel, that he fixes the minds of all who hear him on what he says, while I, after making repeated efforts, can scarcely get out a few dry sentences.[14]

While Marshman could force his way in where he was not wanted, Carey could remain aloof where he was wanted. Marshman could be too narrow, while Ward could be too broad.[15] But Marshman's initiative compensated for Carey's reluctance in taking up new opportunities. And Carey and Ward's irenic nature offset Marshman's polemic nature. This give and take within the Trio, the liberty given to each other to specialize in his respective area of gifting, their willingness to bear with each other in love, and their common mission goal, made possible a sweet unity that transcended their differences. So strong was the bond of love between them, that his unity was preserved in times of peace as well as disagreement.

Peculiar Unity
In March of 1802 Ward describes a Mission incident in which two native brethren, Gokol and Unna, apparently with some complaint, went down to Calcutta to see Carey in order to "take him [Carey] by surprise, I suppose. But he sent them away, declaring he would hear nothing by himself, & that they would only be heard at Serampore."[16] At this stage, the Mission had been bereaved of William Grant, John Fountain, and Daniel Brunsdon. Dr. Thomas' presence was sporadic, and John Chamberlain had not yet arrived. So, Carey's insistence that these brethren would only be heard at Serampore was tantamount to

---

[14] Carey to John Ryland, May 24, 1810 quoted in Marshman, *Life and Times*, 1:433-434. This portion of Carey's letter is also found in Smith, *Serampore Enterprise*, 37 and 37 n14.

[15] As shown in Ward's "Creed of Love," (see p. 99 of this work) his doctrinal imprecision could at times leave the door open for unbiblical interpretation.

[16] Ward, Journal MSS, Friday, March 5, 1802, 215.

Spirituality in Relationships

saying that they would only be heard by the Trio. This is an early, practical example of how Carey, Marshman, and Ward functioned as one. Looking back from a distance of two hundred years, Smith acknowledges their unity:

> They were amazingly close-knit as a leadership team. For several decades they complemented one another in an intricate way. Indeed, very few people in Britain ever realized how dependent Carey was on his partners for insight and a wide range of initiatives.[17]

In a personal letter from 1802, Ward offers his own description of the Trio's unity:

> I have hitherto enjoyed uninterrupted health and good spirits. With my dear brethren Carey and Marshman I live in the closest friendship; we are altogether a happy family, considering our bereavements. All our real wants are abundantly supplied.[18]

Seven years later, Ward's feelings were unchanged:

> My dear brethren Carey and Marshman are well, thanks be to God. We are one heart, and if there were any brethren like them rising up, I should think the Baptist Mission was destined to effect an amazing work indeed.[19]

Interestingly, Ward was not the only one to recognize how much the Mission stood to gain if she could but receive more missionaries of the Trio's ilk. After recording the difficulties

---

[17] Smith, *Serampore Enterprise*, 3.
[18] Ward to an unknown correspondent, January 16, 1802, quoted in Stennett, *Memoirs*, 105.
[19] Ward to an unknown correspondent, January 14, 1809, quoted in Stennett, *Memoirs*, 164.

The Spirituality of William Ward

Carey and Ward had been experiencing with the second wave of missionaries who had arrived in 1803 and 1804, J.C. Marshman records a comment regarding the Trio's comparative worth made by their Anglican friend, the Rev. David Brown:

> I am convinced Fuller ought to have come out. Weakness ruined the missionary efforts of the London Missionary Society, and weakness would have ruined yours, if Carey, yourself, and Ward had not been providentially in the way. You ask for *forty* missionaries; I ask for *five* such as yourselves.[20]

This solidarity on the field was matched by a similar "Trio" in England. Speaking of John Sutcliff's death in 1814, J.C. Marshman writes,

> He had been Mr. Fuller's associate for twenty-two years. The mission appeared to be as much identified with the names of Fuller, Sutcliff, and Ryland, in England, as with those of Carey, Marshman, and Ward, in India. There was the same unison of heart and feeling in the triumvirate at home as in that abroad.[21]

In addition, both Trios were intimately connected. Following Andrew Fuller's death in the following year, the younger Marshman speaks of the intimate bond that united Fuller to the

---

[20] Rev. David Brown to Joshua Marshman, n.d., quoted in Marshman, *Life and Times*, 1:458.

[21] Marshman, *Life and Times*, 2:86. Smith agrees with Marshman's assessment, adding, "Carey would have been horrified to think, for example, that he was being credited with the wisdom of men such as Andrew Fuller, John Ryland, John Sutcliff, or Charles Grant – not to mention his own partners and a host of other expatriates in Bengal. That is why a somewhat 'trinitarian' approach is called for, which sees Carey as one member of a triumvirate, and which recognizes that he was greatly indebted to three immediate groups of people: the Baptist Missionary Society home-base troika of Fuller, Ryland, and Sutcliff; a sizable number of Orientalists and *pandits* (learned men) in Bengal; and his own close colleagues along with their dedicated wives." (Smith, *Serampore Enterprise*, 3)

Spirituality in Relationships

Trio across the miles:

> The connection between the three missionaries at Serampore and Mr. Fuller was characterised by that identity of feeling which seems to belong peculiarly to the early stages of a great undertaking, when congenial minds are absorbed in removing the obstacles which impede the prosecution of it. They began the enterprise together, and they pursued it with unbroken unanimity. Though separated from each other by the distance of half the globe, they appeared to be intuitively acquainted with each other's thought and feelings, and their mutual communications were marked by the total absence of any feeling of reserve.[22]

Marshman's account of Fuller's unity with the Trio is a bit hagiographical. As will be seen in this and the following chapter of this work, the Trio did not always see eye to eye with Fuller or each other on all matters. But compared to the developing friction between the Trio and a growing alliance of recent missionary recruits and an expanding Society back home, the unity of home and foreign Trios is noteworthy. On the field the unity amongst the Trio is seen both when they saw eye to eye as well as when they didn't.

Unity in times of agreement
On the field, given Carey's desire that Marshman and Ward be "united to him in the pastorship," the three served together as co-pastors of the church in Serampore.[23] In January 1809, when the Dissenting chapel opened at Lal Bazaar in Calcutta, the Trio

---

[22] Marshman, *Life and Times*, 2:103.
[23] Ward, Journal MSS, Lord's Day, July 14, 1805, 427. This desire was shortly thereafter fulfilled when Ward was named co-pastor along with Marshman and Carey at the Serampore church on October 5, 1805. Ward, Journal MSS, October 5, 1805, 440.

again served jointly as its pastors.[24] When junior missionary, John Chamberlain, refused to take his turn in superintending the Mission family, Ward writes that "we gave him a verbal answer, & talked to him about refusing to take a part of the burden of the family."[25] Two years later, when a disgruntled Chamberlain threatened to withdraw from the Mission, the Trio was again united in their response. "A letter to Bro. Chamberlain has been agreed to in reply to his; giving him 3 months to consider & pray about the propriety of separating from us."[26]

The depth of the Trio's unity is evident in a poignant excerpt from Ward's Journal when he and Marshman faced the bleak prospects of a Mission bereft of its senior most member:

> While Bro. Carey was ill & his recovery appeared very doubtful, Bro. M & I had one or two conversations on the probable consequences to our work of his removal. Though the blow would have shaken the Mission very seriously, yet I hope we might have carried on most of our works. Oh! that I could see any rising up to stop the gap, but I fear that the removal of Bro. Carey will leave a gulph in the Mission which will never be filled up; and at present I see no single ray of light that promises to dispense the heavy gloom that hangs over this Mission by the removal of its elder members. To depend upon unconverted children or incompetent brethren is a folly that will be rued when too late, I fear.[27]

---

[24] The Trio continued to serve as co-pastors at Lal Bazaar Chapel "until 16 June 1825, when the Survivors of them, the Revd. Dr. Carey and Marshman resigned the Pastorate publicly on the ordination of the Revd. W. Robinson" who served from that day until November the 11, 1838. *Lal Bazar Baptist Church, Calcutta Letter-Book & Records With _____y, December 1876 to April 1885*, 443.

[25] Ward, Journal MSS, Friday, July 15, 1803, 313.

[26] Ward, Journal MSS, Saturday, March 30, 1805, 414.

[27] Ward, Journal MSS, Wednesday, August 9, 1809, 700-701. The context of Carey's illness and Ward's comment on the same is salient. The pages prior to this entry detail Chamberlain and William Robinson's frequent struggles with anger, Robinson's frustrated attempt to enter Bhutan, Felix Carey and James Chater's

Spirituality in Relationships

A few final examples of the Trio's unity will be given from the post-Fuller period in the Mission which was overshadowed by frequent strife with the BMS. During this conflict, known as the Serampore Controversy, different members of the Trio periodically came under attack. And time and again, the band of three responded to accusations as one. A brief summary of the origins of the Serampore Controversy will provide the context for the Trio's stands of solidarity in the face of opposition.[28]

Following Fuller's death, the Trio received a letter from John Ryland indicating a changing climate in the Society with regard to the Trio and larger Mission. In particular, questions began to be raised regarding ownership of property and the direction of the Mission in Serampore. Did it belong to the Serampore Mission or the BMS? After examining all of the pertinent deeds, Ward drew up a "comfortable settlement" which sought to safeguard the Mission's independence, which had been assumed from the beginning when BMS funds were inadequate to support the Mission, and maintain the "confidence of the society." This settlement Ward presented to his colleagues while sending a confidential copy of the same to a friend on the committee. The conflagration began when this private correspondence was made public at the BMS annual meeting in October, 1816. Without waiting to inquire, an unauthorized sub-committee of the BMS "resolved to accept the offer of their brethren at Serampore, to undertake on behalf of the society the direction of the missionaries already under their care," assuming that this included all of the outlying mission stations which Serampore would henceforth manage "on behalf of the society."[29] But in resigning control of

---

difficulty in entering Burma. And all this took place after Richard Mardon's admission that he didn't feel able for the task (of entering Burma), the death of Felix's wife, dissension by one Clark, and frequent backslidings by numerous national believers.

[28] This summary is taken from Marshman, *Life and Times*, 2:137-144.

[29] Marshman, *Life and Times*, 2:139.

missionaries, the Trio had in view only, those European missionaries that the Society supported already.

The news of this resolution was the first correspondence from the Society that the Mission had received following Fuller's death, and it was a harbinger of more acrimonious correspondence to come. Concerns intensified when, unbeknownst to the Trio, Mrs. Ward returned from England with Samuel Pearce's son, William Pearce, whom the Society had taken the liberty to appoint as Ward's assistant in the Printing Office. At another time, the Trio might have welcomed such an able addition to the Mission. But given the current situation and Fuller's prior instruction to outgoing recruits that "they were not to settle at Serampore but on the express invitation of the senior missionaries," his arrival was disconcerting. At this point, Ward wrote a letter to his colleagues in which he exclaimed,

> I repeat it, the property here must not be left in the hands of men at such a distance, whose servants full of envy and ill will are placed all around, and who will never cease to make the lives of our successors a hell upon earth if those successors live on premises belonging to the society in an unqualified sense, or in other words, premises which are common property.[30]

Regrettably, it was Marshman, not Ward, who was tasked with making a reply to the Society. And more regrettable still, his son admitted that "his letter is one of the least happy of his productions. ... The demands of the society were unequivocally rejected, and the spirit of domination to which they were traced was rebuked with no little acerbity."[31] Needless to say, the letter did not go over well in England, and "an attempt was made ... to

---

[30] Marshman, *Life and Times*, 2:142.
[31] Marshman, *Life and Times*, 2:143.

Spirituality in Relationships

attribute it exclusively to Dr. Marshman's machinations," but J.C. Marshman elucidates that Carey claimed full responsibility and argues that the elder Marshman's letter was in agreement with an alternative proposal Ward had already submitted to his colleagues in the letter from which the above extract is taken.[32] Thus the younger Marshman writes, "The letter must therefore be considered as expressing the unanimous opinion of the three colleagues."[33] Though Carey and Ward could have hung Marshman out to dry and secured favor for themselves with the Society by moderating their position, they refused to do so, and chose instead, to stand with their friend in asserting the Mission's right to control the fruits of their labor.

A year later, following the formation by the junior missionaries of a separate union in Calcutta, one new missionary, William Adam "addressed a valedictory letter to the missionaries, containing severe reflections on Dr. Marshman."[34] Again, J.C. Marshman records that Carey and Ward stood by their friend:

> Dr. Carey and Mr. Ward united in replying to it, and stated that they had now lived in the same family with Dr. Marshman for nearly twenty years, and had seen him in all the varied and trying events of this long period, and could not but feel disgust at the wanton and unjust attack on that which to him, at the close of a long and most active and honourable career, must be dearer to him than life itself—his unblemished character. They pronounced these aspersions to be unfounded and calumnious, and stated that they were more likely to know Dr. Marshman's character than Mr. Adam, by all the difference existing between a most intimate union of nearly twenty years, and the distant observation of a few weeks. The letter concluded with these expressions: "It is our earnest wish that, after you

---

[32] Marshman, *Life and Times*, 2:143–144.
[33] Marshman, *Life and Times*, 2:144.
[34] Marshman, *Life and Times*, 2:166.

have lived as long as Dr. Marshman in India, you may find your character as unspotted as his, that your labours have been as incessant and successful as his, that your disinterestedness may prove to have been as great as his, who has from heavy labour devoted what might have been a large fortune to the cause of God, and that in your advanced years you may have the same blessed prospect of glory and immortality as are enjoyed, we doubt not, by our beloved brother.[35]

But even more telling is that their unity was also preserved in times of disagreement.

Unity in times of disagreement
It is not without warrant that Carey, Marshman, and Ward are renowned for their unity. But the following examples demonstrate the Trio's unity was not because of the absence of differing opinions, but rather because of their willingness to compromise and even acquiesce when necessary that they might go forward peaceably. In these efforts, Ward often led the way.

In February of 1803, we find the following frank admission of Ward's desire that Carey would be less with his students at Fort William College in Calcutta and more in Serampore that he might aid them in the work:

> This day brother Carey went down to Calcutta. He has more students this term, & the other teachers teach every day in the week. He is therefore obliged to teach 4 days of the week, & to be one day more at Calcutta. This is rather

---

[35] Marshman, *Life and Times*, 2:166–167. Sadly, time would prove Adam a deserter both to the BMS and the Christian faith as he embraced Unitarianism and "along with Rammohun (Roy) and a few other Indian and European friends, formed the Calcutta Unitarian Society." He would go on to be a Unitarian minister and advocate in the United States. Andrew Hill, "William Adam," *Dictionary of Unitarian & Universalist Biography*, eds. Barry Andrews, et al., accessed November 28, 2018, http://uudb.org/articles/williamadam.html.

Spirituality in Relationships

a painful circumstance, as the affairs of the Mission swell much on our hands, & there is a great necessity for our being often together to consult on the different cases, & the temporal as well as spiritual concerns of the native converts. I am sometimes bowed down with Missionary cares.[36]

A few months later, in a letter to Andrew Fuller, Ward, though showing deference to his older colleague, felt it his duty to write that he differed from Carey's opinion "very much:"

Brother Marshman mentioned to me in conversation a little while ago, that Bro. Carey had written home an opinion that four or five Missionaries were sufficient at once here. You will very properly give much weight to the opinions of Bro. Carey; yet I find it duty to say that I differ from this opinion very much with some explanations which I now give.[37]

In this letter Ward goes on to tell Fuller that he feels instead that they need two or three missionaries for the school, two for the printing office (so that one could print and one could be freed to itinerate), one brother to meet with enquirers and to "adjust the affairs of the family, & of our native brethren," one or two more brethren "constantly itinerating with one or more of the native brethren," plus other brothers to place at other mission stations such as Dinajpur and Goamalty.[38]

On this matter Ward's opinions were decidedly different from Carey's. This difference is significant, for the optimum number of workers and the manner in which these workers

---

[36] Ward, Journal MSS, Monday, February, 21, 1803, 283.

[37] Ward to Fuller, August 24, 1803, *BMS Missionary Correspondence; William Ward; Transcript of Diaries in 2 Books Comprising 4 Volumes; Book 1 (Vols. 1 & 2) 1799-1805; Book 2 (Vols. 3 & 4) 1806-1811*, microfilm; reel 44, publication no. 5350 (London: Baptist Missionary Society Archives, 1981).

[38] Ward to Fuller, August 24, 1803, *BMS Missionary Correspondence*.

should work with native brethren are matters of no mean importance in a mission. Splits and separate missions can easily result over the same. But this was not the result at the Serampore Mission. Ward's forthright but humble posture made possible a unity in diversity.

A month later, there was another disagreement concerning the proper response, "respecting a baptized native's duty if he have more than one wife." But instead of forcing a decision either by submission to the Mission's founder or even by putting the matter to a vote that a majority might be determined, we read, "We were not agreed in opinion, but the subject is to be discussed every sabbath-day after dinner till we are."[39]

Two years later, the members of the Trio were disagreed as to whether it was prudent to allow Ram Mohun, a native convert, to accompany Mr. Maylin and John Fernandez on their trip to England where the latter was to pursue higher studies.[40] Ward's wit adds a comical tone to his case that their native brother should be allowed to go:

> We have this day settled that Ram Mohun shall go with our Brethren to England. ... Bro. Carey is quite averse to any native brother's going. Bro. Marshman & I think it is what we owe to the supporters of the Mission & to you, as a reward for their prayers & subscriptions & your anxiety & labours.—It will be a means of forming a stronger bond of union betwixt Bengalee [Bengali] & English Xns.—It may be a means of strengthening the Mission at home in a wonderful manner, & increase your funds. There never

---

[39] Ward, Journal MSS, Tuesday, March 8, 1803, 286.

[40] John Fernandez is the son of Ignatius Fernandez, a Portuguese convert from Roman Catholicism who was one of the Mission's most successful missionaries, overseeing the outstation at Dinajpur. Sunil Kumar Chatterjee, "Ignatius Fernandez," in *William Carey of Serampore* (Sheoraphuli: Laserplus, 1984, 2004), 134-164 and J.T.K. Daniel, "Ecumenical Pragmatism of the Serampore Mission," *Indian Journal of Theology* 42, no. 2 (2000): 175-176.

Spirituality in Relationships

was a sight like this in England since the world began—a converted brahman. ... The sight of this brahman may stop the mouths of infidels & cold Calvinists. It will electrify whole congregations. Let Fernandez & Ram Mohun sing a Bengalee [Bengali] hymn, after a sermon in behalf of the Mission, & in every place you will be laden with gifts & contributions. Take them with you [on] a Missionary Tour—to Scotland, &c. Don't make a shew of them— Don't be afraid of shewing them. Don't set them on a stool in a chapel. Don't hide God's gift in a napkin.[41]

In the end, Carey had his way, but not because he overruled Marshman and Ward. Rather, "the Capt. was determined not to take our native brother.—I was mortified, & a little chagrined that the Quaker (the Capt. is a worldly quaker) had tricked us."[42]

In another somewhat humorous account, there was disagreement between Marshman and Ward concerning the possible purchase of a horse for use in itinerancy. "Brother Marshman brought forward a plan for a European Brother's itinerating continually, on horseback. I opposed it as being impractical & likely to be very injurious to the health of the brethren, except during the cold season."[43] Though the details are lacking, it appears the Mission did eventually move forward with Marshman's proposal for one reads,

The keeping of a horse, which we felt unwilling to do till our numerous sedentary avocations would permit us to enjoy health no longer without it, enlarged our own sphere of itinerancy; and our native brethren from the beginning of the year, felt much stirred up to seek the salvation of their perishing countrymen.[44]

---

[41] Ward, Journal MSS, Wednesday, December 18, 1805, 462–463.
[42] Ward, Journal MSS, Monday, December 23, 1805, 464.
[43] Ward, Journal MSS, Monday, January 1, 1806, 471.
[44] *Monthly Circular Letters Relative to the Missions In India, Established By a Society In England, Called the "Baptist Missionary Society"* (Serampore: Mission Press,

While the previous two accounts are conveyed with a lighthearted air, this is a testimony to the winsome and witty nature of their author rather than to any insignificance in the matters themselves. These men labored in tropical Bengal before the advent of even electric fans. In such heat and physical discomfort, any disagreement will do to put the best of friends at odds. Carey's wife and Dr. Thomas had bouts with insanity. Bros. Chamberlain and Robinson struggled with outbursts of anger. That Carey, Marshman, and Ward *could* disagree concerning matters involving missions strategy, work location and schedule, discipleship of new converts, contextualization, and transportation, and maintain amicable relations nonetheless, was a work of God's grace. If car-driving church members can argue over a church bus, how much more pedestrian missionaries over a horse! The Trio's much more serious disagreement regarding open vs. closed communion will be addressed in the following chapter. Now, we turn to the outworking of Ward's spirituality in the larger context of ecumenical circles in Bengal.

Beyond Denominational Bounds

It often happens that alliances are formed in war that would not be formed in peacetime, and a common enemy makes friends of those who might otherwise be rivals. Evangelicals in India faced two common challenges—the entrenched native religious systems of Hinduism and Islam and the opposition of the East India Company to unhindered propagation of the gospel. Consequently, Baptists in Bengal found strong allies amongst those of other denominations who were united in religious sentiment and evangelical zeal.

1813), 6:8.

Spirituality in Relationships

Ecumenical harmony in Bengal
Before Ward was even appointed with the BMS, the evangelical giant, John Newton, lent his support to the evangelical cause in India. He and evangelical activist, William Wilberforce successfully lobbied the Archbishop of Canterbury so that "several gospel ministers known to Newton were appointed to the Bengal [Anglican] Mission."[45] Newton would also take a personal interest in Carey, including him regularly in a breakfast group that included fellow ministers and mentees, John Campbell, Claudius Buchanan, and William Jay.[46] In fact, when many ministers in his own denomination had held themselves aloof to Carey's attempts to promote foreign missions, J.C. Marshman remembers, "The only minister from whom Mr. Carey experienced any warmth of sympathy was a member of the Established Church, the venerable John Newton, who 'advised him with the fidelity and tenderness of a father.'"[47] This would not be the end of help Newton would give to the fledgling Baptist missionary endeavor.

But before profiting from Newton's assistance, the missionaries became acquainted with another missions champion en route to Bengal; none other than the captain of their vessel, Benjamin Wickes, a Presbyterian from Providence, Rhode Island and Philadelphia.[48] Regarding his observance of Captain Wickes during "a sweet monthly prayer-meeting" Ward remarked,

> I never saw the power & blessedness of divine grace more highly displayed than in the case of our Capt. His love of the divine character—his tenderness of conscience—his ardour to do good—his humility—his integrity—the prev-

---

[45] Jonathan Aitken, *John Newton; From Disgrace To Amazing Grace* (Wheaton, IL: Crossway, 2007), 314.
[46] Aitken, *John Newton*, 339.
[47] Marshman, *Life and Times*, 1:18.
[48] Smith, *Serampore Enterprise*, 257 n55.

alence of holy temper—his spirituality & savour—his deep insight into many truths of importance—his rich experience, &c. and all this in a sailor—done at sea, or under the Ministry of the Scotch church. I thank our Saviour for Captain Wicks. The divine image, drawn in lively characters on his own, proves more than all the infidel arguments in the world.[49]

The aid Newton gave Ward and his fellows was a letter of introduction to be used upon their arrival in India.[50] But unable legally to travel beyond Danish-controlled Serampore, the missionaries could not deliver it to anyone. So, following their disembarkation from the *Criterion*, while confined to Serampore, the good Captain Wickes personally delivered Newton's letter of introduction to Anglican minister, Rev. David Brown, who served for a time as co-chaplain with Rev. Claudius Buchanan, Carey's fellow in Newton's breakfast group.[51] This was providential aid indeed, coming not from their own denomination or even fellow Dissenters, but from the ranks of the Established Church! This introduction would be the beginning of an amicable and mutually beneficial relationship with the Anglican ministers.

Though he found the state of religion in general to be low in Calcutta, Ward felt that Anglicans Brown and Buchanan "do preach the Gospel."[52] As a result, Marshman and Ward (and we may assume Carey as well) had a standing invitation at Rev. Brown's.[53] J.C. Marshman, commenting on the same, writes,

---

[49] Ward, Journal MSS, Monday, July 1, 1799, 22-23. Roughly a month prior to landing in Serampore, Ward includes a copy of the letter of thanks the missionaries addressed to the Captain which can be found in his entry on Saturday, September 21, 1799, 43-44.

[50] Marshman, *Life and Times*, 1:116.

[51] Marshman, *Life and Times*, 1:116.

[52] Ward, Journal MSS, Saturday June 6, 1801, 157.

[53] Ward, Journal MSS, Friday, August 15, 1806, 499.

Spirituality in Relationships

Mr. Buchanan was a man of liberal feelings, and anxious to promote the cause of religion. At this time [early 1805], moreover, there was less of a sectarian spirit among men of evangelical sentiments in the Church of England in Calcutta and its vicinity, than had perhaps ever been exhibited since the passing of the Act of Uniformity. The Serampore missionaries constantly attended the ministry of the Episcopal Church when in Calcutta with great delight and advantage, and the evangelical clergymen and their families worshipped with the missionaries in their own chapel at Serampore.[54]

Of this state, Ward's spiritual grandfather, Rev. William Grimshaw, would have been proud as he once remarked, "I love Christians, true Christians of all parties; I do love them, I will love them, and none shall make me otherwise."[55] The Christian love between parties in Bengal was seen in shared fellowship, communion, partnership in ministry, and aid received.

---

[54] Marshman, *Life and Times*, 1:231. There were four Acts of Uniformity (1548, 1551, 1558, and 1662). In general, these mandated the use of the Anglican Book of Common Prayer in worship and made church attendance compulsory. J.C. Marshman is likely referring to the Act of Uniformity of 1662, when the English monarchy was reestablished under Charles II, following the period known as the Interregnum, when England was ruled by Lord Protector, Oliver Cromwell. Under this Act, a revised form of the BCP was reintroduced, and "all ministers were required publicly to assent to the Book, from which day its exclusive use was ordered. Ministers not episcopally ordained by that date (Bartholomew's Day, August 24) were to be deprived ... Some 2,000 Presbyterian ministers who refused to conform were ejected from their livings" *The Oxford Dictionary of the Christian Church*, 3rd rev. ed., s.v. "Uniformity, Acts of," eds. F.L. Cross and E. A. Livingstone (Oxford: Oxford University Press, 2009). Of course, Baptists had no "living" to begin with of which they could be deprived.

[55] [John Fawcett, Jr.], *An Account of the Life, Ministry, and Writings of the late Rev. John Fawcett Who Was Minister Of The Gospel Fifty-Four Years, First At Wainsgate, And Afterwards At Hebdenbridge, In The Parish Of Halifax; Comprehending Many Particulars Relative To The Revival And Progress Of Religion In Yorkshire And Lancashire; And Illustrated By Copious Extracts From The Diary Of The Deceased, From His Extensive Correspondence, And Other Documents* (London, 1818), 23.

The Spirituality of William Ward

Shared fellowship

The Trio's shared fellowship with non-Dissenting Evangelicals often took place at Rev. Brown's pagoda. Brief mention has been made of the pagoda prayer meeting. A fuller account will now be given.[56] We read in an 1806 Journal entry,

> Last night we all went down to Mr. Brown's, & had a prayer-meeting in what was once a heathen temple & which happens to be on Mr. Brown's estate. Mr. Brown, Messrs. Carey, Taylor, Marshman, and [Henry] Martyn engaged. We afterwards supped at Mr. Brown's.[57]

And from another entry in early 1807, we gain a fuller sense of the activities that informed these friends' fellowship:

> On Saturday we had a prayer-meeting in Mr. Brown's pagoda on account of Bro. Des Granges from 9 till 12, in the forenoon. Six persons prayed; 7 hymns were sung, & part of a sermon read. A happy meeting. A number of us afterwards dined at Mr. Brown's.[58]

This pattern is often mentioned in Ward's Journal, namely, joint prayer followed by fellowship around a common table. Reports of evangelical activity in Bengal and letters from men of the same stamp were often read.[59] They prayed together at strategic times as when Henry Martyn (1781-1812) was moving progressing in a northwesterly direction in his propagation of the gospel[60]

---

[56] For a detailed account of the history of the pagoda and events that took place there see George Smith, *The Life of William Carey, D. D.: Shoemaker and Missionary* (London: John Murray, 1885), 188-196.

[57] Ward, Journal MSS, Tuesday, July 8, 1806, 495.

[58] Ward, Journal MSS, Lord's Day, January 4, 1807, 533. Des Granges soon embarked for service with the LMS in South India. Marshman, *Life and Times*, 1:395; Smith, *Life of William Carey*, 190.

[59] Ward, Journal MSS, Tuesday, August 4, 1807, 567.

[60] Ward, Journal MSS, Friday, October 10, 1806, 515.

Spirituality in Relationships

and for the general success of the gospel in India.[61] Though all of the Trio were firmly baptistic in their convictions, they joined their Anglican brethren at the pagoda for the christening of Rev. Brown's child[62] and for a wedding he performed, before and after which a Rippon (Baptist) hymn was sung! Of this occasion Ward writes, "Every one seemed pleased & edified. After the ceremony the company proceeded to Mr. Brown's house where a wedding supper was prepared."[63] Of the ecumenical spirit found at Rev. Brown's pagoda, J.C. Marshman comments,

> In that Pagoda, which is yet the first object which meets the eye in sailing up from Calcutta towards Serampore, every denominational feeling was forgotten, and Carey, Marshman, and Ward, joined in the same chorus of praise with Brown, Martyn, and Corrie.[64]

While the Serampore Missionaries often joined Rev. Brown and friends at his pagoda, the High Churchmen often joined their Baptist brethren in worship at the Mission and elsewhere. One Lord's Day "Brother Forsyth preached, & with Bro. Carey's leave, sprinkled Mr. Smith of America's child at our Baptist Meeting at Mr. Lindeman's."[65] On another occasion, possibly regarding the same "Smith," we read, "On Thursday evening

---

[61] Ward, Journal MSS, Tuesday, June 2, 1807, 551.

[62] Ward, Journal MSS, Lord's Day, January 26, 1806, 472.

[63] Ward, Journal MSS, Monday, September 29, 1806, 513.

[64] Marshman, *Life and Times*, 1:247. Daniel Corrie (1777-1837) was an Anglican minister who initially served as chaplain for the East India Company and eventually as archdeacon. See W.H. Carey, *Oriental Christian Biography Containing Biographical Sketches Of Distinguished Christians Who Have Lived And Died In The East* (Calcutta: Baptist Mission Press, 1850), 1:149-169.

[65] Ward, Journal MSS, Lord's Day, March 2, 1806, 478. The "Forsyth" mentioned here is the Scot, Nathaniel Forsyth (1769-1816) who was the Congregational, London Missionary Society's first missionary in India and, like the Serampore Missionaries, arrived without a license. Penelope Carson, *Worlds Of The East India Company*, vol. 7, *The East India Company and Religion, 1698-1858* (Woodbridge, UK: The Boydell Press, 2012), 42.

The Spirituality of William Ward

Mr. Smith, an usher in the Free School, offered to join us, as a Paedobaptist,"[66] and a little over a month later that the same "was admitted into the church at Calcutta on Tuesday night, as a Paedobaptist."[67] We read of the same phenomenon regarding a Mr. Leonard and his wife,[68] a Mr. Warhurst, "a Paedobaptist," whose "experience was very interesting,"[69] and an old gentleman by the name of Shaw.[70]

At this early period of missions in Bengal, when it came to baptism and church membership, Dissenters were in a similar predicament. Dissenting ministers were not permitted to preach in the few Anglican pulpits that existed in Calcutta though they often attended preaching there. [71] The Baptist church in Serampore was one of the only Dissenting churches in the vicinity. And though the missionaries conducted meetings in various Calcutta citizens' homes, it was not until January 1, 1809 that a Dissenting chapel with a permanent structure was opened, on which day the Baptist Carey preached in the morning and the Congregational Forsyth in the evening.[72] In this atmosphere,

---

[66] Ward, Journal MSS, Friday, July 31, 1807, 563.
[67] Ward, Journal MSS, Friday, September 4, 1807, 580.
[68] Ward, Jounral MSS, Friday, October 9, 1807, 600.
[69] Ward, Journal MSS, Lord's Day, October 5, 1806, 514.
[70] Ward, Journal MSS, Monday, December 29, 1806, 532.
[71] For one example of Ward's interest in attending Rev. Brown's sermons and his appreciation of the same, see Ward, Journal MSS, Lord's Day, December 30, 1805, 402.
[72] Ward, Journal MSS, Lord's Day, January 1, 1809, 683. The history of this chapel continuing to the present day is noteworthy, so a brief description will be given from the pages of J.C. Marshman's, *Life and Times*. In 1802 "Mr. Brown, the senior chaplain at the Presidency, called on Mr. Carey in his rooms at the College, and expressed a desire that facilities should be created for communicating religious instruction to the lower classes of Christians in Calcutta, and inquired why the missionaries could not be prevailed on to turn their attention to this subject. He replied that he and his brethren had long wished to establish some place of worship for the benefit of those who, though bearing the Christian name, were too low in the scale of society to intrude into the patrician congregations of the Mission Church and the Presidency Church, but were apprehensive of giving umbrage to Government" (1:174). This encouragement and later aid that would be given, both in the way of ecumenical subscriptions for the building of Lal Bazaar Chapel, as well as timely

Spirituality in Relationships

begging Dissenters could not be choosers, and a liberty was granted to Paedobaptists not only in terms of membership, but also, as will be examined next, in communion.

Communion
The church at the Serampore Mission had not originally practiced open communion. Regarding their beginning as strict communionists, J.C. Marshman relates,

The church at Serampore had, for more than five years, adhered to the practice of what is denominationally called

---

intervention when the architectural plan was opposed at the last minute by Government officials, illustrate the ecumenical spirit that preceded even the opening of the first Dissenting chapel in Calcutta. Of the eventual purpose of the chapel, J C. Marshman writes in 1805, "The object of the missionaries was not to establish a chapel to propagate the peculiar sentiments of their own denomination, but to bring the forlorn beings in Calcutta, who bore the Christian name, and disgraced it by their ignorance and vice, under the influence of religious instruction. They announced, therefore, that the chapel was intended for the worship of all denominations" (1:208). When it opened, it would become the third Protestant and the first Dissenting place of worship in Calcutta (1:406-407; the chapel's opening is described on these pages.). Lal Bazaar Chapel (sometimes called Bow Bazaar Chapel) in time became a "nursery" of the mission because of the way that it supplied native and Asiatic (usually referring to those of mixed Indian and Portuguese descent) laborers such as Mr. Da Cruz mentioned here (1:474). In the year 1816, the chapel became Baptist. The reason for this was two-fold. First, the size of the Congregational congregation meeting at the time allotted to Rev. Forsyth had dwindled as "his ministrations were not popular." When new ministers arrived in Calcutta from the London Missionary Society, they saw the reduced size of the Congregational assembly meeting in the chapel and the established nature of the congregation being shepherded by the Trio and opted to open a separate church on the premises of the Freemason's Hall which became Union Chapel and is still in existence today. Second, the chapel was indebted to the Serampore Mission for money it had advanced the builder. It was decided then that, instead of raising money as a nondenominational Dissenting church to pay off this debt, the mortgage for the property would be retained by the Serampore Mission and the chapel become Baptist in name (2:131-132). It was here that Adoniram Judson was baptized. Here, Rev. Hook ministered for thirty plus years, being sent out by Charles Spurgeon's Pastors' College. Here George Müller spoke. *Lal Bazar Baptist Church, Calcutta Letter-Book & Records With _____ y, December 1876 to April 1885*, accessed in Carey Baptist Church, Kolkata, India. This chapel later became Carey Baptist Church and continues to this day. I had the privilege of first worshipping there with my family in 2003-2005 and then later supplying the pulpit when she was without a pastor from 2015-2016.

The Spirituality of William Ward

"strict communion;" that is, that none but those who had been baptized by immersion, after a personal confession of faith, were admitted to the ordinance of the Lord's Supper.[73]

The younger Marshman goes on to explain that this communion stance was not owing to either Ward's or Marshman's convictions, for they had both been proponents of open communion in England and had enjoyed "communicating" with the Presbyterian Captain Wickes during their voyage to India. It was owing rather to Carey's convictions which were in line with Andrew Fuller and other ministers of the Northamptonshire Baptist Association.[74] J.C. Marshman records that "Mr. Ward, more particularly deplored this rigid, and, as he thought, unlovely proceeding, though he considered it his duty not to disturb the harmony of the church and Mission."[75] So, he and Marshman deferred to their senior colleague, and the Mission church, from its inception, practiced closed communion. As a result, not even their "beloved commander," Captain Wickes, was permitted to commune with them as he had aboard the *Criterion*.[76]

But after more than five years of adhering to the practice of closed communion, the Mission church abandoned it. In an entry containing more personal opinion than most, Ward explains why:

> This alteration of church rules has not been effected by my arguments (tho' I should think it an honour if it had). Mr. & Mrs. Brown seem to have set Bro. Marshman a thinking upon it, & Bro. Marshman converted Bro. Carey, & our new brethren have gone into it cheerfully. All our sisters

---

[73] Marshman, *Life and Times*, 1:214.
[74] Marshman, *Life and Times*, 1:214.
[75] Marshman, *Life and Times*, 1:214.
[76] Marshman, *Life and Times*, 1:214.

Spirituality in Relationships

seem to have been previously on the amiable side of the question. I rejoice that the first Xn. church in Bengal has shaken off that apparent moroseness of temper which has so long made Baptists appear unlovely in the Xn. world. I am glad that this church considers real religion alone as the ground of admission to the Lord's Table ... With respect to a church-state; a stricter union may be required. But to partake of the Lord's Supper worthily it requires only that a man's heart be right with God.[77]

It was, in short, the sweet fellowship the Trio and larger Mission enjoyed with the likes of Rev. Brown and other Churchmen that persuaded Carey and the Mission church to unanimously resolve to open the table to persons of "known piety," upon their request, though they were still considered unbaptized.[78] This broadening of sentiments in Serampore was a local instance of more widespread change that was affecting Particular Baptists in England. W. R. Ward notes,

In England, release from the grip of the hypers, development of the "missionary church," and resistance to the Anglican establishment, all pointed to combined action, especially with the Independents, and combined evangelism, prayer and worship, were bound to lead to demands for open communion.[79]

As the comments in the Journal excerpt above demonstrate, communion, in Ward's mind, represented the union of all who had been put right with God through the redemption in Christ's blood, regardless of their denomination. Therefore, though it was celebrated in the context of a local church, it should be open

---

[77] Ward, Journal MSS, Friday, May 31, 1805, 422.
[78] Ward, Journal MSS, Friday, May 31, 1805, 422.
[79] W.R. Ward, "The Baptists and the Transformation of the Church, 1780-1830," *Baptist Quarterly* 25, no. 4 (1973): 176.

The Spirituality of William Ward

to true saints of the church universal. Interestingly however, Ward, never heedless of doctrinal considerations, drew a line when it came to church membership. If one hoped to join a "Baptist" church, it naturally followed that baptism, as prescribed, should be required of the same. This explains Ward's humorous addition following the above quote: "Mr. Maylin has formally proposed himself for baptism. This will be likely to kick up a dust amongst the good church-folks at Calcutta."[80]

Aid in ministry

The ecumenical fellowship described above paved the way for many instances of mutual aid as Serampore and the Established Church fulfilled their respective ministries. From the side of the Churchmen, this aid was pecuniary and political. From the side of the Mission, it was often the provision of translation services and the supply of religious tracts.

In late 1804, the Mission Press was able to fulfill orders from Fort William College to print two more works in Bangla thanks to Rev. Brown fronting them 5,000 Rupees at twelve percent interest.[81] Around a year and a half later, Carey read in an American newspaper that Captain Wickes had obtained 1,000 Guineas from England for translation works and that he had invited American Christians to "increase the sum."[82] Rev. Brown insisted on giving Ward a 500 Rupees subscription toward the printing of his book, presumably on the Hindus.[83] A year later they received a letter from Rev. Brown informing them of their receipt of a bequest from William Grant of 20,000 Rupees to

---

[80] Ward, Journal MSS, Friday, May 31, 1805, 422. J.C. Marshman notes that Mr. Maylin was a wealthy merchant and presumably Anglican, who loaned the Mission £1,420 toward the total purchase price of £3,000 for "three parcels of ground, which henceforth formed the 'Mission premises.'" Marshman, *Life and Times*, 1:213.

[81] Ward, Journal MSS, Monday, November 19, 1804, 397.

[82] Ward, Journal MSS, Friday, April 11, 1806, 483.

[83] Ward, Journal MSS, Wednesday, September 24, 1806, 513.

Spirituality in Relationships

their translation fund.[84]

The aid mentioned above was, in a sense, routine. But the outpouring of local evangelical support in the aftermath of the devastating fire of 1812 was remarkable.[85] In India, the Anglican Chaplain, T.T. Thomason, "in a day or two raised 800 pounds," from the "members of his own congregation," of which he himself contributed £40. "Six other Christian friends gave 50*l.* each, including one Major Scott Waring who had five years earlier maligned them.[86] And though it took longer to arrive, there was an equal outpouring from evangelical friends in England. The Bible Society contributed 2,000 reams of paper to cover what was lost in that essential commodity. The Congregational London Missionary Society gave one hundred pounds and the editors of the *Evangelical Magazine* gave 50 pounds. The Society in Scotland for Propagating Christian Knowledge contributed two hundred pounds. In addition to the largesse of these evangelical allies, there was such generosity from Baptist churches across England that J.C. Marshman records, "The whole of the loss was made up in sixty days."[87]

But as beneficial as this material help was to Serampore, the political clout the Churchmen lent to the Trio was a greater boon still. In April 1801, at an early stage in the Mission, it was the Anglican Revs. Brown and Buchanan who "were determined, if possible, to secure the services of Mr. Carey in the new Col-

---

[84] Ward, Journal MSS, Tuesday, November 17, 1807, 611.

[85] J.C. Marshman poignantly describes the loss: "During the night of the 11th of March, the printing office at Serampore was totally consumed by fire, and the labour of twelve years destroyed in a few hours." Excepting the premises' deeds and the "records and accounts of the Mission," and some molds for casting type which were later found, the printing office, "a large assortment of types recently received from England," fourteen "founts in the eastern languages," presses, and over 1,200 reams of paper were lost. Marshman, *Life and Times*, 1:468.

[86] Marshman, *Life and Times*, 1:471.

[87] Marshman, *Life and Times*, 1:472.

The Spirituality of William Ward

lege."[88] The College mentioned is Fort William College which Lord Wellesley (1760-1842), then Governor General of the East India Company, had established a year earlier for the training of its civil servants.[89] Rev. David Brown had been appointed as Provost of the College and Rev. Claudius Buchanan nominated as Vice-Provost.[90] Subjects covered at the College were extensive and included the languages and histories of India. But at that time, the Indian *lingua franca* was Persian due to the Muslim conquest of India under Mughal rulers from the early part of the sixteenth century. This was the language of the courts over which English civil servants presided. But it was not the language of the people of Bengal. So, when the College was in need of someone to teach Bangla to its servants "there was but one man in Bengal duly qualified to undertake the office of teaching Bengalee [Bangla], but he was a missionary, and the government was inimical to missionary efforts."[91] The story of the East India Company's opposition to missionary efforts in Bengal will be told in the following chapter, but the point here is that Carey, an avowed missionary, operating from Danish-controlled Serampore, would likely never have been appointed to teach Bengali at Fort William College had it not been for the recommendation of his High Church friends.

But though they had given Carey a good reference, the Churchmen were not oblivious to the religious distinction between themselves and Carey. Buchanan had introduced a clause in the statutes of the College which stated that "'all the superior officers, the professors, and lecturers solemnly and faithfully to promise and declare that they would not maintain publicly or privately any doctrines or opinions contrary to the doctrine or

---

[88] Marshman, *Life and Times*, 1:148.
[89] For more on the genesis of this college, see Marshman, *Life and Times*, 142.
[90] Marshman, *Life and Times*, 1:145.
[91] Marshman, *Life and Times*, 1:148.

Spirituality in Relationships

discipline of the Church of England.'"[92] Carey's appointment, therefore, was made possible by the creation of a lower class of officers, intended for Dissenters and Roman Catholics, for which this clause did not apply. The result was that Carey's pay grade was set at 500 Rupees, that of an inferior teacher. But this was 500 Rupees Carey did not previously have. Following their common purse policy, Carey remitted his salary to the Mission so that he could inform Fuller shortly after his appointment to the College, "Our school has increased, and, together with my allowance from the College, will, we trust, support us without further help from England."[93] In addition, Carey's appointment at the British College elevated his stature in the eyes Calcutta society.[94] Just over five years later, it was again the "influence of Mr. Brown" through which "Bro. Carey ... petitioned the College Council for an increase of salary," as the Persian teacher, "who does not so much as he," earned twice as much as Carey.[95] This petition was granted in 1807 when the College was "remodeled and reduced."[96] One of the reductions was the discriminatory clause mentioned above, and Carey was promoted to professor, receiving a doubled salary of 1,000 Rupees a month.[97] This continued until 1830 when, because of the Government's financial exigency, professorships were abolished, and Carey's salary was reduced from 1,000 Rupees a month to its initial level. So heavy was this blow that coupled with other unexpected losses and mounting debts from the College they had established in Serampore, Marshman and Carey were "dissolved in tears."[98] Clearly, Carey's financial contribution to the Mission from his

---

[92] Marshman, *Life and Times*, 1:149.
[93] Carey to Fuller, June 15, 1802 quoted in Marshman, *Life and Times*, 1:149.
[94] Carson, *The East India Company and Religion*, 59.
[95] Ward, Journal MSS, Monday, August 11, 1806, 498.
[96] Marshman, *Life and Times*, 1:286.
[97] Marshman, *Life and Times*, 1:287.
[98] Marshman, *Life and Times*, 2:423-424.

The Spirituality of William Ward

teaching at Ft. William College was vital and invaluable. And it might never have been had it not been for the recommendation and clout of his Anglican friends.

Another instance in which Rev. Brown's influence prevailed for the missionaries was during the tense standoff between Mission and Government following the Vellore Mutiny. On July 10, 1806, Muslim sepoys,[99] massacred fourteen officers of the garrison, including the colonel, in addition to ninety-nine commissioned officers—while they were asleep and unarmed![100] It seems the mutiny stemmed from an order that sepoys should wear a new turban that was repugnant to them as it bore strong resemblance to an English hat. This repugnance morphed into revolt as family members of the defeated Tipu Sultan spread the report that this was a first step toward full-scale forced conversion of the Indian populace to Christianity.[101] For the antimissionary party in England and India, this horrific slaughter was proof positive of what would happen if missionaries were allowed to excite the religious sentiments of the natives.[102] Just over a month later, on August 23, 1806, two new BMS missionaries, Revs. John Chater and William Robinson, arrived from England. Their arrival could not have been more ill-timed. They were detained in Calcutta by the police, and the Serampore missionaries were confined to Serampore, forcing them to abandon the newly established preaching point in Bow Bazaar, Calcutta as well as their itinerating efforts among Indian nationals in the countryside.[103]

Into this fray jumped Rev. Brown. After a "very long discus-

---

[99] Sepoys were native troops who served under British leadership during their Raj (rule). Sepoy is an anglicization of the Persian (and Urdu) word, *sipahi*, meaning soldier.
[100] Marshman, *Life and Times*, 1:263.
[101] Marshman, *Life and Times*, 1:261–265.
[102] Marshman, *Life and Times*, 1:264.
[103] Ward, Journal MSS, Wednesday, August 27, 1806, 503.

Spirituality in Relationships

sion" that he engaged with the Magistrate, the restrictions on the Missionaries were eased so that they were permitted to "remain at Serampore in full power," circulate the Holy Scriptures, and preach "in their own house [at] Cossitallah, or in the house of any other person," (excepting the preaching point at Bow [sometimes called Lal] Bazaar), and the natives were permitted to "teach & preach wherever they please—provided they be not sent forth as Emissaries from Serampore." This prompted Ward to exude, "The interest he takes in our success & the kinder affection which he & Mr. Martyn & Mrs. B. continually shew towards us calls for our grateful remembrance."[104]

Even when Brown did not intervene directly, he had an inside vantage that enabled him to allay Mission fears which often resulted from the Government's intimidating communiques. After two months of being detained in Calcutta and much prayer, the Mission received a note from Brown containing the joyous intimation that Chater and Robinson would finally be released—only to receive the following day a note from the Calcutta police that the previous orders for Chater and Robinson's deportation to England still held and that they should specify on which ship they would embark![105] A likely nervous Marshman and Ward left Calcutta and made for Brown's home the following evening. Brown's advice? "He advised us not to take the least notice of the police letter. He says the government don't expect to execute their order; but that they were too proud to rescind it."[106]

Ward's Journal is replete with references to a word from Rev. Brown here or a subscription given by an evangelical friend there. He and others were "friends in high places" for the lowly Baptists of Serampore, and the benefit the latter derived from their friendship was incalculable. Understandably, the Serampo-

---

[104] Ward, Journal MSS, Saturday, August 30, 1806, 504–505.
[105] Ward, Journal MSS, Wednesday, November 5, 1806, 521–522.
[106] Ward, Journal MSS, Thursday, November 6, 1806, 522.

The Spirituality of William Ward

re Missionaries were only too happy to return the favors. But ironically, due to the strained relationship between Dissenters and Anglicans back home, they often thought it prudent to extend help clandestinely.

In December 1804, London Missionary Society representative, Rev. Dr. John Taylor landed at Tranquebar, another Danish settlement on the South Indian coast, the site of the first Protestant Mission in India. His intention, along with colleague W. Loveless was to found a mission in Surat, in western India. But before going west, they came north to Bengal.[107] His stay in Bengal was brief, but it afforded him an opportunity to meet the Serampore band and be aided by them. In late 1805 we read that "Dr. Taylor was admitted to our evening council, to see the methods which we observe in doing business," and the following day, that he delivered the message at the Serampore church.[108] Ward regarded him as a "man of the right stamp" and enjoyed sweet fellowship with him on a subsequent visit he made to Calcutta.[109] He was to return to South India shortly en route to Surat, but before embarking for Madras, an evening prayer meeting was held for his sake and for that of Serampore fellows, Mr. Maylin and John Fernandez, who were departing for England for the sake of the latter's studies. As Dr. Taylor left, the Mission gave him a precious gift—"200 copies of the Gospel of Matthew in the Mahratta language, to distribute as he may have opportunity at Surat."[110] Though the Company Government would deny him the opportunity to settle in Surat, he would go on to become the first Protestant missionary to settle in the Bombay

---

[107] Richard Lovett, *The History of the London Missionary Society, 1795-1895*, vol. 2 (London: Henry Frowde/London Missionary Society, 1899), 39.

[108] Ward, Journal MSS, Saturday, December 28 and Lord's Day, December 29, 1805, 465.

[109] Ward, Journal MSS, Friday, December 19, 1806, 530, and Saturday, June 28, 1806, 493.

[110] Ward, Journal MSS, Monday, December 30 and Tuesday, December 31, 1805, 465.

Spirituality in Relationships

Presidency and would remain a friend of the Mission.[111]

Henry Martyn (1781-1812), an East India Company Chaplain of no small notoriety also sojourned in Calcutta before eventually propagating the gospel among Muslims in Persia. And while there, he also made the acquaintance of the Serampore Missionaries and was aided by them as he began his mission. As he prepared to leave Calcutta, we read in Ward's Journal of a prayer meeting, held on his behalf, at Rev. Brown's pagoda,[112] and then a few days later, of another gift resulting from the Mission's translation labors—"50 Hindoostanee [Hindustani] Testaments & 20,000 tracts to begin his Missionary career," followed by the admonition, "Don't publish this."[113] On the field, the Serampore missionaries keenly felt themselves to be part of a larger gospel mission that included ministers and missionaries from various evangelical denominations and sending agencies. But the Trio realized that what was regarded as a beautiful partnership on one side of the world might be seen as suspect on the other. So, lest the readership of the BMS *Periodical Accounts* be disgruntled over that which was truly a cause for rejoicing, Ward requested that Fuller refrain from publishing it.[114]

These are a few examples of the mutual aid shared between

---

[111] Penelope Carson, *The East India Company and Religion*, 63.

[112] Ward, Journal MSS, Friday, October 10, 1806, 515.

[113] Ward, Journal MSS, Wednesday, October 15, 516.

[114] Other admonitions to conceal include news of gifts received and even fellowship enjoyed with Christians of other stripes. On one occasion Ward grants permission to print news of a gift from Portuguese descended partner, Mr. Fernandez, but does not give permission to print news that Miss Rumohr—who would go on to become William Carey's second wife following the death of Dolly—had assigned them a 5,000 Rupee bequest in a will she had just drafted. Ward, Journal MSS, Lord's Day, February 16, 1806, 476. Following the record of a 500 Rupee gift from Judge Harrington toward the building of Lal Bazaar Chapel, Ward warns, "I suppose you'll publish this, but if you do, I'll send you no more news." Ward, Journal MSS, Friday, June 13, 1806, 490. Then, after speaking of news related in a pagoda prayer meeting of Henry Martyn distributing their tracts all the way up to Dinajpur, he writes, "You must not insert any thing respecting these men which I have written on any account whatever." Ward, Journal MSS, Lord's Day, December 7, 1806, 528.

the Trio and their evangelical allies of other denominations. These gospel comrades prayed together regularly at Rev. Brown's pagoda. They worshipped together at the Serampore Church. They enjoyed each other's preaching. They discussed strategies for disseminating the gospel across India.[115] They had a shared interest in the translation of the Holy Scripture into the many languages of the subcontinent. The Serampore missionaries benefitted from the affluence and influence of the Churchmen. And the Anglicans benefitted from the language and printing ability of Serampore. Both sides benefitted from the other's fellowship over and against an East India Company that was often antagonistic to the propagation of the gospel in Bengal. This camaraderie is most notable during the early years of the Missionaries' Bengali tenure. But there were bounds to their ecumenism, and partnership became more challenging after the East India Company's Charter was renewed in 1813. Though the conditions of the new Charter were more favorable to missions in general, they also provided for an official Anglican Episcopate on Indian soil, financed by Indian revenues.[116] With this fortuitous development, the Churchmen would increasingly act to secure their own interests. Though high esteem remained for each other, examples of partnership and fellowship would become less common.

But There Were Bounds!
One area where the Trio both cooperated and butted heads with their Anglican brethren was in the matter of Bible translation, printing, and dissemination. Both wanted to see God's Word go forth across India. But the Churchmen were at the same time loathe to see the credit go to radical Baptist outliers. An early example of this is Revs. Brown and Buchanan's response to a

---

[115] Ward, Journal MSS, Friday, June 25, 1802, 240.
[116] Penelope Carson, *The East India Company and Religion*, 154.

Spirituality in Relationships

letter in July 1804 from the newly formed Bible Society in England. In this letter, the Society requested that a committee of correspondence be formed "relative to the best means of diffusing Christian truth in the Eastern languages."[117] It was also stated that this committee should be comprised of Mr. Udny, Carey's former employer at the indigo factory, Revs. Brown and Buchanan, and the Serampore Trio of Carey, Marshman, and Ward. After receiving the letter, Mr. Udny forwarded it to Buchanan who was expected to share it with the Trio. Instead, Buchanan held the Bible Society letter for many months until Carey himself forced the matter, having inadvertently discovered the letter's existence through conversation with Mr. Udny.

At first glance this seems odd behavior from a minister who had earlier boasted concerning his congregation, "'We have some of all sects ... but a name or a sect is never mentioned in the pulpit.'" But J.C. Marshman explains how such a juxtaposition was possible: "When the idea of being officially associated with the Serampore missionaries, though for the promotion of a great and catholic object, was presented to his mind, he appeared to shrink from the sacrifice of feeling or of dignity which it might involve."[118]

Eventually, Carey, Marshman, and Ward were included on the Corresponding Committee of the Bible Society, but the Anglican effort to ostracize the Trio continued. On June 9, 1810, in a Committee meeting in which Ward was absent, Rev. Brown "proposed that the correspondence should be with the chaplains & company's servants, leaving out every good man not a company's servant & all the Missionaries in the country. Brn. Carey & Marshman resisted this, & Mr. Brown, after a contest of an hour or more, gave up the point."[119] But Brown did not give it up. The

---

[117] Marshman, *Life and Times*, 1:231.
[118] Marshman, *Life and Times*, 1:231.
[119] Ward, Journal MSS, Saturday, June 9, 1810, 728.

semi-annual meeting of the Committee was to happen the following month, but Brown tried to circumvent the meeting by merely requesting the signatures of committee members on a Prospectus he had prepared. The problem, however, was that the Prospectus included a paragraph "again recognizing the [Anglican] chaplains only as the correspondents of the committee."[120] Commenting on this second effort to snub the Trio, Ward jests, "Poor Brown! he is terribly galled, I dare say, that he is so thwarted by these 3 anabaptist dissenters."[121]

So acute was Brown's embarrassment of the presence of Dissenters on the Corresponding Committee of the Bible Society, that half a year later he proposed a complete restructuring. Ward records,

> Mr. Brown & Mr. Thomason called on Bro. Carey this morning at Calcutta, & proposed to him that we should withdraw our names from the Bible Society's Corresponding Committee, & that the Committee should be dissolved, in order to form an Auxilliary Society. Bro. Carey told them he saw no need of dissolving the committee on this account for they might form an Auxiliary Society without dissolving the Committee. It was urged to him that people would not subscribe to the society, under the idea that we were in it.[122]

Revealed here is the fact that Brown's actions were prompted by regard for those Churchmen in England who might not give financial subscriptions to the Bible Society if they observed Baptist Dissenters in positions on par with their own folk. In Brown's defense, however, it is worth noting that he was acting from no different motivation than Ward did when he instructed

---

[120] Ward, Journal MSS, Saturday, July 21, 1810, 731.
[121] Ward, Journal MSS, Saturday, July 21, 1810, 731.
[122] Ward, Journal MSS, Thursday, January 3, 1811, 744.

Spirituality in Relationships

Fuller not to print something he felt might not go over well with their own Baptist subscribers. Though both had adapted to life in Bengal, neither was naïve to political sentiments at home.

To bring the Bible Society saga to its conclusion, Brown eventually had his way. In Ward's entry for February 24, 1811 he writes, "On the 21st (of February) the Auxiliary Bible Society was formed at Calcutta," with Rev. Brown as Secretary. But Ward ruefully adds, "We were not invited."[123] The Trio's exclusion was a clever maneuver on Brown's part. On the one hand, in order to

> preserve the appearance of candour & liberality "Christian Ministers of all persuasions" are allowed to be regular members of the Committee; but, (Oh! ye Serampore Missionaries! I'll be teased with you no longer)—"no person deriving any emolument from the Society shall have that privilege."[124]

So, as the Serampore Mission Press regularly entered into contracts with the Society for the printing of various Scriptures—and was compensated for it—they could not, alas, hold membership on the newly formed Auxiliary Committee. So, Ward wrote around three weeks later, "Sometimes the sky lowers & then comes a fine day.—The ... spirit of Highchurchism, & of Infidelity are all against the progress of truth."[125] Shortly after this, the Trio-absent Calcutta Auxiliary acquiesced to the Advocate-General who had "objected to the latitude" in their resolutions and "avowed that they have nothing to do with Missions."[126] To this the Trio could not have consented.

Another example of Anglican overreach involved Brown and

---

[123] Ward, Journal MSS, Lord's Day, February 24, 1811, 748.
[124] Ward, Journal MSS, Lord's Day, February 24, 1811, 748.
[125] Ward, Journal MSS, Lord's Day, March 17, 1811, 750.
[126] Ward, Journal MSS, Lord's Day, March 17, 1811, 750.

The Spirituality of William Ward

Buchanan's proposal for a "Propaganda College" in May of 1807. The proposed college was thusly named after the Counter-Reformation, Roman Catholic Propaganda College.[127] As described by Ward, the proposal was put to them in a very sudden and brazen manner:

> This day a letter arrived from Mr. Brown inclosing a plan from Dr. Buchanan, for forming a college, to be called the British Propaganda. This college was to be under the superintendence of a Clergyman; to be protected by the Society for promoting Xn. knowledge & His Danish Majesty. The business of translations was to be placed in this College. Our press was to be called the Propaganda press; - no alterations were to be made in the Mission Premises, at present. Bro. Marshman was to sign our consent to this plan directly.—We were alarmed & shocked. Bren. Carey & Marshman called on Mr Brown, & a dreadful collision took place.[128]

So, "the cordial fellowship which had so long subsisted between Mr. Brown and the Serampore missionaries was unhappily interrupted, for a season, in the month of May in the present

---

[127] This college was established by Pope Urban VIII to provide a centralized seminary or college where priests could be trained and equipped for missionary efforts in newly developed states which were not under Roman Catholic sway. The following is from the Catholic Encyclopedia:

But he also saw that it was necessary to establish a central seminary for the missions where young ecclesiastics could be educated, not only for countries which had no national college but also for such as were endowed with such institutions. It seemed very desirable to have, in every country, priests educated in an international college where they could acquire a larger personal acquaintance, and establish in youth relations that might be mutually helpful in after life. Thus arose the seminary of the Propaganda known as the Collegium Urbanum, from the name of its founder, Urban VIII. It was established by the Bull "Immortalis Dei," of 1 Aug., 1627, and placed under the immediate direction of the Congregation of Propaganda. (Umberto Benigni, "Sacred Congregation of Propaganda," *The Catholic Encyclopedia*, vol. 12 [New York: Robert Appleton Company, 1911], accessed December 7, 2018, www.newadvent.org/cathen/12456a.htm).

[128] Ward, Journal MSS, Tuesday, May 5, 1807, 548.

Spirituality in Relationships

year."[129] This was another attempt to become the primary champions of the great catholic project of Bible translation. It appears that Buchanan was the true instigator, and Brown, the meek accomplice. The former, "with all his liberality of feeling, never lost sight of the interests of the Church of England, and the kindness he manifested towards the missionaries at Serampore, however sincere, was too often marked by an exhibition of condescending patronage."[130] A week later, however, the audacious proposal was dropped. Ward wryly concludes the matter, "Dr Buchanan & Mr Brown will not be enemies, I fancy, but they will no doubt remember our non-conformity."[131] Fellowship with Brown and Buchanan was also restored "and the prayer-meetings at the Pagoda were resumed, and their mutual friendship was again cemented by the new difficulties created by the renewed and increased opposition of Government to Missions."[132]

There was also increasing friction in the overlapping mission field of Calcutta. Initially, the work of the Serampore Mission was concentrated in the environs of Serampore and the villages near the Hooghly River that were recipients of their itinerating efforts. Though they were aware of mission opportunities in Calcutta, it was the seat of Company power in Bengal, and as they possessed no proper licenses for their missionary work, labors there were risky. But with Carey's appointment to Fort William College as teacher of Bengali in April 1801, the Mission gained new respect in the eyes of Calcutta society. About this time Ward recorded that

> Creeshnoo proposes to take a small house at Calcutta,

---

[129] Marshman, *Life and Times*, 1:293.
[130] Marshman, *Life and Times*, 1:293.
[131] Ward, Journal MSS, Tuesday, May 12, 1807, 548.
[132] Marshman, *Life and Times*, 1:294–295.

The Spirituality of William Ward

where first one of them & then another may go, to talk about the cause of our Saviour. ... We have told him we will pay the rent, &c. It may open to us a wide field at Calcutta, especially since Bror. Carey is about to be there three days in every week.[133]

In time there was a "meeting for prayer and conversation" with plans to start another meeting the following week that he might "deliver the word at the house of a Portuguese Xn." for the sake of his family and neighbors.[134] Shortly thereafter Brown himself, expressed to Carey his desire "that facilities should be created for communicating religious instruction to the lower classes of Christians in Calcutta, and inquired why the missionaries could not be prevailed on to turn their attention to this subject."[135] On January 3, 1803, a house was secured by Marshman for this purpose, and on the 23rd of the same month the house was "opened for services."[136] Following this auspicious occasion, the Trio wrote to the Society in England:

> God has heard our prayers and has given us an entrance into *Calcutta*. If we should not gather a congregation of Europeans, yet it opens a door to the natives, and we enter at once into the midst of near a million of souls, having the everlasting Gospel to preach.[137]

But within a few years, the Trio did begin to see conversions among European soldiers. And of course, these they baptized by

---

[133] Ward, Journal MSS, Saturday, April 18th, 1801, 151. This and following citations are noted by Edward S. Wenger as he details the early stages of what would become Lal Bazaar Baptist Chapel. Edward S. Wenger, *The Story of the Lall Bazar Baptist Church; Being the History of Carey's Church From 24th April 1800 to the Present Day* (Calcutta: Edinburgh Press, 1908), 21-25.

[134] Ward, Journal MSS, Saturday, February 6, 1802, 207-208.

[135] Marshman, *Life and Times*, 1:174.

[136] Wenger, *The Story of Lall Bazar Baptist Church*, 22.

[137] Wenger, *The Story of Lall Bazar Baptist Church*, 22.

Spirituality in Relationships

immersion. Their zeal for baptism is seen in the response of one Mr. Barlow with whom Ward had shared the gospel, when it dawned on him that he must be baptized. "Well! When I turned from Popery I became a town's talk, & now if I am to be baptized, I shall be a town's talk again, & people will say, he'll become [a] Musselman next."[138] Ward himself performed the first baptism in Calcutta—"a soldier in the artillery in the Fort" named John Axell, and exulted, "I enjoyed much pleasure in these opportunities."[139] From the following entry, it seems the Trio's friends from the Established Church were not amused.

> Our late additions from Calcutta have alarmed our Paedobaptist friends, & Mr. Burney has prefaced & reprinted a pamphlet on baptism written by a [blank]. Lindeman & Warhurst are like men with the cholic. Edmund has been calling Oakey to account for not being content with his own baptism.[140]

In Ward's entry on a Lord's Day in the summer of 1810, we gain a sense of the ferocity of opposition of some anti-baptizers. Ward records that on this day he had baptized seven people in Calcutta, amongst whom were an Englishman and his wife, two native-born persons, two English soldiers, and a "poor blind man born in the country." Then he adds that he would have baptized an eighth, another blind man, "but a Mr. Deronario, one of Mr. Thomason's people, threatened him with starvation if he did; & the poor man preferred his belly to baptism."[141] Ward responded to this aggression *from the baptistry* by telling a crowded congregation that such threatening was comparable to the "burning of

---

[138] Ward, Journal MSS, Monday, March 2, 1807, 541.
[139] Ward, Journal MSS, Lord's Day, August 2, 1807, 564.
[140] Ward, Journal MSS, Lord's Day, August 2, 1807, 564.
[141] Ward, Journal MSS, Lord's Day, July 29, 1810, 731. Mr. Thomason was an Anglican minister at the Mission Church who arrived in Calcutta after Revs. Brown and Buchanan.

The Spirituality of William Ward

Joan Waste a poor blind woman, at Derby, for getting children to read the New Testament to her."[142] Ward continues,

> I attempted to prove at the Baptistry that infant-sprinkling, as bringing the world into the church, had been the fruitful source of the corruptions, the persecutions, & the enormities charged upon the Xn. church. If I was in England I think I should print what I have already given to our congregation—three views of this subject; first that there is not a vestige of scripture proof for infant-sprinkling; that it is essentially deficient in every thing for which baptism was given; & that, instead of being a harmless thing, it is Pandora's box. The above persecution & that at Berhampore, where Bro. Ch. (Chamberlain) has been expelled, & all meetings of the Baptists prohibited, is a tolerable specimen of the blessings of an Ecclesiastical Establishment here: these are the first-fruits.[143]

William Carey, Joshua Marshman, and William Ward are rightly called a Trio. Their unity was not one characterized by domineering strength and cowering diffidence. Each member of the Trio was uniquely gifted. Each personality was gloriously different. At times they disagreed passionately. But the fraternal bonds with which the Trio were bound for more than twenty-three years ensured that foibles were born in love and individual preferences were subjected to the greater missionary cause.

With his Baptist brethren, Carey and Marshman, Ward enjoyed the closest fellowship. But in a real sense, he equally treasured his friendships with any evangelical brother whom he regarded as being of the right stamp. Thus his memoirist could say of him,

---

[142] Ward, Journal MSS, Lord's Day, July 29, 1810, 731.
[143] Ward, Journal MSS, Lord's Day, July 29, 1810, 731-32.

Spirituality in Relationships

He was zealously and experimentally attached to the great doctrines of grace; nor was he indifferent to the ordinances and discipline connected with them; but he had learned, that the bond of christian union is the love of Christ, and where he found this, he recognized the Saviour's image, nor could he withhold his affection. Hence, though in principle and practice he most decidedly held the doctrine of the baptism of believers by immersion; yet he could freely walk with all those christians who conscientiously differed from him in that particular.[144]

And his longtime friend, Marshman, could write when Ward died,

Our brother was not a man who confined his regard for the cause of God to one denomination. He loved all who loved the Redeemer, and sought to promote his cause. Hence his death is a public loss to religion.[145]

---

[144] Stennett, *Memoirs*, 241.
[145] Stennett, *Memoirs*, 226 as preached by Joshua Marshman at a funeral service held for Ward before a large crowd at the Congregational Union Chapel in Calcutta, March 23, 1823.

4
"A soft answer turns away wrath": The Peacemaking Effect of Ward's Piety

William Ward was a natural peacemaker because he was a peaceful man. From birth, he was blessed with an amiable personality; a "mildness and gentleness of temper which insensibly endeared him to all."[1] He could make peace *among* men because he was at peace *with* men. But Ward's irenic nature was transformed and enhanced by the love of Christ with which his spirituality was chiefly animated. His penchant for peacemaking was thus "improved and refined by the power of divine grace."[2]

In general, Ward's peaceful demeanor had a calming effect on those around him. It was like soothing oil that reduced friction in the machinery of the Serampore Mission. It was a balancing force between the polemics of Marshman, and the plodding of Carey. This was true in general and has been highlighted in chapter 3. But in the life of the Mission, there were three critical junctures where things might have gone very badly but for Ward's peacemaking contribution. These involved the Persian Pamphlet Controversy, translation philosophy, and communion decisions.

---

[1] Joshua Marshman, *Divine Grace the Source of All Human Excellence* (Serampore, India: Mission Press, 1823), 35. This work is a funeral sermon that Joshua Marshman preached for his friend and colleague, William Ward.

[2] Joshua Marshman, *Divine Grace*, 35.

The Spirituality of William Ward

"If a ruler's anger rises against you": Ward's Intercession for the Sake of the Press

In the words of *Qoheleth*,[3] "If a ruler's anger rises against you, do not leave your post; calmness can lay great offenses to rest" (Ecclesiastes 10:4, NIV). In the first half of the nineteenth century, the ruler of Bengal was the East India Company. And in 1807, his anger rose against the Mission, and—their Serampore sanctuary notwithstanding—he threatened to seize their press. But Ward did not abandon his post. Neither did he relinquish their press. Instead his calm counsel allayed the wrath of the company, allowing them to retain that tool which was most essential to their missions strategy.

Background of Government Opposition
Government opposition was a frustrating reality for all mission efforts in Bengal. But it was not so much the government of England that opposed them but rather the East India Company which operated increasingly as its own sovereign over the Subcontinent. The East India Company was originally a commercial enterprise of London merchants. Wanting to trade locally in foreign commodities such as "spices, cotton piece-goods, and China tea," they first obtained a royal charter which granted them "exclusive rights over the Asian trade." Second, they raised money for their commercial ventures and safeguarded against potential loss due to pirates or storms on the open seas through numerous investors who purchased shares of stock in the Company in return for a share in the profits.[4]

In time, however, its quest for profit led to conflict with other colonial powers in the area who sought the same as well as with

---

[3] Sometimes rendered, "Preacher" (ESV) or "Teacher" (NIV).
[4] Ian Copland, s.v. "East India Company," *An Oxford Companion to the Romantic Age*, eds. Iain McCalman, et al. (Oxford: Oxford University Press, 2009).

Spirituality in Peacemaking

local Indian rulers. The Company soon found itself in need of both arms and army that it might protect its interests against such competitors. But compared to local militaries, it had nowhere near the manpower for such competition. So, the East India Company made up the difference by raising up and training a sepoy army comprised of local soldiers, sometimes recruited courtesy of the favor of local allied rulers.[5] As the Company and its sepoy army met with success on the battlefield, treaties were made with existing Muslim Mughal rulers that were mutually beneficial. Germaine to this thesis is the Battle of Plassey in 1757 in which a *sepoy* army led by Robert Clive defeated a much larger French supported Mughal army led by Siraj-ud-Daula.[6] Then in 1765,

> The Mughal Emperor, Shah Alam II, granted Clive the *diwani* of Bengal and the Company thus became a revenue collector and territorial administrator as a trader. The Company now had effective control of the provinces of Bengal, Bihar and Orissa in addition to the Madras and Bombay Presidencies.[7]

So, by the time Carey arrived in Bengal in 1793, the East India Company had not only firmly secured its commercial interests but had begun acting as a sovereign power over a large portion of the subcontinent. Hailing from England, the Company was, in a sense, Christian. By contrast, the subcontinent over which it ruled was a mixture of predominantly Hindu sects and a minority of Muslims that were part of the waning Mughal empire. In such an environment, the Company could ill afford to offend local

---

[5] Penelope Carson, *Worlds Of The East India Company*, vol. 7, *The East India Company and Religion, 1698–1858* (Woodbridge, UK: Boydell Press, 2012), 2, 23.

[6] *A Dictionary of British History*, 3rd ed., s.v. "Plassey, Battle of," eds. John Cannon and Robert Crowcroft (Oxford: Oxford University Press, 2015).

[7] Carson, *The East India Company and Religion*, 19.

religious sentiments—especially its *sepoys*. So, in India the Company followed a shrewd policy of religious neutrality and toleration.[8]

In England, however, it behooved the Company to show a Christian face. In the arena of missions, this meant the Company tolerated the few Protestant Lutheran missionaries (mostly in South India) that still operated under the patronage of the SPCK (Society for the Promotion of Christian Knowledge).[9] But the thought of radical Dissenters exciting the passions of the natives through their itinerancy was a frightening and intolerable prospect. The attitude of the Company is exemplified in the words of Warren Hastings (1732-1818), the first Governor-General of India. In words reminiscent of John Ryland Senior's infamous "Sit down young man!" statement to Carey, Hastings believed it was Britain's duty "to protect their [Indian] persons from wrong and to leave their religious creed to the Being who has so long endured it and who will in his own time reform it."[10] In such a delicate environment, it is no wonder Carey was not a welcomed guest when he landed in Calcutta on November 11, 1793. He and others after him found that they could be tolerated by the Company as long as they did not make any waves, but the following confrontations demonstrate the "colonial dance" in which they

---

[8] Carson, *The East India Company and Religion*, 14.

[9] The SPCK was established in 1699 and "can be regarded as a halfway house between the government-patronised Catholic societies of continental Europe and the Protestant voluntary societies of late eighteenth-century Britain." Carson, *The East India Company and Religion*, 10. Its patronage of Lutheran missionaries under the Royal Danish Mission arose through the influence of Anton Böhme, chaplain of Queen Anne's husband, Prince George, who hailed from Denmark.

[10] A. Wild, *The East India Company, Trade and Conquest from 1600* (London, 1999), 162 quoted in Carson, *The East India Company and Religion*, 15. At a meeting of the Northamptonshire Association around 1788, when Carey had proposed that they discuss "The duty of Christians to attempt the spread of the Gospel among heathen nations," John Ryland Sr. chastised Carey, "Young man, sit down. When God pleases to convert the heathen, he will do it without your aid or mine." J.C. Marshman, *The Life and Times of Carey, Marshman, and Ward* (1859; repr., Serampore: Council of Serampore College, 2005), 1:10.

were constantly engaged.

General Examples of Government Opposition

In late 1801, Ward, Felix Carey, and Creeshnoo were itinerating and distributing tracts in the midst of a crowd at a Bengali fair in a village named Khardah, two miles downriver from Serampore. After emerging from a discussion in one man's home, he was confronted by an English police officer "who had arrived from Calcutta, & who was come up with a number of sea-poys to keep the peace, take up thieves, & c." Ward continues,

> I went back to this man, & was interrogated by him, whether I had not been distributing papers among the natives? Answering in the affirmative, he asked if I had any license from government? I then told him of my connections & of our errand & of Bro. C.'s appointment, & assured him that the papers were entirely about Jesus Xt. He said he would not let me go until a native should read it before him, & declare the contents. He got a man, who read very poorly. Another man said there were bad things in them; that we said that Creeshnoo [Krishna] was a liar, & Ganga a murderer, &c. &c. I promised to write my name on the papers. A pen & ink being procured, I signed my name, after which he consented to let me go, declaring that he should send the papers to the Police Office immediately. We parted tolerably friendly. It was rather late when we got home.[11]

A little over three weeks later, Ward records of a similar encounter that Carey endured:

> This evening Brother Carey arrived late. He had been detained in translating two pieces in Bengalee [Bangla] which had been given away by us amongst the natives. It seems

---

[11] William Ward, Journal MSS, Friday, November 20, 1801, 188.

these papers had been put into the hands of one of the Judges, who had talked of bringing the business forward at the Levee. Mr. Buchannon had said he was persuaded there was nothing but what was innocent in these papers; but he sent them to Bro. Carey to get him to translate them, which he did & sent them to Mr. Buchannon. The Judges Bengalee [Bengali] Sircar, when he carried these papers to his master, enquired if the Company had given orders for the natives to lose Cast [Caste], as these papers went to persuade people to lose cast [caste]. There is not a sentiment, however, in them, but what is perfectly inoffensive, & infinitely removed from civil affairs.[12]

These two accounts, taken together, display the complex, muddled nature of relations between the Company Government and the Serampore missionaries. To begin with, as seen in both excerpts, neither Ward nor Carey denied that they distributed gospel pamphlets among the natives. That which they were careful to distance themselves from was any notion that they had disparaged Hindu deities or assaulted the deeply ingrained social structure of caste. The Government feared that comments of this nature would inflame local passions and endanger their trade and rule. The missionaries knew this; hence Ward's unequivocal disavowal, "There is not a sentiment, however, in them, but what is perfectly inoffensive, & infinitely removed from civil affairs." This is representative of the Mission's local public stance. They eschewed any acknowledgement of that which they knew the Company Government considered out of bounds.

But in Serampore and in news communicated to the evangelical public back home, Ward spoke much more sanguinely regarding the breaking of caste. For example, a couple of years prior to his statement above, Ward rejoiced when the Mission's first two converts, Krishna Pal and Gokol, publicly broke caste by eating

---

[12] Ward, Journal MSS, Friday, December 4, 1801, 190.

Spirituality in Peacemaking

lunch with the missionaries, exulting, "Thus the door of faith is opened to the Hindoos [Hindus]- who shall shut it? Thus the chain of the cast [caste] is broken—Who shall mend it?"[13] The very next day, a mob of 2,000 was in an uproar precisely because Krishna had lost his caste.[14] But for the protection of the Danish magistrate, the light of his witness would likely have been snuffed out ere it had an opportunity to shine. Gokol was unwilling to proceed with baptism at that time, but six days later, Krishna Pal, along with William Carey's son, Felix, testified publicly of their faith by being immersed in water baptism. Following that momentous event, Ward boasted over the Hindu gods, "Ye gods of stone & clay did ye not tremble, when, in the name of the Father, Son, & Holy Ghost, one individual shook you as the dust from his foot?"[15]

On the one hand, the Company was right in its understanding of the potential unrest that could occur if local religious sentiments were offended. On the other hand, the missionaries rightly understood that there would be no true conversion among Hindus *without* breaking caste. In the above excerpts and elsewhere, the missionaries regularly celebrated each breaking of caste as a victory of Christ over the powers of heathen darkness. Fully aware of the insults, slander, riots, and even martyrdom that might result from such breaking of caste, the missionaries were willing to risk such hazards for the sake of the Kingdom of Christ

---

[13] Ward, Journal MSS, Monday, December 22, 1800, 125. The version published in the Periodical Accounts of the BMS is only slightly different, but the feeling regarding caste is the same e.g. "Thus the door of faith is opened to the gentiles; Who shall shut it? The chain of the cast is broken; Who shall ment it?" *Periodical Accounts Relative to the Baptist Missionary Society. Baptist Missionary Society Archives, 1792-1914*, microfilm, reels 1-9 (London: Baptist Missionary Archives, 1981), 2:124.

[14] Ward, Journal MSS, Tuesday, December 23, 1800, 126.

[15] Ward, Journal MSS, Lord's Day, December 28, 1800, 129. Ward's taunt as recorded in the *PA* for subscribers in England, is worded more strongly than Ward's Journal, describing Krishna not merely as an "individual" who shook off the Hindu gods as one shakes dust off of his foot, but as "one of [the god's] votaries" who did the same. *PA*, 2:127.

in Bengal. The Company, for the sake of the preservation of its kingdom, was not.

Returning to the above examples of government opposition, it is also noteworthy that when questioned about their itinerating activities, Ward mentioned his "connections ... & Bro. C.'s appointment." The "connections" in view were undoubtedly Ward's connections with the Danish colony of Serampore. It was under the protection of a Danish passport that Ward, shortly after arriving in India, was able to travel safely to Carey's bungalow near the indigo factory in Malda District, Bengal.[16] Once there, he explained to Carey that at Serampore they would be "under the protection of the Danish flag" and would be "free from molestation by the British authorities; they might establish a press, and receive additional missionaries."[17] With only a "small garrison of forty native soldiers, and the few honeycombed guns which had been used as a saluting battery," Serampore offered the missionaries no martial protection to speak of. This is evident from the effortless manner in which British forces occupied Serampore from 1808–1814. What these "connections" did offer was enough respect from Company officials to prevent their immediate arrest or seizure of property.

They did not, however, shield them from ongoing interrogation and harassment. In September 1803, Ward's journey to Dinajpur in north Bengal was delayed for five days due to lack of a passport as the Government, then at war with the Mahrattas in western India, was "very cautious & [required] every person going out of Calcutta to get a pass from the police."[18] A couple of years later, after journeying to Sahebgunge, Ward was denied land he desired to purchase for a new mission station near Jessore because of the Collector's concern over a mob Marsh-

---

[16] Marshman, *Life and Times*, 1:121.
[17] Marshman, *Life and Times*, 1:121.
[18] Ward, Journal MSS, Monday, September 19, 1803, 322.

man's preaching had once raised in that place.[19] In early 1806, colleague John Biss was unable to accompany Fernandez on a trip to the interior because of a law stating that he had not yet been in the country for a sufficient amount of time.[20] Later that year, as mentioned in chapter 3, it appeared new recruits Chater and Robinson would be sent back to England shortly after arriving in Bengal. In the midst of that saga that lasted over two months, the Calcutta Police queried at one point "whether the Missionaries were not at Serampore as refugees rather than under the protection & patronage of the Danish Crown." A perturbed Ward records, "You see they want to root us out here, if possible, but God has shut us in."[21] In their plans to build a chapel for Dissenters in Calcutta, the police objected that they needed government permission as it would be a "public edifice." On this occasion, Ward writes, "We had thoughts of complying, with this, but have been persuaded not to do it, as it is not likely that government would grant leave."[22]

In late 1810, after originally seeking permission to settle near the Punjab, John Chamberlain and his Asiatic partner, Mr. Peacock were given official permission to proceed instead to Agra where they hoped to set up a new mission station.[23] Christopher Smith writes that this change of location was mandated so that Chamberlain and Peacock would be "under the watchful eye of the Magistrate."[24] Consequently, though they were successful in opening the new station, the process to gain such approval was so vexing, Ward quipped to Fuller, "Now we are likely to get stations fixed with the public permission of Government, and we

---

[19] Ward, Journal MSS, November 16-20, 1805, 453–456.
[20] Ward, Journal MSS, Wednesday, February 19, 1806, 476.
[21] Ward, Journal MSS, October 13-14, 1806, 516.
[22] Ward, Journal MSS, Monday, March 16, 1807, 542.
[23] Ward, Journal MSS, Tuesday, September 11, 1810, 735-36 and Monday November 26, 1810, 739.
[24] A. Christopher Smith, *The Serampore Enterprise* (Bangalore, India: Centre for Contemporary Christianity, 2006), 174.

shall be tolerated like toads, and not hunted down like wild beasts."[25] In early 1811, Brn. and Sisters Chamberlain and Peacock embarked for Agra with "a good cargo of parts of the Scripture & Tracts in Persian & Hindoostanee [Hindustani], & some tracts in the Sikh. ... in good spirits."[26] But sadly, by September of that year, Bengal Government Chief Secretary, Neil Edmonstone was compelled to write to Marshman concerning Chamberlain's aggressive attempts to convert locals by means of, "declamatory harangues, and Challenges to Controversy on points of Religious Faith, in publicly reviling the Koraun, and the Shasters and the Religious Ceremonies of the Hindoos [Hindus], and in diffusing tracts obnoxious to the religions of the Country."[27]

This is a brief snapshot of the colonial dance in which Ward and his band were constantly engaged. In times of war or unrest, Government scrutiny increased and the missionaries had to tiptoe as it were, in their itinerancy and printing. At other times, Company officials looked the other way, and the missionaries were tolerated in overt ministry efforts. For the East India Company's part, because they were wary of the damage evangelical missionaries' unchecked zeal could do to their trade and rule in India, they felt obliged to keep a watchful eye on Dissenters and Churchmen alike and, when needed, put them in their place. But they were careful not to be overtly tyrannical when they did so, knowing that an anti-mission reputation in Christian England would also not serve their interests. For the Mission's part,

---

[25] Marshman, *Life and Times*, 1:432. This quote is also found in Ward to Fuller, October 21, 1810, BMS MSS, quoted in E. Daniel Potts, *British Baptist Missionaries in India 1793-1837; The History of Serampore And Its Missions* (Cambridge: Cambridge University Press, 1967), 195. The larger episode is also described in Ward, Journal MSS, 735-39.

[26] Ward, Journal MSS, Monday, January 21, 1811, 746.

[27] N.B. Edmonstone to Joshua Marshman, September 13, 1811, "Rev. J. Marshman's Correspondence, 1799-1826," BMS MSS, quoted in Potts, *British Baptist Missionaries in India*, 195. "Shaster" is a variant of the Sanskrit *shastra* referring to the Hindu scriptures.

Spirituality in Peacemaking

though they were often frustrated in their missionary efforts by the Company's interference, they and their converts enjoyed their protection, and they often sought to establish new mission stations in the "colonial shadow."[28] Though tensions in their relationship would ease somewhat with the revision and renewal of the East India Company's Charter in 1813, a full-blown crisis occurred in what came to be known as "The Persian Pamphlet Controversy."

The Persian Pamphlet Controversy

As the Persian Pamphlet Controversy consisted of company efforts to silence the Mission Press, it will be helpful to review its origin and the early history of the Government's relationship to it.

History of Serampore's Mission Press

When Carey arrived in India, printing was in its infancy in Bengal and presses were few. In 1778, the Orientalist and Company civil servant, Charles Wilkins, with the aid of a native blacksmith named Punchanon, had printed *Halhed's Bengalee Grammar*, the first work of any kind printed in the Bangla language, at a press in nearby Hooghly from punches that he made with his own hands. Then, in 1785, Jonathan Duncan, eventual governor of Bombay, completed a Bangla translation of *Regulations* which "became the basis of all subsequent legislation."[29]

The Baptists obtained their first printing press in 1797, courtesy of a forty pound gift from Mr. Udny, the owner of the indigo factory in Mudnabatty which Carey oversaw.[30] In 1800, this press was moved to Serampore and set up in a side building of

---

[28] A. Christopher Smith, *The Serampore Mission Enterprise* (Bangalore, India: Centre for Contemporary Christianity, 2006), 165, 178.

[29] Marshman, *Life and Times*, 1:70–71.

[30] Marshman, *Life and Times*, 1:80.

the newly purchased premises there.[31] The smaller and neater Bengali font that Ward would prepare here would supersede the earlier fonts mentioned above.[32] Thus, the earliest printing efforts were very primitive and were, in some way, affiliated with the East India Company. The superior press at Serampore was not. In addition, it was operated by a professional printer who had served as editor for two British newspapers and had had some connection there with radicals. The Company Government recognized the rival power represented by the Serampore Press and was determined to keep it under their watchful eye. The Mission was also aware that their ability to exercise their press for the sake of reaching the lost in Bengal was dependent on Government favor.

Though both parties were wary of the other, there was also mutual benefit in their relationship. When it came to translation of vernacular works and superior printing, the Company had no better option than Serampore. And the print jobs that the Company and especially Fort William College gave to the Mission provided them with much needed revenue. So, from 1801, the Company supplied two of their three main sources of revenue—a regular salary to Carey for his teaching services at Fort William College and regular printing orders which were fulfilled by Ward.[33] The primary aim of the press was to print evangelistic literature and translations of Holy Scripture for distribution in Bengal and beyond. But ideally this aim could be pursued without endangering lucrative Government contracts.

Tens of thousands of tracts and religious tracts and pam-

---

[31] Marshman, *Life and Times*, 1:128-29.
[32] Marshman, *Life and Times*, 1:71.
[33] The third main income source was tuition from students in the schools that Joshua and Hannah Marshman ran. The role of the school and press in accomplishing their pecuniary and ministry needs is discussed in the Trio's letter to the Society, January 1805 as printed in *PA*, 3:26.

Spirituality in Peacemaking

phlets regularly rolled off of the presses at Serampore.[34] These "paper missionaries" were distributed liberally by the Serampore missionaries and their national partners as they itinerated amongst villages throughout the Bengali countryside.[35] The fruit of Ward's press was two-fold. First, enquirers, with appetites whetted by a tract, began to journey to Serampore to hear more of the gospel message.[36] Second, as they journeyed further afield from their home base at Serampore, Ward and his national partners often found that their printed tracts had preceded them, paving the way for a verbal proclamation of the gospel.[37]

---

[34] Regarding the massive amounts of tracts that were distributed by the Serampore missionaries, Ward, just a few years into his ministry, while explaining the Mission's methods of ministry to an emissary from a particular guru that advocated a type of native monotheism, informed them that "we had already distributed 22,000 pamphlets or small tracts amongst the people." Ward, Journal MSS, Monday, October 18, 1802, 261. For a discussion on distribution methods and cost of production of smaller tracts and pamphlets compared with Bibles and Scripture portions, see James Ryan West, "Evangelizing Bengali Muslims, 1793-1813; William Carey, William Ward, and Islam" (PhD diss., The Southern Baptist Theological Seminary, 2014), 159.

[35] For a fuller discussion of the missiological significance of the Serampore Press via the "paper missionaries" it sent forth, see West, "Evangelizing Bengali Muslims," 154.

[36] The following quotes are examples of this: In the summer of 1802 Ward records, "During our journey [from Calcutta to Serampore] a man from Belleah (see my Journal of Oct. 19 & 20) had arrived to enquire about the Gospel. He had seen one of our tracts, having read it he was come for more knowledge." Ward, Journal MSS, Saturday, January 23, 1802, 205. In a similar vein, Ward writes about a week later, "We had two men from Jess[ore], a journey of three or four days, to hear & get the scriptures to-day. This is another fruit of our first journey out, when Creeshnoo & I went with Mr. Short. We had much talk with them during the day. They staid & heard preaching at night, & afterwards went to Creeshnoo's & talked wt. Petumber, &c. almost all night." Ward, Journal MSS, Lord's Day, January 31, 1802, 206-207.

[37] After receiving a warm reception in a village called Ogradeep [Agradwip], Ward records that, among twenty Testaments distributed there, one was "for Dacca [Dhaka; the capital of present-day Bangladesh], another for Beerbhoom [Birbhum; a district of Bengal almost 200 km. north of Kolkata], another for Shoomadragheer; another for Kallepore, & the rest went into Ogradeepe or its immediate neighborhood. ... Several persons in this & other places have enquired for Persian & Nagaree books. The news of Jesus Christ & of the church at Serampore seems to have gone much further than I expected. It appears to be known in most villages to a few." Ward, Journal MSS, Friday, September 30, 1803, 328. Of this encounter, West perceives, "These inquirers knew of Ward's product and sought out their own copies of

The Spirituality of William Ward

Early example of government opposition to the Mission Press

But the Company recognized that if such pamphlets contained language of a religiously incendiary nature, the results could be perilous to their rule and profits. From the inception of the Mission Press, the Government was uneasy. And it seems the Mission did not always act prudently in its zeal to print mission-related literature. On March 18, 1800, shortly after the press' arrival in Serampore, Ward presented Carey "the first sheet of the [Bengali] Testament."[38] They then proposed to raise money for the publishing of the Bengali Bible by way of subscriptions.[39] Without fanfare, they placed an advertisement for these subscriptions in the Calcutta newspaper. And so, upon reading his newspaper one day, Marquess Wellesley, the Governor General of Bengal, came to know of the Mission's press! This was especially disconcerting because, as will be seen shortly, he was in the habit of censoring news before it was printed. Upon hearing of its existence, Governor Wellesley first thought to inquire in writing of his Danish counterpart in Serampore. "Of what use is it for one to read every paper before it is printed at Calcutta & watch every press there, if a press, over which I have no control, exists at Serampoor?" he reasoned.[40]

But on second thought, he opted to have his secretary write a similar letter instead to Rev. Brown. But before receiving the letter, Rev. Brown reached out in person to the Governor General—with a proposal from the Mission Press to print the Bible

---

testaments and pamphlets, which was a direct result of his work. This particular entry—September 30, 1803—was a summary of his encounter in Ogradeep, a village from which a resident heard Ward preach in nearby Gayakalee and took some of his materials eighteen months earlier on January 20, 1802." West, "Evangelizing Bengali Muslims," 157 n25.

[38] Marshman, *Life and Times*, 1:129.

[39] The following account of the Mission's proposal and its interaction with the Governor General concerning the same as well as related citations are found in Ward, Journal MSS, Tuesday, June 24, 1800, 89 and Lord's Day, June 29, 1800, 89-90.

[40] Ward, Journal MSS, Lord's Day, June 29, 1800, 90.

Spirituality in Peacemaking

in Bangla![41] It appears the Mission was operating from an "It's easier to ask forgiveness than permission" mindset. If so, their strategy worked. In this personal meeting, Brown was able calmly to allay the Governor's concerns. Ward records salient points of their conversation:

> Mr. Brown assured his Lordship that we should print nothing on the subject of politics. His Lordship asked Mr. Brown if he thought it were safe to publish the Bible without a commentary, seeing it taught the doctrine of Xn. equality? Mr. Brown promised that he would be answerable for all the harm which the Bible would do. His Lordship acknowledged that he was a friend to making men Xns. Mr. Brown told his Lordship that this work would be particularly useful in the College which his Lordship intended to establish for Oriental Literature. He asked if the translation were a good one. Mr. Brown replied, that if he did not think it were he would not recommend it. His Lordship said he would consult a gentleman well versed in Bengallee [Bengali], & the Subscription-book might remain with him a little longer.[42]

The Trio subsequently received a letter from Brown in which he assured his friends that they would "come to no harm since he answered them all [that is, the Governor's inquiries concerning the press], & made some promise on our account."[43] Ward then concludes, "Such are the jealousies which our press excites in the minds of the English government, tho' we are under the jurisdiction of a foreign power. How long would it have stood at Mudnabatty?"[44] Yet, a little over a month later, Ward mentions

---

[41] Ward's journal entry records the proposal being made to "Lord Mornington." This is the same person as Marquess Wellesley, the Governor General of Bengal. Ward, Journal MSS, Tuesday, June 24, 1800, 89.

[42] Ward, Journal MSS, Lord's Day, June 29, 1800, 89-90.

[43] Ward, Journal MSS, Tuesday, June 24, 1800, 89.

[44] Ward, Journal MSS, Tuesday, June 24, 1800, 89.

that Brother Brunsdon, while in Calcutta, had heard from Rev. Brown that "the Governor had talked of taking all the presses in India under his own direction & pay."[45] At this juncture the threat proved idle. But the threat was to be reissued seven years later with passionate vigor.

Details of the Persian Pamphlet Controversy

Following the Vellore Mutiny in July 1806, when, understandably, the Government was on high alert to anything that might excite the native population, a disturbance arose concerning one pamphlet concerning the life of the Prophet Muhammad. It all began with a seemingly mundane piece of official correspondence from the Governor General, Lord Minto, which was sent, not to the Serampore missionaries, but to Danish Governor Krefting:

> This evening Mr. Krefting, our Governor, sent for our perusal an official letter signed by Lord Minto, Sir Geo. Barlow & Mr. Lumsden, complaining of one of our Persian pamphlets as very inflammatory & calculated to inflame the Musulmans. We promised to wait on the Governor in the morning.[46]

The next day the brothers at Serampore received a letter on the same subject from Carey, who was at his post at Fort William College in Calcutta. He had been summoned "to attend immediately at the Government House."[47] Before he arrived, he came to know of the matter at hand from Rev. Brown who asked if he knew anything about a "publication in the Persian language at

---

[45] Ward, Journal MSS, Friday, August 1, 1800, 92.
[46] Ward, Journal MSS, Wednesday, September 2, 1807, 579.
[47] This and following quotes in this paragraph taken from Carey to Serampore Brethren, September 3, 1807, quoted in Ward, Journal MSS, Thursday, September 3, 1807, 579-580.

Spirituality in Peacemaking

our press, which was calculated to inflame the minds of the Mussulmans." Carey answered Brown that he was unaware of anything "being published in that language" but acknowledged that a pamphlet might have slipped through the press without his knowledge. Brown then produced the pamphlet in question, and its contents were indeed inflammatory and ominous.

The Persian pamphlet gave "a history of the life of Mahomet" and contrasted "the mild genius of the Gospel with his impostures." The pamphlet repeatedly referred to the Prophet Muhammad as a "tyrant" and to the *Qur'an* as an "imposture"—i.e., a work which is intended to deceive. Because of such language, the Government deemed this pamphlet "sufficient to excite rebellion among the Mussulmans." And why not? Just over a year prior to this pamphlet, Muslim sepoys had murdered over one hundred British officers while they slept because they felt their religion had been endangered by news that the sepoys were to be forced to wear new headgear resembling a British hat![48] If rumor of a military wardrobe change had effected such horrific consequences, what might be the result of a pamphlet that overtly disparaged their Prophet and Holy Book?

Carey first, and then the rest of the Trio tried to contain the damage. Carey "promised to furnish Government with the history of this pamphlet, and to what extent it had been circulated." Then he instructed Ward and Marshman,

> You will therefore greatly oblige me by sending immediately to me an account [of] how many were printed, whether it has gone through more editions than one, and if so how many—whether any have been sent to places at a distance from Serampore, and where, and how many. You had better not let any more of it to be distributed till you see me. I hope none have been sent to Martyn and Corrie, as Gt.

---
[48] Marshman, *Life and Times*, 1:263.

Seems to be peculiarly suspicious of them. I was asked whether we were engaged in any places with any clergyman to carry on our schemes. I could say no, and for their sakes am glad I could. I think irritating epithets should be expunged from all our pamphlets—we lie open to animadversions here.[49]

Thus began the crisis known as the "Persian Pamphlet Affair." Ward's Journal entries are consumed with the matter for an entire month. And for good reason. When Marshman and Ward went to wait on Governor Krefting, he "expressed a good deal of alarm on the subject of the letter from the Governor-General & Council at Calcutta." The conversation between Ward, Marshman, and their Danish protector was cordial, but he emphasized that he was unable to protect them if they "pushed things to extremities; as what could he do with 50 sepoys." The two junior Trio members responded by apologizing for the "irritating expressions in the pamphlet, declared [their] sorrow, & gave him the most solemn assurance of [their] desire to please him, & utter aversion to do any thing to offend him."[50] Following this interview, Governor Krefting sent the Brethren an official letter "in strong terms, ordering the Persian pamphlets to be sent to him, & desiring us to avoid all inflaming things in future."[51]

It turned out that the inflammatory contents of the pamphlet had come to the Calcutta Government's attention via Secretary Lumsden's Persian Moonshee.[52] Someone had put a copy of the pamphlet in his hands and "challenged him to write an answer to it."[53] By the time the Mission replied to Governor Krefting's

---

[49] Ward, Journal MSS, Thursday, September 3, 1807, 580.
[50] Ward, Journal MSS, Thursday, September 3, 1807, 582.
[51] Ward, Journal MSS, Lord's Day, September 6, 1807, 582-583.
[52] A *moonshee* was a native Indian language tutor.
[53] Ward, Journal MSS, Friday, September 4, 1807, 582.

Spirituality in Peacemaking

letter, a fuller picture of the origins of the pamphlet had emerged. The Trio explained that about three months prior, they had asked a moonshee, converted from a Muslim background, to translate a "short abstract (in the Bengalee [Bengali] language,) of the life of Mahomet taken almost verbatim from Sales' preliminary discourse prefixed to his translation [of] the Koran, desiring him to translate it into Persian."[54] In their haste, the pamphlet went to press without sufficient editing, and only later did they find that the over-zealous convert had inserted the derogatory comments under question. They owned the fault as their own and offered to supply the Serampore Governor the original pamphlet or an English translation of the same should he so desire.[55]

As for the circulation of the pamphlet, the Serampore Brethren reported that only two thousand had been printed, of which, one thousand seven hundred were still in their hands. They were confident that the remaining three hundred pamphlets had been distributed in Serampore, Calcutta, and nearby former Dutch colony, Chinsurah. Then, contrary to Ward's previous journal entries describing the persuasive effect on those who read their tracts, they downplayed any potential negative impact from the Persian pamphlet, claiming that such literature usually met with "indifference and disregard" among the natives, and that it was likely that "the greater part of them are thrown away or destroyed."[56] In other obsequities, the missionaries stated that they were turning over all undistributed Persian pamphlets to his "Excellency" and that it would "never more issue from [their]

---

[54] Ward, Journal MSS, Tuesday, September 8, 1807, 584. The *Qur'anic* translation mentioned here is that of George Sale who translated the *Qur'an* from Arabic to English in 1734. This translation contained a defense of Muhammad that earned him a "reputation as a secret Muslim convert, or at least as a freethinker." *Encyclopedia of the Enlightenment*, s.v. "North Africa and the Levant," ed. Alan Charles Kors (Oxford University Press, 2005).

[55] Ward, Journal MSS, Tuesday, September 8, 1807, 584.

[56] Ward, Journal MSS, Tuesday, September 8, 1807, 584.

press in any form whatever," and that the way of conversion by coercion and irritation was not one they espoused. They reminded him of the clean track record that they had maintained during the eight years of Danish patronage they had enjoyed, and in almost groveling language, acknowledged that they recognized as he did that their "very existence in this a heathen country is suspended on the prosperity of the British Empire in India."[57]

Ever the draftsman, it is likely that Ward himself wrote this letter. Its wording is shrewd, expedient, and obsequious. The pamphlet may well have been the work of an over-zealous moonshee/convert, but previously the Trio had used wording in itinerancy and tracts that would surely have evoked similar alarm from British and Danish authorities as the Journal excerpts in the footnote below demonstrate.[58] It is a fine line between disparagement and truth telling. And it is understandable that an eager evangelist and unconverted interlocutor might disagree regarding the proper positioning of this line. But Carey felt such force

---

[57] Ward, Journal MSS, Tuesday, September 8, 1807, 585–586.

[58] In a letter from the Trio to BMS Society, July 16, 1802 (likely drafted by Ward), it is mentioned that "an unknown number of small tracts purely on the way of salvation, and against the Hindoo and Mussulman errors, have been dispersed." *PA*, 3:290. This wording was likely intended to assure Society members that they were not meddling in political affairs. They spoke "purely on the way of salvation." But they readily acknowledged that their tracts also confronted what they believed to be false in local religious teachings. The tone is even more combative in conversations Ward recorded during early itinerating trips: "In the evening a Brahman invited Brother Carey to go to his village, and 'talk of these things there.' Brother C. fixed a time. One man, during the discourse, walked off, declaring he would stay no longer to hear his gods abused." Ward, Journal MSS, Lord's Day, March 2, 1800, 71. On another occasion, Ward records that Carey was "very earnest in his intreaties on this occasion. He told the Mussulmans that Mohammed was a servant, who married his mistress, & afterwards murdered those who did not believe as he did. ... To the Hindoos he said the incarnation of Ram was to destroy Raabin the man-eater—but there was no salvation for them in all this. Whereas the salvation of Xt. was for them, for the salvation of their souls." Ward, Journal MSS, Lord's Day, August 31, 1800, 96. Of another of Carey's contests with Brahmins, Ward writes, "With the last he contended till near dark, when the Brahman asked leave to go to worship. Bro. C. told him, if he was anything of a Brahman he might order the evening to stay for him, as a Brahman was said to have done formerly, when he had overslept himself. ... Bro. C. said he despised his gods." Ward, Journal MSS, Friday, September 5, 1800, 97.

Spirituality in Peacemaking

was justified. He reasoned that "he was like a man who should find his neighbor asleep with his house on fire. He might fetch him two or three hard thumps, but it was only to warn him of danger, & promote his escape."[59] Truly, once saved, many look back and see how God worked through many witnesses, both kind and brusque, to bring them to Christ. God, in his grace, may well have worked through the Trio's early combative witness, but the following comment demonstrates that the frontal attack sometimes achieved the opposite effect. "The Mussulmans are fond of hearing the Hindoo [Hindu] gods run down. Bro. C. frequently produces some pointed ridicule against the heathen customs. The Brahmans are generally shy of hearing now."[60] From their safe vantage at Serampore, the Baptist missionaries delighted in proclaiming the truths of Christianity and the falsehood of Hinduism and Islam without reserve. But they were not naïve. And in times of exigency, they walked another fine line (i.e. the line between sagacity and compromise).

And this was certainly a time of great exigency. On September 11 an alarming express letter arrived for Carey from the Company Government in Calcutta. In their eyes, the pamphlet was "detrimental to the tranquility of the British dominions in India," and they avowed their intention to "arrest the progress of any proceedings of that nature." Theirs was an obligation "to leave the native subjects of the Company in India, in the full, free & undisturbed exercise of their respective religions."[61] To these ends, they demanded that the house of worship in Calcutta be closed, and worst of all that the Mission Press "productions should be subject to the immediate countroul of the Officers of Government." Then, explaining the control that they had in mind, they continued, "With this view I am directed to desire

---

[59] Ward, Journal MSS, Lord's Day, October 5, 1800, 105.
[60] Ward, Journal MSS, Lord's Day, September 14, 1800, 98.
[61] Ward, Journal MSS, Friday, September 11, 1807, 588.

that you will signify to the Missionaries the expectation of the Governor General in Council, that the press be transferred to this Presidency where alone the same Controul that is established over presses sanctioned by Government, can be duly exercised."[62]

This letter brought the Mission very low. They called a special prayer meeting. And then they agreed it would be best for the present for Carey to make a short, general reply to Secretary Edmonstone and later present a more detailed "memoir" to Lord Minto. This Carey did, but the crisis was taking a heavy toll. Ward records,

> Bro. Carey dines today with Lord Minto. We have never been so heavily oppressed in mind by any thing as by Edmundstone's letter. Bro. Carey wept like a child on Saturday morning at the prayer—meeting. The natives are triumphing over us, and it is reported all over this place & neighbourhood that the Governor of Calcutta is driving us out of the country.[63]

Before the Trio could compose their memoir, another letter arrived from the Company Government expressing their thanks to Governor Krefting for suppressing and handing over the "obnoxious" Persian pamphlets and their hope that he would comply in their desire for the removal of the press to Calcutta.[64] The following day, the Serampore band held another prayer meeting. Meanwhile, it seems local clergyman, Dr. Buchanan visited Governor Krefting and Ward records that he "no doubt spoke a word for us."[65] Perhaps with this encouragement, an emboldened Krefting "declared his determination not to part with the

---

[62] Ward, Journal MSS, Friday, September 11, 1807, 589.
[63] Ward, Journal MSS, Tuesday, September 15, 1807, 592.
[64] Ward, Journal MSS, Friday, September 18, 1807, 593.
[65] Ward, Journal MSS, Lord's Day, September 20, 1807, 594.

Spirituality in Peacemaking

press. He said, if they came to compel him, he would strike the flag, & surrender himself a prisoner, but that he would not give up the press."[66]

Danish Government, Serampore Mission, and East India Company officials were at an impasse. Though the brethren in response "agreed with him to leave the whole in his hands" Ward, after hearing of their conversation was "full of thought" about their situation.[67] Drawing from his years of editorial experience, Ward drafted a letter to his colleagues in which he made an irenic proposal aimed at pacifying the wrath of the British rulers—and keeping the Mission's press!

Ward's pacific reply

Ward began by expressing his "great deal of hesitation" regarding their "sullen silence" in the face of the English Government's recent communique to Carey and Governor Krefting.[68] Though the Government had not yet compelled them to come down to Calcutta, the situation was dire in Ward's eyes as "the having them as our avowed and exasperated enemies is no small calamity." So, before laying out his proposal, Ward argued, point by point, just how calamitous it would be if they remained in the Company's ire:

> They may deprive us of Bro. Carey's salary, with which we can hardly get on now, & without which we must put an end to the translations, and go to gaol in debt; they can shut up the new meeting at Calcutta; they can stop the circulation of our grammars, Dictionaries and every thing issued from this press in their dominions; they can prohibit

---

[66] Ward, Journal MSS, Monday, September 21, 1807, 594.

[67] Ward, Journal MSS, Monday, September 21, 1807, 594.

[68] Ward, Journal MSS, Monday, September 21, 1807, 595. Ward reprints his entire letter to "Bren. Carey, Marshman, Chamberlain, Chater, Rowe, Robinseon, &c," on this and the following page of his journal.

our entering their territories, &ca.[69]

In other words, if the Company Government remained opposed to the Serampore Mission, and so desired, they could put a complete and immediate end not only to all their missionary endeavors, but to their very presence in Bengal. They were facing nothing less than the potential end of the Serampore Mission. His case made for the dire nature of their situation, Ward began laying his counsel before his brethren.

With regard to Governor Krefting, he deprecated the idea of "embroiling him with the English Government" if they could possibly avoid it. Instead, they should speak to the British Government *through* Governor Krefting as they were—for the moment—still free subjects under a Danish sovereign:

> We should entreat their clemency, & try to soften them. Tender words, with the consciences of men on our side, go a long way. We can tell them to take the press to Calcutta would involve us in a heavy and unbearable expence, break up our family, &ca. & ca. &ca. and that we will give them every security which they would wish, by subjecting our press to the absolute control and inspection of the Government here, nay that we are willing to do every thing they wish us, except that of renouncing our work and character as Ministers of the Saviour of the world. To this Mr. Krefting can add what he likes. If they listen to this we are secured, with all the advantages of their sufferance. If they are obstinate, we are still at Serampore. I entreat you dear Brethren, to consider these things, and give them all the attention that our awful circumstances [require].[70]

Ward's proposal met with the approbation of his brothers, and they decided, according to his previous counsel, personally to present a "supplicatory & explanatory address to the Gover-

---

[69] Ward, Journal MSS, Monday, September 21, 1807, 595.

[70] Ward, Journal MSS, Monday, September 21, 1807, 595-596.

Spirituality in Peacemaking

nor in Council." Ward felt that by plainly "unfolding their whole conduct" they would "invariably cultivate a good understanding" with the Governor as had their Moravian forebearers. "In this case," Ward writes, "prejudices are disarmed, & enemies prevented from prejudicing the mind of Governors."[71]

The next day a Dr. Leyden called, and "offered his services" if the missionaries "wished to call upon Governor General Lord Minto." Dr. Leyden was "acquainted with one of his Lordship's aid-de-camps" and counseled that a friendly visit to the Governor, eschewing any mention of their "situation & mission" would plainly demonstrate that they were not hiding themselves "as guilty persons." Marshman and Ward consulted, and the former set off with Dr. Leyden to propose the plan to Carey, and "if it were thought best, to wait on his lordship" the following day when he gave "private audiences."[72]

Ward's description of Carey and Marshman's visit to Lord Minto is humorous, revealing Ward's wit that surfaces again and again in his journal. Marshman, having no proper coat, borrowed one from Mr. Rolt. Then, with a gift of their English translation of the Hindu epic, *Ramayana*, they called on Lord Minto, Governor General of the Company's dominion in India. Ward writes that "it was lucky for Bro. Carey, that the form required him to leave his hat in the passage, or he would most likely have stuck it under his left arm-pit; bro. Marshman would by a dreadful squeeze, have made his hat shrink into the size of black pocket-handkerchief."[73] They declared their intention of presenting to him a private memorial, apparently along the lines of the "supplicatory & explanatory address" Ward had recommended. In the course of their conversation, Lord Minto indicated that he would welcome and read the memorial though such a "private

---

[71] Ward, Journal MSS, Monday September 21, 1807, 596.
[72] Ward, Journal MSS, Thursday, September 24, 1807, 596-97.
[73] Ward, Journal MSS, Friday, September 25, 1807, 597.

memorial could not be brought into the measures of government." The Governor assured them that "he had no hostility" towards them or their work, and that he "thought the conversion of the natives, in a peaceable way, a desirable object, but that he was afraid there was danger of provoking the Musulmans." He "hinted that it was expected that Missionaries should have a little enthusiasm in them; that they should feel warmer on the subject of converting the heathen than worldly men; & that they should be able to bear the frowns of men in power sometimes."[74]

Bear them they did for a couple of more weeks. Marshman wrote and submitted their explanatory memorial. Meanwhile, Governor Krefting "added" a letter favorable to their cause. Then, on October 10, the Danish Governor's secretary delivered a letter from Governor Minto "revoking their decree about the press."[75] Ward's pacific counsel had won the day.

Although Ward's counsel succeeding in retaining the Mission's press, there was a cost. Though they were free to print and distribute their Bengali translation of the Bible, the missionaries were to observe certain "restrictions imposed upon them" by the Government "relative to the publication of works offensive to the religious prejudices of the natives." As the missionaries might have different thoughts than the Government regarding what was prudent to publish in the Company's Indian realm, the missionaries were henceforth required to, submit other types of literature "to the inspection of the Officers of the British Government" before publishing it.[76] In addition, a relieved but still nervous Governor Krefting requested that

> such publications as might tend to develop the errors of the religions of the Natives, and which you intend to distribute either at this place or within the territories under

---

[74] Ward, Journal MSS, Friday, September 25, 1807, 598.
[75] Ward, Journal MSS, Saturday, October 10, 1807, 600–601.
[76] Ward, Journal MSS, Saturday, October 10, 1807, 601–602.

Spirituality in Peacemaking

the British Authority may not only be as few as possible, but be also previously submitted to my inspection, and that nothing of the kind may be printed without being first approved of ... [as he was] very anxious not to give any cause of offence to the British Government.[77]

As he looked back on the controversy, Joshua Marshman's son, John Clark Marshman, interpreted the final outcome as a "favourable change" attributable to

> peaceable and judicious conduct of the three at Serampore in bending to the necessity of circumstances, and endeavouring to conciliate those who possessed despotic power, and were at one time disposed to use it tyrannically. It was the irresitble might of Christian meekness which carried them safely through this crisis.[78]

Ward, however, was aware that such a resolution, though celebrated by the missionaries in India, might be deprecated by their sending society in England and particularly by its secretary, Andrew Fuller who considered confinement in the gaol preferable to restrictions of liberty in itinerating. In a portion of his Journal published neither by J.C. Marshman nor by the edited *Periodical Accounts* in his own day, Ward offers his own defense to Fuller and any who might cast aspersions on the compromise they had accepted to retain their press:

> It may be right to take Bro. Fuller's advice, to go to gaol, when the putting one man in gaol will not be putting the whole cause at once in gaol, but in present circumstances I think it much better that we should give way in some instance, to secure objects which we may retain. Any *one* of us, I suppose, is ready to go to gaol, but we are none of us

---

[77] Ward, Journal MSS, Saturday, October 10, 1807, 603.
[78] Marshman, *Life and Times*, 1:327.

willing to put the whole Gospel interest in Bengal in gaol at once. I suppose, for the sake of preaching at the bull-ring in the market-place, you would not think it right to quarrel with the mayor of Northampton, if you knew that the result of this quarrel would be the silencing of all the Gospel Ministers in England. "If they persecute you in one city, flee," &c. Mr. Brown concurred in the idea of our softening Government.[79]

Ward's words are witty, insightful, and poignant. Such dilemmas are still faced by missionaries today. What constitutes wisdom and shrewdness, and what constitutes compromise? It is a difficult question to answer, both for those who are far removed from the situation and culture and for those who are near and heavily invested. This question will be further considered in chapter 5.

---

[79] Ward, Journal MSS, Monday, September 21, 1807, 596. In E. Daniel Potts' typewritten transcription of Ward's Journal MSS, the account of the Persian Pamphlet Controversy spans twenty-four pages (579-603). Similarly, J.C. Marshman devotes twenty-five pages (307-332) to the ordeal and its repercussions in England in volume 1 of his 1859 work. In striking contrast, the heavily edited version presented in the *Periodical Accounts* to financial supporters in England, consists of a mere paragraph: "The difficulties which had arisen from the offensive terms in the Persian tract occasioned great distress to the missionaries during the whole month of September. They were not allowed to preach to the Armenians and Portuguese in Calcutta, and all preaching among the soldiers in Fort William, by ministers not episcopally ordained, was forbidden. The enemies of religion triumphed, its friends were discouraged, and common report went that the missionaries would be driven out of the country. This cloud however was dissipated, and things went on pretty much as before" (*PA*, 3:397)." To some degree, each author recorded what suited his purposes. In his Journal account, Ward's primary concern was the possible seizure of his press by the British. Therefore, he was careful to relate events highlighting the threat to the press and the eventual resolution which allowed them to keep it. British and Danish Governors are presented in a favorable light, and he offers a brief apology for the compromise they were willing to accept in order to keep their press. J.C. Marshman, in keeping with the aim of his first volume, devotes much space to the explanatory memorial written by his father as well as to a dispatch sent by the Company to its governing body in England in order to emphasize the aberration of the incident with the Persian pamphlet compared to the general congenial manner of the Trio's mission. The *PA*'s purpose was simple i.e. paint the Serampore missionaries as victims of an irascible East India Company that stood opposed to English evangelical aims abroad.

Spirituality in Peacemaking

However, regardless of how this question is answered, we see in Ward's letter to his colleagues the impact of Ward's spirituality at a critical time in the life of the Serampore Mission. This is not a proud letter. A proud, defensive letter might well have resulted in the immediate British occupation and surrender of Serampore and the seizure of the Mission Press. Instead it is a *humble* letter, forthrightly confessing their desperate situation and acknowledging their need of clemency from the Government, aid of "the consciences of men on our side," (which were surely their Churchmen friends, Brown and Buchanan who were both sympathetic to their plight and politically more powerful than they), and of Governor Krefting to "add what he likes." It is not a timorous letter. The easiest path to placating the wrath of their rulers would have been to surrender the press to Calcutta posthaste. It is rather a hopeful letter born on the wings of much *prayer*. It is not an unrealistic letter, but eminently *useful* and expedient. It is not a polemic work. On the contrary, it is a peacemaking letter, an outworking of the *love* of Christ for the sake of his fellows in the Mission. This is the pacific power of Ward's piety availing for the preservation of the Serampore Mission.

"Look Not Only to Your Own Interests": Ward's Acquiescence in Translation Matters[80]

The ninth guiding principle of the 1805 *Serampore Form of Agreement* begins:

> It becomes us too to labour with all our might in forwarding translations of the sacred scriptures in the languages of Hindoostan [Hindustan]. The help which God has afforded us already in this work is a loud call to us to "go for-

---

[80] This phrase from Philippians 2:4 which reads, "Each of you should look not only to your own interests, but also to the interests of others" (NIV).

ward." So far, therefore, as God has qualified us to learn those languages which are necessary, we consider it our bounden duty to apply with unwearied assiduity in acquiring them. We consider the publication of the divine Word throughout India as an object which we ought never to give up till accomplished, looking to the Fountain of all knowledge and strength, to qualify us for this great work, and to carry us through it to the praise of his holy name.[81]

A testimony to the Trio's assiduity in learning, translating, and printing Holy Scripture in the languages of India is found in the William Carey Museum a couple of hundred feet in front of the original classroom building of Serampore College. Along the inside wall of that museum, framed and encased in glass, are single-page copies of Scripture translations into thirty-five different Indian languages! With special permission, one can enter the translation room of the Archives where entire original and early printings of the same translations are held, including the world's oldest extant translation of the Bible in Chinese![82]

But though the Trio was in agreement concerning the general translation aims expressed in the *SFA*, Ward differed with Carey

---

[81] *PA*, 3:208–209. "Agreed upon at a Meeting of the Brethren, at Serampore, on Monday, October 7, 1805." *PA*, 3:198.

[82] The translation room at the CLRC contains, ironically enough, the oldest extant translation of the Bible in Chinese. Former Vice Principal Subhro Sekhar Sircar told me about an official visit from the Chinese Embassy to view the same. Translation was central to the Mission's overall strategy. In the 1815 report of the Mission that arrived in England shortly after Fuller's death, they stated their conviction that "the work of planting the Gospel in any heathen land, required three distinct agencies," viz., 1) the formation of new mission stations, 2) "the translation of Scriptures," and 3) "the instruction of youth in the knowledge of the Bible and of the literature suited to the state of the country." Marshman, *Life and Times*, 2:97. In an address Ward drew up for the British public in 1819 on his voyage to England, he set forth three departments of labor which had existed since the beginning of the Serampore Mission, namely, preaching, translation, and schools. Part of the reason for Ward's return to England was to raise support for a new, fourth labor of the Mission in the establishment of a college "intended chiefly for the instruction of native teachers and pastors in secular and Christian knowledge." Marshman, *Life and Times*, 2:197.

Spirituality in Peacemaking

and Marshman concerning the best way to achieve them. In addition, the difference in cost and time required for their respective translation philosophies was considerable. As in any enterprise, time and money were limited commodities, and therefore, potential for conflict was great. Ward's spirituality, however, effected a more peaceful outcome.

The Grand Translation Project

William Carey studied Bangla en route to Calcutta, and just over two months after arriving on November 11, 1793, he records in his journal that he "began the Correction of Genesis."[83] On the twenty-seventh of January, he notes, "This day finished the correction of the first chapter of Genesis, which Munshi says is rendered into very good Bengali."[84] This reveals the manner in which Carey was able to begin translating the Bible so early in his tenure. While he and the rest of the Trio labored assiduously in acquiring the native Bangla tongue, Carey employed the services of *munshis*, or native tutors who could "understand a Considerable deal of English" and eventually of learned *pandits* in order to expedite Bible translation.[85] Carey also had the benefit of a rudimentary translation of Genesis that Dr. Thomas had rendered.[86] Remarkably, in a letter that reached the Society in the summer of 1797, Carey informed them that "the translation of the New Testament ... would be completed before his letter reached Eng-

---

[83] Carey, Journal MSS, January 22, 1794 as found in William Carey, *The Journal and Selected Letters of William Carey*, ed. Terry G. Carter (Macon, Ga: Smyth & Helwys, 2000), 10. Compared to Ward's Journal, William Carey kept a journal for a very short period from June 13, 1793 to June 14, 1795. Terry Carter has necessarily made minor editions to Carey's handwritten copy, but includes his journal in its entirety (xi–xiv).

[84] Carey, Journal MSS, January 27, 1794 as found in Carey, *Journal and Selected Letters*, 13.

[85] Carey, Journal MSS, March 21, 1794, as found in Carey, *Journal and Selected Letters*, 19.

[86] Carey, Journal MSS, March 21, 1794, as found in Carey, *Journal and Selected Letters*, 20.

land."[87] And amazingly, by the time the press was moved to Serampore from Mudnabatty in early 1800 "with the exception of two books of the Old Testament, the translation of the whole bible into Bengalee [Bangla] had been completed."[88] As mentioned before, on March 18, 1800, Ward "presented the first sheet of the Testament to Mr. Carey."[89] Thus began the translation and printing efforts of the Serampore Mission.

In four years' time, ambition for translating and printing the Scriptures had grown to the extent that the missionaries made a proposal to the BMS "to translate and publish the Bible, or portions of it, in seven of the chief languages of India, if they could obtain aid to the extent of 1000*l* a year." The proposal met with Fuller's approbation, and he began a preaching tour of England and Scotland to raise the necessary funds. The catholicity of such a project appealed to all denominations, enabling him to raise 1,300*l* in England, to which another 700*l* was added in America through which the gift passed on its way to India.[90] But about the same time, the primarily Anglican British and Foreign Bible Society was formed for essentially the same purpose on a larger scale. As mentioned in chapter 3, a rivalry between the two groups developed from the start, but it would be seven years before the Baptists would be excluded from the Bible Society.

Meanwhile, unaware of Fuller's fundraising efforts, the missionaries began their own. As was so often the case, these were raised by way of solicitation of subscriptions from the evangelical and general public. To this end, Joshua Marshman wrote a "Memoir on the Translation of the Holy Scriptures into the languages of the East" which proposed translations into the Sanskrit, the "Latin" of Indian languages, and six other languages

---

[87] Carey to Society, n.d., quoted in Marshman, *Life and Times*, 1:79. The Society passed a resolution in response to this letter on August 29, 1797 (78).
[88] Marshman, *Life and Times*, 1:129.
[89] Marshman, *Life and Times*, 1:129.
[90] Marshman, *Life and Times*, 1:230.

Spirituality in Peacemaking

including "Persian, the Hindostanee [Hindustani], the Bengalee [Bengali], the Mahratta, the Ooriya [Oriya], and the Telinga."[91] Marshman conceived this grand translation scheme would cost 36,700 Rupees and proposed to fund it over the nine years required for the translation with the interest from an initial target sum of 60,000 Rupees. By any measure, this was a handsome sum of money. The mission house that the missionaries purchased in Serampore just four years earlier cost 6,000 Rupees.[92] The following year, because of a burgeoning school, they were constrained to purchase the adjoining house and grounds, described by Ward as "one of the finest in Serampore, for 10,340 Rs."[93] Or compared to Carey's salary as teacher of Bangla at Fort William College, Marshman's goal represented five years' worth of Carey's salary as he began receiving it in 1807 or ten years' worth of his salary as he was then receiving it.[94]

But so strong was evangelical support for such a project, the large budget did not prove a hindrance. Rev. Brown "expressed the strongest approbation of it" but recommended some revisions that it might go over better with an "infidel public."[95] Rev. Buchanan was also supportive but thought that the "Chinese language should be added to the list, and that Mr Marshman himself should forthwith enter on the study of that language."[96] Buchanan sweetened the deal by offering to supply a tutor, one Johannes Lassar, an Armenian, born at Macao, who had facility in spoken Chinese and less facility in the written language.[97]

Buchanan wanted to submit the Memorial first to the Government in hopes of securing its patronage. To this end, Buchan-

---

[91] Marshman, *Life and Times*, 1:232-233.
[92] Marshman, *Life and Times*, 1:128.
[93] Marshman, *Life and Times*, 1:152.
[94] Carey received 500 Rs./month for his teaching services at the college and in 1807 began receiving double that. Marshman, *Life and Times*, 1:149, 286.
[95] Marshman, *Life and Times*, 1:234.
[96] Marshman, *Life and Times*, 1:234.
[97] Marshman, *Life and Times*, 1:244.

an affixed an image of Britannia, "presenting a New Testament to a Hindoo [Hindu]," to the front of the, "proposals for printing the scriptures in the different languages of India."[98] Ward was dubious the Governor General would give it his approval and thought instead that the proposal would be carried on by subscriptions.[99] Ward was right, and the Government, true to its cautious stance, was unwilling to align itself with a Christian effort as benign as Scripture translation. However, determined to gain some credit for his proposal, Buchanan required the Serampore band to attest in writing at the close of the memoir, the dependence of their success on the College's patronage.[100] Such a confession would boost the reputation of the Establishment via the College as Buchanan was then serving as Vice Provost. In England, Andrew Fuller heard and was concerned:

> I must repeat to you that I and some others are under strong apprehensions that the friendship of Mr. Buchanan to you and the Mission is purchased too dear, and that you are in great danger of being drawn into his worldly political religion. ... Beware, my brethren, of the counsel of Mr. Worldly Wiseman. He will draw you off from the simplicity of Christ, and, under pretence of liberality, &c., you will be shorn like Samson of his locks.[101]

In Fuller's mind, the financial support and public commendation the missionaries stood to receive from Buchanan and Brown were not worth the price they would have to pay in terms of concessions and additions to the Memorial. As mentioned above, Brown had suggested revisions to make the Memorial more palatable to an "infidel public." Left to themselves, the Serampore

---

[98] Ward, Journal MSS, Wednesday, March 19, 1806, 479.
[99] Ward, Journal MSS, Friday, December 27, 1805, 464.
[100] Marshman, *Life and Times*, 1:234–235.
[101] Fuller to Missionaries, n.d. quoted in Marshman, *Life and Times*, 1:237.

Spirituality in Peacemaking

missionaries tended to state their aims with explicit evangelistic language. But such language would make the government nervous and would not endear the Baptists to a more broad-minded Christian public. Aware of this reality, the Trio reluctantly accepted these revisions. Buchanan's request for a Chinese translation of Scripture likely stemmed from similar motives. Certain Orientalists were likely to support a literary project involving an exotic Eastern language if it were not too enthusiastic.[102]

A valiant effort was made to raise sufficient funds, but far less than Marshman's 60,000 Rupee target were realized. Had it not been for Buchanan and Brown's generous gifts of 5,000 and 1,000 Rupees respectively, they would not have raised even 10,000 Rupees. Nevertheless, the Trio went forward with the grand translation plan, and it was agreed that 300 Rupees a month would be given to them to for their labors.[103]

Marshman's Chinese translations

As many Indian languages share a common Sanskrit root, the missionaries could at least make an argument that such translations were not far removed from their Bengali bailiwick. But Chinese? None of the Trio were even remotely familiar with the language, nor was it routinely spoken by any community then residing in Serampore or Calcutta. The attempt was only made possible by the Chinese-speaking Armenian tutor that Buchanan provided. But so ardent was Buchanan's desire for a Chinese translation that he offered Marshman a 300 Rupee a month stipend from his own purse to take up the work.[104] Apparently Marshman was much pleased with Buchanan's offer, for Ward

---

[102] Marshman, *Life and Times*, 1:235.

[103] Marshman, *Life and Times*, 1:235.

[104] Ward, Journal MSS, Saturday, February 16, 1805, 409–410; Friday, December 27, 1805, 464; Marshman, *Life and Times*, 1:244.

wryly writes, "Bro. Marshman stands with open mouth to receive him."[105]

Marshman would eventually spend fifteen years in what his own son calls a "wearisome employment."[106] Yet his academic ardour and hawklike zeal enabled him to pursue the work with alacrity.[107] Ward, however, was not so keen on the project and often referred to it with sarcasm. Once, when a new convert (Gorachund) was being forcibly carried off the Mission premises by some determined opponents, Ward secured Marshman's help after waking him from his "Chinese revery."[108] On another occasion, some friends arrived at the Mission with a Chinese man with whom "Bro. Mardon spluttered Chinese" over tea.[109] A year and a half after beginning the project, Marshman had completed the translation of the Gospel according to Matthew and sent it through Dr. Buchanan to the Archbishop of Canterbury.[110]

In early 1808 funds for the grand translation project were exhausted, and Marshman determined to approach the Governor General himself for subscriptions. Pleased with two pages of Matthew's Gospel account that Marshman had recently printed in Chinese, renowned linguist Dr. John Leyden (1775–1811), encouraged him to call on Lord Minto with the same. Marshman and Carey followed Leyden's advice, and Lord Minto was indeed impressed by Marshman's "singular instance of public spirit and perseverance" in the exotic Chinese tongue. But he was not so impressed as to overcome his political reservations to publicly associate himself with the Baptists' translation project.

---

[105] Ward, Journal MSS, Friday, December 27, 1805, 464.

[106] Marshman, *Life and Times*, 1:244.

[107] Regarding Marshman's hawklike zeal, see Carey to John Ryland, May 24, 1810, letter no. 33 in the College Street Baptist Church's (Northampton) collection of BMS manuscripts, quoted in Smith, *Serampore Enterprise*, 37.

[108] Ward, Journal MSS, Friday, August 22, 1806, 501.

[109] Ward, Journal MSS, Tuesday, December 23, 1806, 531.

[110] Ward, Journal MSS, Monday, June 1, 1807, 551.

Spirituality in Peacemaking

However, if Marshman would be willing to also undertake a translation of Confucius' writings into English, "the most liberal encouragement might be expected, and he and his colleagues would thus be furnished with an early supply of funds."[111] In this manner, "profits derived from the sale of Confucius would be applied to the publication of the Scriptures." Now, with the inclusion of the writings of Confucius and the endorsement of the Governor-General, Ward records that "Bro. Marshman is beginning to beg for the translations in Calcutta, & for subscriptions towards the translation of a work of Confucius's."[112] In this manner, Marshman was able, in a short time, to raise two thousand pounds "which were destined collaterally to aid the publication of the translations."[113]

About two years later, Marshman "published the first volume of his English translation of the works of Confucius, with a preliminary dissertation on the language of China" which was heartily commended by Lord Minto.[114] In 1814, Marshman's "'Clavis Sinica,' or key to the Chinese language," rolled off the Serampore Press after "eight years of labour and study."[115] And in the first week of December 1822, Marshman had the satisfaction of seeing the completion of the printing of the Scriptures in Chinese. His son notes, "This was the first complete edition of the Sacred Scriptures in the Chinese language, perhaps also the first Chinese work ever printed from moveable metallic types."[116] Throughout his chronicle of the progress of translations involving the Chinese language, John Marshman frequently lauds his father's assiduity, perseverance, and amazing progress given the scant resources at his disposal. But his chronicle is also

---

[111] Marshman, *Life and Times*, 1:389-390.
[112] Ward, Journal MSS, Tuesday, April 19, 1808, 657.
[113] Marshman, *Life and Times*, 1:390-391.
[114] Marshman, *Life and Times*, 1:440.
[115] Marshman, *Life and Times*, 2:88.
[116] Marshman, *Life and Times*, 2:253.

replete with admissions of its shortcomings and of the "more idiomatic, perspicuous, and acceptable" translations that others completed after him.[117]

Marshman's Chinese translations, though astonishing, were accomplished at a great cost. In the beginning, Buchanan suggested its inclusion, not out of concern for the Chinese people, but in hopes of widening the memorial's appeal to a broad-minded, "infidel public." Then when funds ran short, Carey and Marshman employed the same tactic, agreeing to translate the works of Confucius into English in hopes of securing funds for the larger translation project. This was the cart of financial need and political expediency driving the horse of the Mission's translation strategy.[118]

Ward's concerns

Ward had numerous concerns regarding the scheme to translate the Bible into all the languages of India. First, on the financial front, Ward notes in his journal that the subscriptions raised fell "far short of what was hoped, & will, instead of forming a permanent fund, be exhausted at 300 rupees a month in two years."[119] This shortfall would be realized just over a year later,

---

[117] Marshman, *Life and Times*, 2:253.

[118] Marshman was in fact, doing no differently than his senior colleague had done in 1805 when he agreed to translate the Hindu epic, *Ramayana* into English. Though it was "a most arduous undertaking ... the toil was lightened by the reflection that, 'means would thus be obtained of supporting at least one missionary station.'" The initial amount for the project was raised again by subscriptions which Carey solicited from Fort William College and the Asiatic Society. Marshman, *Life and Times*, 1:220-221. Even the solicitation effort was expensive. Ward notes, "Bro. Carey is sending proposals for subscriptions for the Ramyun all over the country. The postage of all these letters comes to a great sum." Ward, Journal MSS, Wednesday, April 9, 1806.

[119] Ward, Journal MSS, Lord's Day, April 27, 1806, 484. The subscription amounts recorded by Ward (12,000 Rupees total, 5,000 of which were given by Rev. Buchanan, 2,000 by Rev. Brown, and an unnamed amount by Mr. Udney) are slightly different than those recorded by John Clark Marshman (10,000 Rupees total, 5,000 of which were given by Rev. Buchanan, and 1,000 by Rev. Brown). Marshman, *Life*

Spirituality in Peacemaking

when, during the Persian Pamphlet Controversy, Ward warned his colleagues they would go to jail on account of translation debt if they lost Carey's salary from the College.[120] But Ward had other concerns of a missiological and linguistic nature—concerns which Carey and Marshman, in their enthusiasm for the grand translation scheme, did not share:

> I think, however, that a person is in a great measure disqualified for becoming a translator into a new language unless he know the force & bendings both of that <u>from</u> which he translates & that <u>into</u> which he translates. Perhaps it is enough to justify the work that the substance of the divine will would be made known in such a translation. I know that these translations will be, & must be worse than the first Bengalee [Bengali], because in the Bengalee [Bengali] Brother Carey knew something of the language but in these comparatively little can be known; respecting the construction, shades of meaning, words to convey spiritual ideas, &c. &c. great dependence must be placed on the pundits.[121]

From a linguistic standpoint, Ward was concerned the Trio was getting out of their depth. Closely related to these were missiological concerns:

> I recommend to Bren. Carey & Marshman to enter upon translations which we, with our hands, can distribute, & which may be fitted for stations which we ourselves can occupy. As to making Bibles for other Missionaries, into languages which we ourselves do not really understand, I recommend them to be cautious; lest they should be wasting time & life on that which every vicissitude may frus-

---

and Times, 1:235.
[120] Ward, Journal MSS, Monday, September 21, 1807, 595.
[121] Ward, Journal MSS, Lord's Day, April 27, 1806, 484–485.

trate. I tell them that the Jesuit Missionaries have made grammars, dictionaries & translations in abundance, which are now rotting in the Libraries at Rome. I remind them that life is short; that this life may evaporate in schemes of translations for China, Bootan, Mahratta, &c. while the good in our hands & at our hands is left undone. I urge them to push things which are in our own power, &, under Providence, at our own command. I tell them that the natural & common-sense-way is for Missionaries to settle in a country—get its language—pick out a learned native or two & then begin to translate. When then books are printed he is on the spot to distribute them. Whereas if we had at this moment the scriptures in Chinese, Bootan, &c. &c. on our shelves—what then—would this convert the people. By spending so much of our time on translations which we can never distribute, we may leave undone translations nearer home, & leave the Mission at our deaths in such an unestablished state, that all may come to nothing; whereas if it be once well established & pretty extensively spread in Bengal, this will secure in their proper time all these translations, & everything else.[122]

In Ward's estimation, not only would the grand translation project encumber them financially, but it would be a poor stewardship of the time and gospel with which they had been entrusted. He recognized that though Holy Scripture was vital to the missionary task, their mission would not be accomplished merely by sending Bibles to peoples whose languages they could not speak and whose lands they could not occupy. Instead, Ward advised his colleagues that it would be more profitable to spend their time and energies closer to home where their gifts were best suited.

So, did Ward's domestic bent intone a lack of concern for reaching the rest of India? On the contrary, the following excerpt

---

[122] Ward, Journal MSS, Lord's Day, April 27, 1806, 484-485.

Spirituality in Peacemaking

demonstrates that Ward simply had a different fundamental translation philosophy in order to do so:

> We have begun to print the Shanscrit Testament. I have urged Bren. C. & M. to urge this forward, as a faithful translation into the Shanscrit will render all the translations into the other Eastern languages easy & certain; for all the eastern pundits know the Shanscrit; &, making the Shanscrit the original, every real pundit in the East could make from this a good translation into his own vernacular tongue. I have told them that by translating the scriptures into Shanscrit they at once, in a sense, translate the Scriptures into all the languages of Asia.[123]

Ward recognized, as his memoirist would later state, that Sanskrit "occupies the same place among the eastern natives, that the Latin does amongst us; it is the vehicle, by which the learned communicate their literary information from one to another, through the numerous nations that people that vast continent," and he desired that the missionaries prioritize this vehicle for the distribution of the Bible throughout the subcontinent.[124]

The common and missiological sense of Ward's proposals is obvious. It represented a far more responsible stewardship of time, money, and linguistic gifts than the grand translation project. It held forth more promise of long-term fruit. But it lacked the sizzle and notoriety of a proposal for a "Translation of the Holy Scriptures into the languages of the East."[125] However, good sense and superior stewardship notwithstanding, Carey and Marshman were apparently not convinced, for the grand translation project moved forward.

Given his translation convictions and his close friendships

---

[123] Ward, Journal MSS, Friday, June 6, 1806, 489–490.
[124] Stennett, *Memoirs*, 150.
[125] Marshman, *Life and Times*, 1:232.

with Carey and Marshman, Ward was in a quandary. A. Christopher Smith surmises that Carey and Marshman sought to allay Ward's misgivings but notes that

> special pleading in itself did nothing to resolve the problems that such a wide-ranging scheme imposed on Ward. He was unhappy that work in the mission's printing office gobbled up so much of his time, at the expense of other forms of ministry. Nevertheless, he deferred to his colleagues who were in the majority—as each member of the Trio occasionally did in other matters—because of the bond of loyalty that bound them together. After all, if they did not hold together, their mission would disintegrate.[126]

Ironically, and presumably to maintain a united front to those holding the ropes, Ward later came to defend the system he originally opposed. On August 15, 1807, he "proposed that Bro. Marshman should draw up an account of the Translations, which should be sent home as soon as possible, without any reference to Dr. B[uchanan], or Mr. B[rown]."[127] A little over two years later, Ward writes, "We have begun to print the Sikh Testament, & to cut the Tailingu types. The Sikh will be very easy. Our Sikh has understood his Shanscrit original very well, & the language to those who knew the Bengalee [Bengali] & Hindoost'hanee [Hindustani] is quite [easy]," and then proceeds to describe the manner in which he proofs translations in the various Indian languages. He then concludes, "Our friends need be under no pain as though we were printing the sacred volume in languages without thoroughly understanding them."[128] No pain indeed—unless they had read his journal entry from three years prior! In a span of two years, it is amazing how much confidence

---

[126] Smith, *Serampore Enterprise*, 319 n2.
[127] Ward, Journal MSS, Saturday, August 15, 1807, 571.
[128] Ward, Journal MSS, Monday, December 4, 1809, 709-10.

Spirituality in Peacemaking

Ward gained in their own language abilities and in the prowess of their pandits![129]

As translations were completed—even in part—they became a selling point as they solicited or "begged" new subscriptions for the mammoth translation project. Thus, Ward writes,

> Brn. Carey & Marshman waited on Lord Minto on Saturday with a copy of the Sanscrit Gospels, & Specimens of our other translations; & they solicited his Lordship for leave to go a begging thro' Calcutta in favour of these translations, & expressed their desire to get his Lordship's subscription.[130]

But with insufficient funds and their translation aspirations known to the public in India and abroad, they had little choice but to beg further subscriptions. In Ward's *Circular Letters* of

---

[129] Similar sanguinity is seen in a letter Ward wrote to Fuller on March 24, 1813. While Ward originally rued the dependence upon native pandits a grand translation scheme would impose on them "respecting the construction, shades of meaning, words to convey spiritual ideas," (Ward, Journal MSS, Lord's Day, April 27, 1806, 484-485), he revels in the boon of the pandits seven years later: "It may appear a matter of doubt with some at home, how one or two individuals are able to translate so difficult a book as the Bible, into so many languages. It would be impossible for Europeans alone to do this. It would be very difficult for a European of the very best talents to translate, without any native assistance, into one language so as to make a good translation; but that wherein the difficulty of foreign translation lies, the idiom and construction, is here overcome, by their flowing from the pen of learned natives; so that the European translator has little else to do than rigidly keep his eye on the meaning, and see that that is unequivocally given." (Ward to Fuller, March 24, 1813, quoted in *PA*, 5:218-219). In addition, in this same account, contrary to his earlier assertion that missionary bodies were needed to distribute and press home the message of the Bible, Ward exudes optimism in the power of Scripture to effect salvation apart from any missionary involvement, mentioning one man who was "converted entirely by reading the scriptures and other books without having heard a sermon, or seen a Missionary." After citing another example of someone who requested baptism after reading of his need in Scripture from some booklets distributed by Bren. Moore and Carey years before, Ward proclaims, "Besides these remarkable instances of the power of the word alone, in its silent progress through this immense population, we observe a great and very visible change on the minds of great bodies of the natives where the light has been shining for any considerable time." *PA*, 5:219-220.

[130] Ward, Journal MSS, Monday, April 11, 1808, 656.

The Spirituality of William Ward

1813, he reports on translation progress in eighteen Indian languages.[131] Despite the progress in translations and press, in echoes of his original concern, Ward wrote to a friend in the same year:

> I know not how it would be if conversions among the natives were very numerous, our hands are so full with translating and other foundation work. I am encouraged to hope, that the foundation is not thus laying, to such an extent and to such a depth, without reason.[132]

Yet, the translation project continued. Of the progress of translations in 1822, John Clark Marshman records that "the New Testament had been published in twenty of the languages of India" with an "experimental translation of the New Testament" begun in "nine other dialects." In addition, "the sixth edition of the Scriptures in Bengalee [Bangla], and a second and revised edition of the Hindee, Sanscrit, Orissa, and Mahratta Scriptures" were then in the press.[133] Regarding the immense labor that had been expended in translation efforts thus far, he continues, "Of these versions, some had been twelve years in progress, but seven years was the shortest period occupied in translating and printing any version of the New Testament." And towards the close of that year, Marshman notes that it was also necessary for the missionaries to solicit yet more money by publishing "another memoir of the translations."[134] This was a year before Ward's untimely death, and the missionaries were still running short of funds for the grand translation project.

---

[131] *Monthly Circular Letters Relative to the Missions In India, Established By a Society In England, Called the "Baptist Missionary Society"* (Serampore: Mission Press 1813), 6:153-161.

[132] Ward to an unknown correspondent, December 28, 1813, quoted in Stennett, *Memoirs*, 183-184.

[133] Marshman, *Life and Times*, 2:254-255.

[134] Marshman, *Life and Times*, 2:254.

Spirituality in Peacemaking

Ward's original counsel had proven prophetic.[135]

What shall we make of Ward's original translation convictions, his acquiescence to his colleagues, and his changed tone in the years that followed? A full evaluation of the merits of the Serampore Mission's translation efforts is beyond the scope of this work. And a fuller assessment of Ward's legacy will be undertaken in chapter 5. It is a fact that their efforts at translation and press reduced the time the Trio was able to spend in itinerancy and personal evangelism.[136] Ward also wondered in 1813 if this would negatively impact the Mission and whether they were laying an elaborate foundation that would not pay off in the end.[137] What would have happened had the Trio followed Ward's translation advice? Would his Bengalcentric, Sanskrit-priority strategy have resulted in a more strongly established Mission? Would it have freed up the Trio to spend more time with national partners in itinerancy and mentoring? Would it have yielded more native conversions? We can only wonder.

But had Ward's colleagues followed his counsel, the Mission's course would have been affected in two important ways. First, their translation selection would have been shaped more by theology and missiology than by economic and political concerns. In his original counsel in 1806, Ward considered the "grammars, dictionaries & translations" of Jesuit Missionaries that were then "rotting in the Libraries of Rome" and applied the lesson to their own situation, reminding his colleagues that "life is short; that this life may evaporate in schemes of translations for China, Bootan, Mahratta, &c. while the good in our

---

[135] A. Christopher Smith refers to Ward's initial misgivings over the grand translation project as an "appallingly prescient warning." Smith, *Serampore Enterprise*, 272 n10.

[136] See *PA*, 5:220: "We have often deplored our inability to pursue the work of itinerancy, (the proper business of a Missionary,) on account of our heavy labours at home."

[137] Ward to an unknown correspondent, December 28, 1813, quoted in Stennett, *Memoirs*, 183–184.

The Spirituality of William Ward

hands & at our hands is left undone."[138] A. Christopher Smith notes that this is William Ward doing missiology, and that in this discipline, he was likely well ahead of his colleagues.[139] Ward's missiological thinking is also more in line with translation guidelines they had set forth in the *Serampore Form of Agreement* just a couple of months before embarking down the grand translation road. Second, the Mission would not have embroiled themselves in the financial quagmire that resulted from their ongoing support of the memoir.

In the grand translation saga, Ward's spirituality is seen both in terms of his counsel and in terms of his acquiescence. His counsel was sensible, useful, and missiologically sound. When he did express opinions that were decidedly different from his closest colleagues, he did so with humility and love. In the case of the Persian Pamphlet Controversy, Carey and Marshman had heeded Ward's counsel, and both press and Mission had been preserved. In the scheme of the grand translation, however, they did not. Despite significant misgivings, Ward's *love* and *humility* compelled him to yield to his friends, rather than risk fracturing the Trio's inner peace. But, in the end, much time, money, and energy were wasted. Was Ward right in this case to compromise? For his part, A. Christopher Smith argues that had he not done so, the entire Mission may have disintegrated.[140] We will return to this discussion in the final chapter.

---

[138] Ward, Journal MSS, Lord's Day, April 27, 1806, 484–485.
[139] Smith, *Serampore Enterprise*, 272 n10.
[140] Smith, *Serampore Enterprise*, 319 n2.

Spirituality in Peacemaking

"I throw away the guns to save the ship": Ward's Concession in Communion[141]

The difference of opinion that Ward and his colleagues held with regard to translation philosophy represented two different ways of fulfilling their mission. Similarly, differences concerning the number of missionaries needed at the Serampore Mission, whether a horse was needed for itinerancy, and whether a native convert should accompany returning missionaries to England related to the missions modus operandi. Nonetheless, any of these differences could easily have occasioned a more serious falling out within the Trio. In addition, many of these matters involving money could easily have escalated in bitter disputes and even a split in the Mission. In fact, this is exactly what happened in 1818 when some of the newer missionaries seceded from the Serampore Mission and established a separate church and boarding schools in Calcutta more closely aligned with the BMS.[142]

But the matter of communion was different. In particular, the question was whether the Mission church should observe open or closed communion. This lay close to Ward's heart, and his feelings regarding this subject were much stronger than those

---

[141] This phrase from the letter, Ward to John Ryland, November 14, 1815, *BMS Missionary Correspondence; William Ward; Transcript of Diaries in 2 Books Comprising 4 Volumes; Book 1 (Vols. 1 & 2) 1799-1805; Book 2 (Vols. 3 & 4) 1806-1811*, microfilm; reel 44, publication no. 5350 (London: Baptist Missionary Society Archives, 1981). It is also the title of an article E. Daniel Potts has written on the disagreement within the Trio of whether to practice open or closed communion. E. Daniel Potts, "'I Throw Away the Guns to Preserve the Ship': a Note on the Serampore Trio," *The Baptist Quarterly* 20, no. 3 (July 1963): 115-117.

[142] Marshman, *Life and Times*, 2:166-167. This split took place following Andrew Fuller's death in 1815, from which time a widening gulf developed between Serampore and the BMS. Newer missionaries resented the prestige and key positions in the Mission held by the Trio in particular and preferred what was in their minds a more equitable system of remuneration in set salaries from the BMS that each missionary could use as he or she saw fit as opposed to the common purse system the Serampore Missionaries had followed from the beginning.

other areas in which the Trio differed from time to time. From the earliest days, in keeping with the position of Fuller and others in the Northamptonshire Association, the Serampore Church practiced closed or strict communion.[143] But onboard Captain Wickes' *Criterion*, the missionaries—to Ward's delight—enjoyed open communion. After arriving at Serampore, Ward, in order to maintain the "harmony of the church and Mission," conformed to their custom of closed communion though he "deplored this rigid, and ... unlovely proceeding."[144] Then he rejoiced when, due to the influence of extra-denominational brothers like Rev. Brown, Carey reneged, and by unanimous vote, the Mission agreed to occasionally open their table to "persons of known piety" though they were, in their estimation, unbaptized. This much has been covered in the previous chapter in the section on Communion. This was in 1805. But in 1811, the Mission Church again resumed the practice of closed communion. This would strike at Ward's heart and try his allegiance to the other members of the Trio as would nothing else.

Communion Background in Particular Baptist Life

Baptists had been divided over the matter of open and closed communion for centuries. In the seventeenth century, *The Pilgrim's Progress* author and Baptist pastor, John Bunyan "insisted baptism should not be made a condition for participation at the Lord's Supper," but he was opposed by Baptist contemporaries including William Kiffen (1616-1701) who favored closed communion. In the eighteenth century, Abingdon pastor and hymn writer, Daniel Turner (1710-1798), "maintained that the Lord's Table must be kept open to all, 'who appear to love our Lord Jesus Christ in sincerity.'" He was joined in his opinion by John Collett Ryland (Sr.). Together they pseudonymously wrote *A*

---

[143] Marshman, *Life and Times*, 1:214.
[144] Marshman, *Life and Times*, 1:214.

Spirituality in Peacemaking

Modest Plea for Free Communion at the Lord's Table.[145] On the other side in their day was General turned Particular Baptist, Abraham Booth (1734-1806), who unashamedly stated, "I believe that baptism is an immersion in water, in the name of the Father, and of the Son, and of the Holy Ghost, ... and is previously *necessary* to the Lord's Supper."[146] Then in the early part of the in the nineteenth century, alongside William Ward, Particular Baptist Mission Society founding member, John Ryland Jr. and Robert Hall Jr. favored open communion while William Carey; PBMS founding member and Secretary, Andrew Fuller; and Norwich minister, Joseph Kinghorn (1766-1832) did not. Hall and Kinghorn debated the matter with their pens, the former championing open communion in *A Short Statement Of The Reasons For Christian, In Opposition To Party Communion* (1826) and the latter replying with a defense of closed communion in his *Baptism, A Term Of Communion At The Lord's Supper* (1816) and *Arguments Against The Practice Of Mixed Communion, And In Support Of Communion On The Plan Of The Apostolic Church* (1827).

In his work, Hall maintained that "the sacrament of the Lord's supper is of perpetual obligation, and that it was designed by its Founder for one of the principal indications and expressions of that fraternal affection which ought to distinguish his followers."[147] So, the main question in his mind when it came to admitting someone to the Lord's Table was "whether all real Christians are entitled to share in this privilege, whether it forms a part of that spiritual provision which belongs to the whole family of the faithful, or whether it is the exclusive patrimony of a

---

[145] Raymond Brown, *The English Baptists of the Eighteenth Century* (London: Baptist Historical Society, 1986), 130.

[146] Samuel H. Ford, "Abraham Booth; The Great And Learned Weaver," *The Christian Repository and Home Circle* 67, no. 3 (April 1889): 245.

[147] Robert Hall Jr., *A Short Statement Of The Reasons For Christian, In Opposition To Party Communion* (London: Hamilton, Adams, & Co., 1826), 1.

sect."[148] By contrast, Kinghorn felt the whole controversy hinged

> on the question, whether we ought to obey the direct law of Christ, and the explanation given of it in the conduct of the apostles;—or, whether we are justified in being guided by inferences, which ... are not correctly drawn from New Testament premises.[149]

A full consideration of Hall's and Kinghorn's central questions and their subsequent answers in the debate is beyond the scope of this chapter. This brief exposure to them, however, will provide a general familiarity with the perceptions that informed both open and closed communion positions. But before going forward, it will be helpful to visit two additional prerequisites for communion that were raised by Trio member, Joshua Marshman, aboard the *Criterion*:

> We have been discussing the Conference Meeting & the question,—Whether we shall have the Lord's Supper on board.—Bro. M. objects as it would establish an irregular precedent—we are not in a church state—we have no ordained Minister amongst us. All the rest are unanimous. We have given an hour's time to consider of it. Alas, how difficult it is to bear with each other in maintaining opposite opinions. The Lord preserve us in the comity of the Spirit, & the bonds of peace.[150]

Five days later, Ward records, "Our Bro. M. has signified his consent to join in sitting at the table of our Saviour on board the

---

[148] Hall, *A Short Statement*, 2.

[149] Joseph Kinghorn, *Baptism, A Term of Communion at the Lord's Supper*, 2nd ed. (Norwich, 1816), iv.

[150] Ward, Journal MSS, Tuesday, June 11, 1799, 12-13.

Spirituality in Peacemaking

ship."[151] It appears that all the participants in this conversation were Baptists. Open communion as such was not under discussion. But when they observed the Lord's Supper at the end of the month, a surprised Captain Wickes was admitted:

> In the afternoon we enjoyed the Lord's Supper in company with our dear Capt. He was willing to sit down with us, but he asked before we began whether it were not contrary to our discipline to admit; & whether we had not sacrificed something to oblige him. We satisfied him on this subject. Our brethren imposed upon me the administration; but I am afraid they suffered thro' my inability.[152]

This was an inter-Particular Baptist debate. Proponents of both sides were members of the Mission in Serampore and of the Society in England. Desiring to continue the open table they had enjoyed on the *Criterion*, Ward asked Fuller, "Do not the bounds of Scriptural communion extend to all who are real Xns, except they have embraced immorality, or dangerous heresy?" to which Fuller replied that "anyone who was not 'properly' baptized was not a genuine Christian."[153] In Fuller's understanding, non-Baptists should not be admitted to communion at the Serampore church.[154] Therefore the practice of open communion was abandoned, and Ward conformed to closed communion in the Serampore Church.

But on the foreign mission field, two unique realities pressed for open communion. On the one hand, the Baptist missionaries

---

[151] Ward, Journal MSS, Lord's Day, June 16, 1799, 17.

[152] Ward, Journal MSS, Lord's Day, June 30, 1799, 22.

[153] This correspondence between Ward and Fuller is related in E. Daniel Potts, "'I Throw Away the Guns to Preserve the Ship': a Note on the Serampore Trio," *The Baptist Quarterly* 20, no. 3 (July 1963): 115. It seems that Potts attributes Fuller's remark to a letter he wrote to Ward, September 21, 1800, but Potts gives no footnote as to the date of Ward's letter to Fuller.

[154] Potts, "I Throw Away the Guns," 115.

were denied in India the expansive fellowship with brothers and sisters of their own denomination that they had enjoyed in England. On the other hand, they found that in terms of Christian fellowship and missionary labor among the heathen, beggars could not be choosers. For reasons mentioned in the previous chapter, Anglican chaplains, David Brown and Claudius Buchanan, quickly became fast friends and allies. In this case the Trio's "near neighbors" were of more value to them than their "brothers" far away (Prov. 27:10). So, in 1805, as mentioned in Chapter 4, due to the winsome influence of Brothers Brown and Buchanan, Carey relented and opened the table to non-Baptists of known piety. Following this change, the Serampore missionaries wrote to the Society explaining their conviction that

> no one has a right to debar a true Christian from the Lord's table, nor refuse to communicate with a real Christian in commemorating the death of their common Lord, without being guilty of a breach of the law of Love, which law is addressed to us as Christians, and not as Baptists or Paedobaptists.[155]

Ward could not have been happier.

Convictions Concerning Closed and Open Communion

The staunchness of his convictions concerning open communion and the rationale for his abhorrence of closed communion is seen in a letter that he wrote to a friend in March of 1810:

> I think you cannot abstain from communion with any real christian whose moral conduct substantiates the truth of his faith in Christ, without a *positive crime* ... I think the shutting out from communion such a man as Doddridge, a

---

[155] Carey *et. al.* to the BMS, August 6, 1805, BMS MSS, quoted in Potts, "I Throw Away the Guns," 116.

Spirituality in Peacemaking

Baxter, because he was a paedobaptist, arises from the same spirit as that, which burnt men alive.[156]

As seen in the previous chapter, Ward was not an advocate for admitting as members of Baptist churches those who had not been baptized—which included their dear Anglican brothers whose infant baptisms they did not recognize. He recognized that a "stricter union" might be required "with respect to a church-state."[157] But as with Bunyan and Turner in centuries prior, Ward could not bear the implementation of baptism as a requirement for participation in the Lord's Supper. He felt that the Lord's Table was that symbol which united all believers and therefore, should not be withheld from those exhibiting a sincere love for the Savior. But then in words full of prescience, Ward speaks of his intentions should the Mission ever depart from its open policy:

> We admit paedobaptists to communion with us; but should the Serampore church change its practice, which, in my opinion, is its glory, I would take all proper occasions to protest against its spirit; but should I abandon all means of doing good, because they acted wrong? Would not my opinions, mildly and properly urged, be more likely to do good, than if I left the church, and placed myself at a greater distance from my fellow-christians?[158]

Return to Closed Communion

But though Ward spoke candidly regarding his views on communion, it was not enough to sway Fuller. Carey already held Fuller's position, and over time, Marshman also was won over, and related his changed position to Ward in a letter. Then on

---

[156] Ward to a friend, March 3, 1810, in Stennett, *Memoirs*, 243–244.
[157] Ward, Journal MSS, Friday, May 31, 1805, 422.
[158] Ward to a friend, March 3, 1810 in Stennett, *Memoirs*, 245.

The Spirituality of William Ward

March 3, 1811, we read that while Ward was in Calcutta "Bro. Marshman interdicted him [that is, Bro. Pritchett, an independent missionary, who seems to have been preaching that day] the Lord's Supper."[159] Despite his restraint in the above letter, Ward's immediate response to the Mission's return to closed communion was that "he would rather die than go into such a measure."[160] In the end, however, Ward regained composure and pursued a course in keeping with the prudent resolve expressed in the letter he had written a year earlier.

Four years later in November 1815, shortly after hearing news of their dear friend Fuller's death, Ward expressed his willingness to surrender his own position for the sake of the larger Mission in a poignant way. Ward told Ryland that Marshman had been "deeply wounded" by his letter of severe censure regarding Serampore's return to strict communion. Ward lamented what he considered to be his brethren's mistake in the matter, but he reminded Ryland that Marshman had "committed no crime by differing from [him] on the subject, and that the right of private judgment is sacred." He continues to exhort Ryland: "This is not a time for us now to be at a distance, but unite all our energies to supply the want of the colossus we have lost." Then he concludes, "But I throw away the guns to preserve the ship."[161]

Ward's Spirituality in the Communion Crisis

Was Ward's willingness to "throw away the guns" merely a way to cloak his convictional compromise? Was he motivated primarily by a desire to please others or by fear of letting them down? The excerpts from the above letters and journal entries suggest not. Did Ward's conviction change with the winds of public

---

[159] Ward, Journal MSS, Lord's Day, March 3, 1811, 749. Mr. Pritchett is called an "independent missionary" in Marshman, *Life and Times*, 1:461.

[160] Marshman, *Life and Times*, 1:460.

[161] Ward to Ryland, November 14, 1815, BMS MSS.

Spirituality in Peacemaking

opinion? Instead, as with his willingness to subject his opinions on Bible translation to those of his colleagues, Ward's compliance with closed communion was motivated by Christ's *love* in him and his *love* for Christ and those who bore the divine stamp. As Stennett notes, Ward was not "indifferent to the ordinances and discipline connected with them; but he had learned, that the bond of christian union is the *love* of Christ, and where he found this, he recognized the Saviour's image, nor could he withhold his affection."[162]

The peace and harmony that the Mission was able to maintain at this time was also due to the *humble* nature of Ward's spirituality. Paul instructed the Philippians,

> Do nothing from rivalry or conceit, but in humility count others more significant than yourselves. Let each of you look not only to his own interests, but also to the interests of others. Have this mind among yourselves, which is yours in Christ Jesus (Phil. 2:3–5).

It often happens in ministry—whether in the sending church or on the mission field—that friction, divisions, splits, and bitterness arise because our "passions are at war" within us. We fight and quarrel when we fail to receive even petty things that we have desired and coveted (Jas. 4:1–3). How much greater the risk of quarrelling when something of great import—such as the type of communion observed—is at stake? James goes on to remind that "God opposes the proud, but gives grace to the humble" (Jas. 4:6).

When love and humility are absent strife and bickering will not be far behind. In the communion crisis, Ward's *love* and *humility* again preserved the unity of the Mission. Ward's *love* tempered his tongue even when disagreeing passionately with oth-

---

[162] Stennett, *Memoirs*, 241.

ers. Ward's *love* enabled him to take up for Marshman though he was an enemy in the debate. Ward's *usefulness* helped him see the futility of leaving the church and separating himself from his fellow-Christians.[163] Ward's *humility* helped him stay.

---

[163] Stennett, *Memoirs*, 245.

6
Conclusion

In December 1817, for the sake of his health, William Ward embarked on a journey to England. The trip did prove a boon to his health but offered little rest. Ever desirous to be useful, Ward composed his two-volume, *Reflections on the Word of God for Every Day of the Year* in seventy days while en route to England.[1] Ward was the first missionary to the east to ever return to England, and after a brief time of convalescence, was busy speaking to eager audiences for the cause of missions in India.[2] Ever the peacemaker, he interacted frequently with Society members during his time in England in hopes of "healing the breach" that had developed since Andrew Fuller's death between the BMS and the Serampore Mission over ownership of property, missionary remuneration, and management of mission stations.[3] After his stay in England, Ward journeyed first to Holland to promote missions among Mennonite brethren, and then had a profitable tour of America, raising $10,000 for the new college at Serampore.[4] Then on his return trip to England, he wrote his *Farewell Letters*

---

[1] Marshman, *The Life And Times of Carey, Marshman And Ward* (1859; repr., Serampore: Council of Serampore College, 2005), 2:189.

[2] Marshman, *Life and Times*, 2:196-197. While it is technically true that Ward was the first missionary to the east to return to England, in a recent conversation with the author, Peter de Vries notes that John Thomas, though professionally a surgeon and not called a missionary at the time, did return from Bengal to England in 1799. And since he was a colleague of Carey, he was able to communicate to others the needs of Carey and the Mission on his visit. Additionally, though John and Hannah Biss, BMS missionaries, left Serampore in January,1807 for the sake of his health, it was for America, not England. John died at sea, and Hannah returned to Serampore in August 1809 and later married fellow missionary and widower, William Moore in February, 1812" (*Friend of India* (Monthly) I, (1818): 16-17 [regarding info on John and Hannah Biss]). (WhatsApp thread from September 2-3, 2023).

[3] Marshman, *Life and Times*, 2:188.

[4] Marshman, *Life and Times*, 2:219-221.

*to a Few Friends in Britain and America on Returning to Bengal in 1821.*⁵ Then, on October 20, 1822, after almost five years away, he reached Serampore once again, in better health than when he had left.

But Ward's reinvigorated state was short-lived, and he succumbed unexpectedly to a virulent strain of cholera and died March 7, 1823, at the age of fifty-three. Sudden as it was, his death in Serampore was, in one way, Ward's wish come true. On the first leg of his international tour, he was pained as he pondered the possibility of dying away from the Mission and colleagues that he so dearly loved. He confessed then, "'There seems a propriety that persons who have engaged in such a way as we have done should die at their posts.'"⁶ And so it was.

Legacy of William Ward

How should William Ward be remembered? What is his legacy for those that follow? Did his spirituality of love, prayer, humility, and usefulness combine to preserve the harmony of the Serampore Trio and the peace of the Mission? Or did his piety result in costly compromise? These are fair questions, but they are not peculiar to Ward's day.

As with the opposition of the East India Company in the early nineteenth century, many missionaries today, because of governments that are hostile to the gospel, are forced to think creatively and cleverly to find ways to fulfill their mission. Like Ward and his companions, they are painfully aware of two competing realities. On the one hand, millions around them are dying daily and will spend eternity in hell without Christ. Feeling an obliga-

---

⁵ William Ward, *Farewell Letters to A Few Friends In Britain and America On Returning to Bengal In 1821* (New York: E. Bliss and E. White, 1821). J.C. Marshman writes that Ward wrote *Farewell Letters* "during the voyage from America." Marshman, *Life and Times*, 2:245.

⁶ Marshman, *Life and Times*, 2:189.

Spirituality in Peacemaking

tion, like Carey, to use means for their conversion, there is an urgency to find a way to deliver the gospel to those who have not heard that they may believe on Jesus and be saved. But, on the other hand, they are equally aware that their residence in a foreign country is at all times owing to the good will of their governing host. If the missionaries are too overt in their evangelistic efforts, or if they are unable to comply with any number of visa regulations, the government may turn them out in an instant, and all of their labors in the country—including efforts to raise up national leaders to carry on the work when they are gone—will come to a sudden end. Therefore, many missionaries today can say, as Ward did to his parent society,

> It is difficult for us to ascertain the present path of duty. We are in much the same situation as the apostles were, when commanded not to preach in His name. They, it is true, replied, "whether it be right in the sight of God to obey you rather than God, judge ye." Would it be right for us to make the same reply in the first instance? To act in open defiance of the will of the Governor-General might occasion a positive law against evangelising the heathen, and at once break up the Mission, which has been settled at so great an expense. On the other hand, if we yield a little to the present storm, it may soon blow over, and we may not only preserve our present privileges, but obtain the liberty which we have so long wished for.[7]

It is easy to stand at a distance of two hundred years and thousands of miles and criticize the practices of the Serampore Mission. If put to it, Ward and his brethren were ready go to jail and even die for their faith. But knowing when one is "put to it" is not easy. The line between shrewdness and compromising

---

[7] Ward to BMS Society, n.d., quoted in Marshman, *Life and Times*, 1:260.

one's faith or mission is a fine one. But all things considered, Ward walked it well.

Many a missionary, who departed for the field with intentions of serving a lifetime, has returned a short time later because of team conflict. Consequently, mission fields and agencies are in sore need of William Wards today. Unlike the independent trailblazer, William Ward is a missionary hero of a different kind. His heroism is displayed in his spirituality, marked by love, humility, prayerfulness, and usefulness. These qualities may not arrest the attention of missionary-biographer publishers, but they win friends at every turn. And they might just make for a good biography as well.

Appendix 1
The Lost Devotion of Question Meetings

Ward began his journal on May 25, 1799 aboard the American vessel, the *Criterion*. And from the beginning of Ward and his companions' journey to India, the intentional manner in which they lived out their faith is striking. But equally if not more striking is the fact that their manner of life aboard the *Criterion* was essentially the same as it would be in Serampore. Missionary activities which would become routine in Serampore—corporate worship, personal devotions, evangelism, and discipleship—were begun at sea, shortly after leaving England. Thus far, these activities are still staples of missionary efforts today.

But one activity, practiced religiously by the missionaries, both on board the *Criterion*, and after they disembarked, is virtually unheard of today, namely, the "question meeting." Punctually, but without fanfare or explanation, the reader of Ward's journal frequently encounters record of a question meeting sandwiched between other unrelated and mundane events:

> Good wind thro' the day. Found closet exercises this [morning] comfortable. Thank God for a closet on board a ship.—This evening we had our Question meeting. The enquiry was "What are those dispositions which we ought to cultivate towards each other in present circumstances?"—self-annihilation—forebearance & patience—Avoid rash measures—comfort each other—forgiveness—Avoid whispering—bring forward profitable subjects. ... A three-mast vessel passes us.[1]

---

[1] Ward, Journal MSS, Thursday, June 13, 1799, 15.

It is apparent that readers in Ward's day needed no explanation as to what a question meeting was. But to the modern reader of Ward's journal, the question meeting will likely first appear novel and strange, then his attention will be piqued by the recurring nature of the phenomenon, and then gradually, from repeated observation of both the nature of the questions and their surrounding context, an appealing picture will emerge of a corporate devotional practice that is largely nonexistent today.

I am not contesting that questions are absent in modern-day devotional practice. Bible study groups abound in which various questions are put forth for discussion. In these discussions, questions tend to begin with a verse or passage of Scripture and then focus on personal impressions received or personal application warranted. Examples of the first type of question include: "What was your favorite thing about this passage?"; "What did you like/not like about this passage?"; "What came to your mind when you read ...?"; or "How do you feel about ...?" Examples of the second type of question include "What are some idols that we worship today?"; "How might this truth be an encouragement to single mothers?"; or "Is there an immigrant or sojourner in your sphere of influence to whom God may be calling you to show hospitality?" These questions aim to stimulate self-reflection and internal processing with reference to teaching from God's Word, and used conscientiously, they have value for personal sanctification.

But these questions are qualitatively different from the questions found in the question meetings of Ward and his colleagues. Consider the following:

Thursday, June 20, 1799—"The question discussed tonight was, 'What is that conduct which most tends to

The Lost Devotion of Question Meetings

grieve the Holy Spirit.'"[2]

Thursday, July 4, 1799—"Question to-night – 'What are the best evidences of Union with Xt?'"[3]

Thursday, July 11, 1799—"Question to-night: 'Why was divine Revelation necessary?'"[4]

First, the aim of these questions is not *personal* but *corporate* reflection and discussion. Second, the goal is not inspiration or application for one's own life, but rather, with the aid of other saints, to sharpen and grow in one's practical knowledge of a particular doctrine. Third, these questions do not invite pat or *prima facie* answers. One cannot merely turn to a particular passage in Scripture and read the answer. Nor can one merely offer his opinion. Rather, these questions require respondents to *search* related Scripture passages, *synthesize* or distill pertinent truth from the whole counsel of God's Word pertaining to the question at hand, and then to *resolve* or settle the matter in one's mind for the present that it might be implemented in everyday life—all in a corporate, iron-sharpening-iron-setting.

Put another way, question meetings aimed at the stuff of piety or spirituality—the meeting point of doctrine and practice. They were an earnest attempt by the body to *do* theology together and grow in useful knowledge for the Christian life. They were common in Ward's day. They are conspicuously absent in ours.

Following is a comprehensive list of questions from such meetings mentioned in Ward's journal from May 25, 1799 to October 30, 1811. Many more are recorded aboard the *Criterion* and in the early years of the mission than in subsequent years. But the regularity of their occurrence and their eventual imple-

---

[2] Ward, Journal MSS, Thursday, June 20, 1799, 18.
[3] Ward, Journal MSS, Thursday, July 4, 1799, 24.
[4] Ward, Journal MSS, Thursday, July 11, 1799, 26.

mentation by national believers suggests that the practice continued in the intervening years despite the absence of such record. This appendix is included in hopes that this devotional practice may be recovered in our day.

Thursday, June 13, 1799—This evening we had our Question meeting. The enquiry was "What are those dispositions which we ought to cultivate towards each other in present circumstances?"—self-annihilation—forebearance & patience—Avoid rash measures—comfort each other—forgiveness—Avoid whispering—bring forward profitable subjects.

Thursday, June 20, 1799—The question discussed to-night was, "What is that conduct which most tends to grieve the Holy Spirit."

Thursday, July 4, 1799—Question to-night - "What are the best evidences of Union with Xt?" I believe several of our friends found it profitable.

Thursday, July 11, 1799—Question to-night: "Why was divine Revelation necessary?"

Thursday, July 18, 1799—Question to night—"What are the best evidences of a tender conscience?" Comfortable. At the close we sung—["Guide Us, O Thou Great Jehovah"].

Thursday, July 25, 1799—Question to-night: "What are the evidences of a justified state?"

Thursday, August 1, 1799—We had a tolerably comfortable discussion of this question to-night: "What is the nature of Xt's intercession?"

The Lost Devotion of Question Meetings

Thursday, August 8, 1799—Question to-night: "What ought to be our feelings under a sense of daily depravity?"

Thursday, August 15, 1799—Question discussed to-night: "What are the effects on the mind from a believing view of Xt.'s blood?"

Thursday, August 22, 1799—Question discussed this evening "What is the nature, content, and usefulness of Xn. watchfulness?"

Thursday, August 29, 1799—Question to-night: "What are the supports which God hath afforded to a Missionary under his trials and discouragements."

Thursday, September 5, 1799—Last night we discussed this question: "What is the meaning of 'We are not ignorant of his [de]vices[']?"[5]

Thursday, September 19, 1799—Question discussed to-night: "What is it to ask amiss in prayer?"

Friday, January 3, 1806—In the evening we held a meeting for prayer on account of our two brethren's journey, & at the close we discussed the question, "How personal godliness might best be preserved on board ship, & how a person might be likely to do most good while there."[6]

Lord's Day, May 25, 1806—Mr. Brown & Mr. [Henry] Martyn spoke at our conference on Friday evening. The question[:] "Why could not God pardon sin without the death of Xt."

---

[5] The first set of brackets is mine while the second set was inserted by E. Daniel Potts.

[6] The two brethren in question here are John Fernandez, son of Asiatic colleague and Dinajpur mission station director, Ignatius Fernandez, and Mr. Maylin who were traveling to England where John would pursue further studies.

Lord's Day, November 27, 1808—Having begun an experience-meeting at Calcutta on a Tuesday evening, I go down every Tuesday with Bro. Carey. At these meetings I get from Krishnu an account of what he is doing. These meetings I find very useful, especially to the members born in this country, who have had little knowledge of the Xn. life.

Tuesday, August 22, 1809—The question at our conference this evening was "Why are we Dissenters."

Tuesday, November 7, 1809—We had a large meeting at the conference. The subject was, Is it lawful for Xns. To engage in lotteries.

Tuesday, December 26, 1809—The experience meeting was attended but thinly; the conference better. The question. "May a christian marry an unconverted person?" Mr. Maylin gave it.[7]

Tuesday, January 2, 1810—Our question at the conference was "How should a Xn. treat refractory & dishonest servants?" The common practice of beating servants was severely reprobated by the three speakers, Carey, Marshman & Ward. Such a question is never discussed in England. The Tuesday night before the question was "May a Xn. marry an unconverted person?"

---

[7] Aboard the *Criterion*, experience meetings were often held on Wednesday with question meetings on Thursday. As their name implies, in experience meetings, different people shared testimonies of their Christian experience for the benefit and edification of others present. The second to last entry is noteworthy for the last sentence, "Mr. Maylin gave it." He offers a similar comment in the final excerpt regarding the question, "How should a Xn. treat refractory & dishonest servants?" It seems that in both cases, Ward wanted readers to know that he and his colleagues did not propose or approve of such questions whose answers were clearly given in Scripture.

Appendix 2
The Winsome Wit of Ward

Though there are invaluable treasures within William Ward's journal, it does not make for the most entertaining reading. This is not due to mundaneness of events for most of what is recorded is consequential in one way or another. Rather, it is often laborious for two reasons. First, journals are not constructed as a novel, history, or biography with predetermined plot lines and supporting literary devices. Stories and events therefore, must be reconstructed from multiple journal entries that may be out of sequence, overlap, and be separated and surrounded by other completely unrelated material. Second, even that which is consequential can become mundane to the reader from sheer repetition.

But one element of the journal which makes reading much more enjoyable is the winsome wit of Ward which meets the reader when he is least suspecting it. Ward's contemporaries however, would not have been surprised, for he was known for his wit. Speaking of Ward's early days in the printing business, while still apprenticed to Mr. Drury, J.C. Marshman remarked, "He was endowed by nature with a lively imagination and pregnant wit."[1] Ward's primary memoirist, Samuel Stennett recognized the same, noting that, along with other marketable qualities, Ward's "ardent imagination" and "lively wit ... made him a valuable assistant in the conducting of a provincial journal."[2]

The following journal excerpts, contain some of the more

---

[1] John Clark Marshman, *The Life And Times of Carey, Marshman And Ward* (1859; repr., Serampore: Council of Serampore College, 2005), 1:93.

[2] Samuel Stennett, *Memoirs of the Life of the Rev. William Ward, Late Baptist Missionary in India; Containing A Few Of His Early Poetical Productions, And Monody to His Memory* (London: Simpkin and Marshall, 1825), 11-12.

noteworthy examples of Ward's wit and are presented that the reader may become better acquainted with this winsome aspect of Ward's personality.

Baptism

Lord's Day, June 14, 1801—Rowland Hill's zeal agst baptism made us smile. Poor Man. Bror. Carey has rendered baptize <u>dip</u>.

Lord's Day, June 13, 1802—After sermon we went down to the tank, for an alligator having destroyed two or three people who were bathing in the river near our house, we thought it hardly prudent to baptize in the river.

Monday, March 2, 1807—[In the context of an attempt to persuade the Derozio family of the necessity of baptism.] This excited their attention very much & the old man & Barlow were busy a good part of the day searching dictionaries & the testament whether these things were so or not. The old man could not master the evidence, & at length broke out—well: when I turned from Popery I became a town's talk, & now if I am to be baptized, I shall be a town's talk again, & people will say, he'll become [a] Musselman next.

Lord's Day, August 2, 1807—I got up at 5 and bathed in Mr. Derozio's tank to get acquainted with the nature of the steps before baptizing.

Friday, August 14, 1807—[The following quote involves the wife of Sabat, a convert from a Muslim background, and her objection to the impropriety of public baptism by immersion.] When Sabat was at Viziagapatam he wanted his wife to become a Xn; but there were no Xns. there at that time but the Armenians. The Armenian priest was spoken to; the baptistry was prepared, & the time fixed;

but when this woman saw that she was to be baptized by immersion <u>before</u> a <u>number of people</u>, she said (Sabat's words) She was willing to go to hell, but she would never expose herself in that way.—Sabat used this as an argument why public baptism by immersion would not be right: the Asiatic women would never submit to it. Yet Sabat is nearly convinced of baptism. He is sure both cannot be right. He asked me to lend him my book. I told him to consult with Dr. Buchanan & Mr. Brown first, & then if he wished I would lend it him. He said he had consulted Mr. B[<u>rown</u>] but he had no arguments.

Anglicans/Roman Catholics

Tuesday, May 12, 1807—The Propaganda is given up. Dr. Buchanan & Mr. Brown will not be enemies, I fancy, but they will no doubt remember our non-conformity. [Following the defeat of an attempt to bring their translation work and press under Anglican control via a new Propaganda College that the Anglican ministers proposed to establish.]

Lord's Day, February 2, 1806—On Friday evening Mrs. Brown sent 16 rupees, a gift to the poor of the church, or in English her sacrament money.

Lord's day, August 3, 1806—Three Catholic Missionaries lately came out from Europe. One went to Delhi & was murdered by the Musulmans; another went into Assam, where he is since dead; the third (an Irishman) returned to Europe, so says this young man. ... Here, as in Europe, in the Catholic church, all is in Latin. Bengalese learn to mutter a few words in Latin before they are christened! What a blessed way of making Xns.

Missions

Lord's Day, November 10, 1805—A dull sabbath. I said a few things in the boat to our native brethren, but we had no opportunity of preaching to any but monkies.

Wednesday, December 18, 1805—[Regarding native convert, Ram Mohun whom Ward thought should accompany Mr. Maylin and John Fernandez to England.] We have this day settled that Ram Mohun shall go with our Brethren to England. ... Bro. Carey is quite averse to any native brother's going. Bro. Marshman & I think it is what we owe to the supporters of the Mission & to you, as a reward for their prayers & subscriptions & your anxiety & labours. ... There never was a sight like this in England since the world began—a converted brahman. ... The sight of this brahman may stop the mouths of infidels & cold Calvinists. It will electrify whole congregations. Let Fernandez & Ram Mohun sing a Bengalee hymn, after a sermon in behalf of the Mission, & in every place you will be laden with gifts & contributions. Take them with you [on] a Missionary Tour—to Scotland, &c. Don't make a shew of them— Don't be afraid of shewing them. Don't set them on a stool in a chapel. Don't hide God's gift in a napkin.

Language Learning

Wednesday, May 14, 1806—Our new brethren have begun to go out into the adjoining villages: they begin to stammer a little. Bro. Mardon seems to stand first & Bro. Biss next. They will none of them be pundits [i.e. teachers].

Sabbath-breaking

Lord's Day, April 28, 1805—I spoke at night at home in Bengalee. Felix was twice at the Bengalee school. In the intermediate parts of the day Bro. C. & I were busy reading Bible proofs. Is this Sabbath-breaking?

Lord's Day, October 27, 1805—Five of the seven Boxes arrived in the night. We were almost guilty of Sabbath-breaking in opening them, but who could forbear?

Natives/local Culture

Friday, April 11, 1800—The other day a man came to our gate with his arm erect & his finger nails grown several inches long. I have since heard that he has held his arm in that posture 12 years, and that he has been silent so long, in consequence of a curse of the Brahmans. Oh! if this man, with his stiff arm, was converted to Xt. what a striking preacher he would make.

Lord's Day, October 20, 1805—[Regarding an episode from brother Juggernaut's life before his baptism.] One day they run short of wood to cook with. What was to be done? One of them (either the husband or wife) advised to cut up the god & teach him to boil the pot. The other objected & advised to get rid of him in a more honourable way, viz., by throwing him into the river. The other argued that they really were short of fuel; that Jaggernaut was good dry wood & would burn well, & therefore it was best to turn him to some useful account. This argument prevailed, & Jaggernaut (the Lord of the world) was cut in two, & half of him was used in boiling the rice of his once devoted worshippers. To this very image these two had prostrated themselves, & they had performed his worship, & regarded him as a god. I hope to preach in this brother's house on Lord's-Day, & if I can lay hold of the other half of Jaggernaut I will send him in triumph to Bristol.

Monday, December 1, 1806—Some of our younger native brethren among the least conscientious have lately begun to drink spirits, & in one or two instances have been overcome. This is one of the bad effects of our drinking spirits, for we are hardly able to forbid them what we do ourselves; & they even quote scripture in favour of drinking; not being use[d] to drink any thing except water they know not how to take little enough. We are now laboring to put an effectual check to this, before worse come o[f] it.

Hygiene

Thursday November 8, 1804—[In a conversation with a Muslim man.] Amongst other questions, he asked me whether I washed my backside after doing my business? It seems our using paper is a great offence to Musselmans. A brahman, after washing his backside, washes the fingers of his left hand 21 times, & repeats a munter [muntra], then he is clean.

Weather/heat/sweat

Lord's Day, May 18, 1800—It has been very hot within these few days, & the rains are coming on, yet in passing thro' the fire & the water we are not materially affected. We have felt the greatest heat now, & though a person sweats profusely, it neither sets aside business nor destroys health.

Friday, May 30, 1800—It is so hot that in sitting still with nothing but a very thin white waistcoat & jacket on my shirt is quite wet in a few minutes. We are all in very merciful circumstances, however.

Lord's Day, September 4, 1803—I have lately fallen off in my flesh & spirits a good deal. I believe the present sultry weather produces an unfavourable effect upon my constant habit, flatulency & indigestion.

Tuesday, June 4, 1805—It is impossible to bustle about as with the frost at one's fingers and nose.

Wit of Ward

Lord's Day, June 17, 1810—Preaching in black clothes in this climate is a sad burthen [*sic*]. My clothes have been three times as wet as dung to-day, & the very papers in my pockets have been dyed black with sweat.

Lord's Day, August 12, 1810—At ten I preached; then baptized; at ½ past 3 I preached at the jail in English, & afterwards in Bengalee; at 7 I preached again at the Fort; & at 9 I met a number of friends at Mr. Thompson's. The skeleton's of two of these sermons I had to prepare also during the day. You see the heat of the climate does not prevent a hard day's work, as I this day composed 2 sermons; preached 4; baptized, & held two meetings besides.

Collegial Jabs

Saturday, June 28, 1806—The head-pundit said to me one day, I do not know what kind of a body Carey Saheb's is? He is never sensible of fatigue, or of hunger, and never leaves a thing till it is finished.

Friday, July 4, 1806—Bro. Biss will be able to go up directly. ... Bro. Biss is a most wretched coward & confines himself like a lying-in [pregnant] woman, terribly afraid of death.

Lord's Day, November 16, 1806—Bro. Biss seems better. I think he is getting fat: still he is not without very strong fears that he is dying. He is at Mr. Lindeman's, & gets the advice of Dr. Hare.

Lord's Day, December 7, 1806—Mr. Brown has called upon Dr. Hare respecting Bro. Biss's complaint. After seeing Dr. H[are], he sent Bro. Biss the following letter, which decides upon Bro. B[iss],'s returning home, as if we were not now to send him he would actually die with fear.

The Spirituality of William Ward

Lord's Day, December 28, 1806—[Shortly before Bro. and Mrs. Biss returned to England on account of Bro. Biss' health.] Bro. Marshman preached at Calcutta. It was Bro. Rowe's turn, but Bro. Marshman came down to try to prevail upon Sister Biss to give up her white clothes & the children's & receive an equivalent for them, instead of taking them to England, where people will wonder to see a Missionary's wife so fine. Bro. Marshman's a good hand in getting thro' a disagreeable job, though I fancy Sister Biss is none so fond of his arguments against her thin clothes.

Friday, September 25, 1807—[When Carey and Marshman called on Lord Minto to seek his favor in the midst of the Persian Pamphlet Controversy.] Bren. Carey & Marshman having settled their plan, & Bro. M. having borrowed Mr. Rolt's coat, they set off to wait on his lordship. They had sent their names on the preceding evening, according to etiquette, but some how or other their note had miscarried; the aid-de-camp, however, introduced them, with the Ramayunu under their arm; & these two brethren [making very awkward bows, no doubt: it was lucky for Bro. Carey, that the form required him to leave his hat in the passage, or he would most likely have stuck it under his left arm-pit; bro. Marshman would, by a dreadful squeeze, have made his hat shrink into the size of a black pocket-handkerchief.] ventured into the presence of the Governor-General of India.[3]

Saturday, October 3, 1807—Robinson declared his resolution not to go to Cutwa; these two Brethren however dissatisfied with Serampore, would live together like two Cats tied together by the tails.

Lord's Day, October 18, 1807—[In describing fellow BMS missionary, William Robinson.] This Bro. has a great facili-

---

[3] The first bracketed text is mine. The second bracketed text appears to be Ward's own as text added by Potts typically consists of names and alternate spellings.

Wit of Ward

ty in acquiring languages. I heard him (secretly) in the Bengallee school, the other night with surprise. He is far very far before Moore & Rowe in Bengallee. He is very acceptable in English, and has much originality in his preaching, but he is infinitely obstinate, and capable of shaking down the whole Mission House.

Timeline

Oct. 20, 1769	Birth at Derby
1789–1793	Editor of the Derby *Mercury*
Dec. 25, 1792	Ward's "Address of July 16" is published in the *Morning Chronicle* which causes editor and printer to be prosecuted for sedition
Mar. 31, 1793	Meets William Carey in London; Carey urges him to India to print the Bible for him
Oct. 1794	Leaves Derby for London to learn the art of printing
Jan. 1795	Move to Staffordshire to write prospectuses for the *Staffordshire Advertiser*
Late 1795	Move to Hull to serve as editor for the *Hull Adviser and Gazette Exchange*; begins attending Baptist church
Aug. 28, 1796	Baptized at church meeting in Hull
Mar. 20, 1797	Ward, without permission, admits John Thelwall to the Baptist chapel in

	Derby who delivers a political lecture which incites a mob to riot
Late 1796-1797	Ward preaches in villages around Hull
Summer 1797	Call to ministry
Aug. 1797	Moves to Ewood Hall, Yorkshire for theological education under John Fawcett
	Itinerant preaching in hamlets around Ewood Hall
Autumn 1798	PBMS member visits Ewood Hall to talk about printing
May 7, 1799	Ward formally accepted as a missionary of the PBMS
May 24, 1799	Ward departs for India on the *Criterion* along with fellow PBMS Missionaries, Joshua and Hannah Marshman, Daniel Brunsdon and William Grant and their spouses; begins his missionary *Journal*
Oct. 13, 1799	Ward and companions arrive in Serampore
Jan. 10, 1800	Carey joins Ward and campanions in Serampore

Timeline

Mar. 18, 1800	Ward presents Carey with first sheet of The Bengali Bible
April 24, 1800	Church constituted at Serampore; practice closed communion
Dec. 28, 1800	Baptism of Krishna Pal
May 10, 1802	Marriage to John Fountain's widow, Mary Tidd
1803 and 1805	Second wave of BMS missionaries arrive in Serampore
Oct. 7, 1805	Missionaries sign *Serampore Form of Agreement* which was drafted by Ward
1805	Serampore Trio embark on the "Grand Translation Project"
1805	Serampore Church begins to practice open communion
1806	Ward publishes first edition of *A View of the History, Literature, and Mythology of the Hindoos*
Sept.–Oct. 1807	Persian Pamphlet Affair
Dec. 1807	Ward begins writing *Circular Letters* to convey news to England

The Spirituality of William Ward

Jan. 1, 1809	Opening of Lal Bazaar Chapel in Calcutta
Mar. 3, 1811	Serampore Church returns to closed communion
Oct. 30, 1811	Last entry of Ward's *Journal*
Mar. 11, 1812	Devastating fire at Serampore printing office
May 7, 1815	Death of Andrew Fuller; beginning of the Serampore Controversy which is not resolved until 1837 around the time of Joshua Marshman's death.
July 15, 1818	Missionaries found Serampore College for the spiritual and intellectual improvement of native students
1818–1821	Ward's tour of England, Holland, and America
Dec. 1818	Begins writing *Reflection on the Word of God for Every Day in the Year* as he sails from to England
1821	Ward writes *Farewell Letters* on his return journey from America to Serampore, where he arrives in October
Mar. 7, 1823	Death at Serampore

Bibliography

Primary Sources
Published/Archived Works by Ward

Ward, William. "Bengal." In *The Baptist Mission in India: Containing a Narrative of Its Rise, Progress*, by William Staughton, 199-258. Philadelphia: Hellings and Aitken, 1811. (Ward's authorship mentioned on pp. iii-iv of the preface.)

_____. *The Blessedness of the Righteous Dead. A Sermon preached at Mission House, Serampore, Bengal: On Lord's Day, April 12, 1806 After Receiving the Afflictive Intelligence of the Death of Mr. William Sedgwick, Deacon of the Baptist Church, Meeting In George Street, Hull. Who Died February 14, 1805. Aged 41 Years*. London: Dunstable, 1807.

_____. *BMS Missionary Correspondence; William Ward; Transcript of Diaries in 2 Books Comprising 4 Volumes; Book 1 (Vols. 1 & 2) 1799-1805; Book 2 (Vols. 3 & 4) 1806-1811*. Microfilm; Reel 44. Publication No. 5350. London: Baptist Missionary Society Archives, 1981.

_____. *Brief Memoir of Krishna Pal, the First Hindoo, in Bengal, who broke the Chain of the Cast, By embracing the Gospel*. 2nd ed. London: John Offer, 1823.

_____. *The Design of the Death of Christ Explained, a Sermon by William Ward*. Serampore: Mission Press, 1820.

_____. *Farewell Letters to A Few Friends In Britain and America On Returning to Bengal In 1821*. New York: E. Bliss and E. White, 1821.

_____. *The First Hindoo Convert: A Memoir Of Krishna Pal, A Preacher of the Gospel To His Countrymen More Than Twenty Years*. Philadelphia: American Baptist Publication Society, 1852.

The Spirituality of William Ward

_____. "Letter to the Ladies of Liverpool, and of the United Kingdom." *The Times* 3 (January 1821): n.p. (This bibliographic entry is cited on p. 90n26 of [Gleadle, Kathryn and Sarah Richardson, eds. *Women in British Politics, 1760–1860: The Power of the Petticoat.* Houndmills, UK: Palgrave Macmillan, 2000].)

_____. *A Letter To The Right Honorable J. C. Villiers, On The Education Of The Natives Of India: To Which Are Added An Account Of Hindoo Widows, Recently Burnt Alive In Bengal; And Also Some Extracts From The Reports Of The Native Schools, Published By The Serampore Missionaries.* London, 1820.

_____. *The Love of Christ Beareth Us Away.* London, 1820.

_____. *Reflections On The Word of God For Every Day In The Year: In Two Volumes.* 2 vols. Serampore: Mission Press, 1822.

_____. *Serampore Form of Agreement.* Found in *Periodical Accounts Relative to the Baptist Missionary Society. Baptist Missionary Society Archives, 1792–1914. (London, England).* Vol. 3, pages 198-11. Nashville, TN: Historical Commission, Southern Baptist Convention, 1981. Microfilm.

_____. *Sermon Preached on the 1st of August, 1813, in the Settlement Church at Serampore on Occasion of the Erection of a Monument to the Memory of the Lady of N. Wallich, Esq.* Serampore: Mission Press, 1813.

_____. *A View of All Religions; And the Religious Ceremonies of All Nations.* 2nd ed. Hartford, CT: Oliver D. Cooke & Sons, 1824.

_____. *A View of the History, Literature, and Religion of the Hindoos: Including A Minute Description of Their Manners and Customs, And Translations From Their Principal Works, In Two Volumes,* 2nd ed. Serampore: Mission Press, 1815.

_____. *A View Of The History, Literature, And Religion Of The Hindoos: Including A Minute Description Of Their Manners And Customs, And Translations From Their Principal Works.* 5th ed. Madras: J. Higginbotham, 1863.

Bibliography

Other Primary Sources

Carey, William. *Carey's Covenant for the Church at Moulton.* N.p., n.d.

———. *An Enquiry into the Obligations of Christians, to Use Means for the Conversion of the Heathens: In Which the Religious State of the Different Nations of the World, the Success of Former Undertakings, and the Practicability of Further Undertakings Are Considered.* Leicester: A. Ireland, 1792.

———. "Jishur Prem." In *Hallelujah Sangeet.* Calcutta: Hriday Ranjan Samaddar, 1949.

———. *The Journal and Selected Letters of William Carey.* Edited by Terry G. Carter. Macon, GA: Smyth & Helwys, 2000.

———. "'Letters From The Rev. Dr. Carey, Relative to Certain Statements Contained in Three Pamphlets Lately Published by the Rev. John Dyer, Secretary to The Baptist Missionary Society: W. Johns, M.D. and The Rev. E. Carey and W. Yates.; The Third Edition, Enlarged from Seventeen to Thirty-Two Letters, Containing Dr. Carey's Ideas Respecting the Mission from the Year 1815 to the Present Time.'" In *Serampore Bound Pamphlets.* Edited by Joshua Marshman. 135:9. Serampore, 1828.

Edwards, Jonathan. *A Careful And Strict Inquiry Into The Modern Prevailing Notions Of That Freedom of the Will, Which Is Supposed To Be Essential To Moral Agency, Virtue And Vice, Reward And Punishment, Praise And Blame.* In *The Works of President Edwards, In Four Volumes With Valuable Additions And A Copious General Index, And A Complete Index Of Scripture Texts.* Vol. 2. New York: Robert Carter and Brothers, 1881.

———. *An Humble Attempt to Promote Explicit Agreement and Visible Union of God's People, in Extraordinary Prayer, for the Revival of Religion and the Advancement of Christ's Kingdom on Earth, Pursuant to Scripture Promises and Prophecies Concerning the Last Time.* In *The Works of Jonathan Edwards.* Edited by John E. Smith. Vol. 5, *Apocalyptic Writings*, edited by Stephen J. Stein. New Haven and London: Yale University Press, 1977.

Fuller, Andrew. *Andrew Fuller's Confession of Faith (Delivered by Mr. Fuller, on the occasion of his installation as pastor of the First Baptist Church at Kettering), October 7, 1783.* As found in Ryland, John. *The Work of Faith, the Labour of Love, and the Patience of Hope Illustrated In The Life and Death Of The Reverend Andrew Fuller, Late Pastor Of The Baptist Church at Kettering, And Secretary to the Baptist Missionary Society From It's Commencement, In 1792.* London: Button & Son, 1816. 99-109.

_____. *The Gospel of Christ Worthy of All Acceptation, Or The Duty Of Sinners To Believe In Jesus Christ, With Corrections And Additions; To Which Is Added An Appendix, On The Necessity Of A Holy Disposition In Order To Believing In Christ* (1801). In *The Complete Works Of The Rev. Andrew Fuller: With A Memoir Of His Life, By Andrew Gunton Fuller.* Vol. 2. Third London Edition. Reprint, Harrisonburg, VA: Sprinkle Publications, 1988.

Fuller, Andrew Gunton. "Memoir." In *The Complete Works Of The Rev. Andrew Fuller: With A Memoir Of His Life, By Andrew Gunton Fuller.* Vol. 1. Third London Edition. Reprint, Harrisonburg, VA: Sprinkle Publications, 1988.

Hall, Robert Sr. *Help to Zion's Travelers: Being An Attempt To Remove Various Stumbling Blocks Out Of The Way, Relating To Doctrinal, Experiemental And Practical Religion.* 3rd ed. 1824. Reprint, Whitefish, MT: Kessinger Legacy Reprints, n.d.

_____. *Help to Zion's Travellers: Being an Attempt to Remove Various Stumbling Blocks out of the Way, Relating to Doctrinal, Experimental and Practical Religion.* Edited by Finn, Nathan A. 1781. Reprint, Mountain Home, AR: Borderstone Press, 2011.

Ivimey, Joseph. "Memoir of the Late Rev. W. Ward, Extracted from a larger Account contained in the Appendix to Mr. Ivimey's Funeral Sermon for him." In *The Baptist Magazine.* London: J. Barfield, 1823, 15:405-11.

Lal Bazar Baptist Church, Calcutta Letter-Book & Records With _____y, December 1876 to April 1885. Carey Baptist Church Historical Papers. Carey Baptist Church, Kolkata, India.

Bibliography

Lewis, C. B. *The Life of John Thomas, Surgeon of The Earl of Oxford East Indiaman, And First Baptist Missionary To Bengal.* London: Macmillan and Co., 1873.

Lumpkin, William Latane. *Baptist Confessions of Faith.* Chicago: Judson Press, 1959.

Marshman, John Clark. *The Life And Times of Carey, Marshman And Ward.* 2 Vols. 1859. Reprint, Serampore: Council of Serampore College, 2005.

Marshman, Joshua. *Divine Grace the Source of All Human Excellence.* Serampore: Mission Press, 1823.

Marshman, Joshua. *The Efficiency of Divine Grace; A Funeral Sermon for the Late Rev. William Carey, D.D.* Serampore: Mission Press, 1834.

Memoir Of The Rev. William Ward, One Of The Serampore Missionaries. Philadelphia: American Sunday School Union, 1828.

Monthly Circular Letters Relative to the Missions In India, Established By a Society In England, Called the "Baptist Missionary Society." Vols. 4, 6. Serampore: Mission Press, 1811, 1813.

Periodical Accounts Relative to the Baptist Missionary Society. Baptist Missionary Society Archives, 1792-1914. Microfilm; reels 1-9. London: Baptist Missionary Archives, 1981.

"Record of Petition and Subcription for Lal Bazar Dissenting Chapel." Edited by Lal Bazaar Chapel Trustees. Ca. 1809. Carey Baptist Church Historical Papers. Carey Baptist Church, Kolkata, India.

Rennell, James. *A Bengal Atlas: Containing Maps Of The Theatre Of War And Commerce On That Side Of Hindoostan.* N.p., 1781.

Sargent, J. *The Life Of The Rev. T.T. Thomason, M.A.; Late Chaplain To The Honourable East India Company.* London: R. B. Seeley and W. Burnside, 1833.

Stennett, Samuel. *Memoirs of the Life of the Rev. William Ward, Late Baptist Missionary in India; Containing A Few Of His Early Poetical Productions, And Monody to His Memory.* London: Simpkin and Marshall, 1825.

The Spirituality of William Ward

Yates, William. *Memoirs of Mr. John Chamberlain, Late Missionary in India*. Calcutta: The Baptist Mission Press, 1826.

Secondary Sources
Books

"Abstract of Title Deeds of Ground & Building." *Lal Bazaar Baptist Church, Calcutta; Letter-Book & Records With _____ y, December 1876 to April 1885.* Carey Baptist Church Historical Papers. Carey Baptist Church, Kolkata, India.

Aitken, Jonathan. *John Newton; From Disgrace to Amazing Grace*. Wheaton, IL: Crossway, 2007.

Bebbington, David. *Baptists through the Centuries: A History of a Global People*. Waco, TX: Baylor University Press, 2010.

_____. *Evangelicalism in Modern Britain: A History from the 1730s to the 1980s*. Grand Rapids: Baker Book House, 1992.

Bradley, James E. *Religion, Revolution, and English Radicalism: Nonconformity in eighteenth-century Politics and Society*. Cambridge: Cambridge University Press, 1990.

Briggs, J. H. Y. *The English Baptists of the 19th Century*. Oxford: The Baptist Historical Society, 1994.

Brine, John. *A Refutation of Arminian Principles*. London, 1743.

Brown, Raymond. *The English Baptists of the Eighteenth Century*. London: Baptist Historical Society, 1986.

Burns, Evan. *Monographs in Baptist History*. Vol. 4, *A Supreme Desire to Please Him; The Spirituality of Adoniram Judson*. Eugene, OR: Pickwick Publications, 2016.

Calvin, John. *Institutes of the Christian Religion*. Translated by John Allen. Philadelphia: Presbyterian Board of Publication, 1909.

Carey, Samuel Pearce. *William Carey D.D., Fellow of Linnaean Society*. 8th ed. London: The Carey Press, 1923.

_____. *William Carey D.D., Fellow of Linnaean Society*. 3rd ed. London: Hodder and Stoughton, 1924.

Bibliography

Carey, W. H. *Oriental Christian Biography Containing Biographical Sketches Of Distinguished Christians Who Have Lived And Died In The East*. 2 vols. Calcutta: Baptist Mission Press, 1850.

Carson, Penelope. *Worlds Of The East India Company*. Vol. 7, *The East India Company and Religion, 1698-1858*. Woodbridge, UK: Boydell Press, 2012.

Chatterjee, S. K. "Ignatius Fernandez" in *William Carey of Serampore*. Sheoraphuli, India: Laserplus, 2004. 134-64.

_____. *William Carey and His Associates in the Renaissance of Bengal*. Calcutta: Rachna Prakashan, 1974.

_____. *William Carey and Serampore*. Sheoraphuli: Laserplus, 2004.

Cowper, William. *Olney Hymns in Three Books*. "Praise for the Fountain Opened," Book 1, Hymn 79. Buckinghamshire, England: Arthur Gordon Hugh Osborn, 1979. Accessed October 16, 2018. http://www.ccel.org/ccel/newton/olneyhymns.html.

Crosby, Thomas. *The History of the English Baptists*. 4 vols. 1738-1740. Reprint, Paris, AR: The Baptist Standard Bearer, Inc., 2015.

Culross, James. *William Carey*. London: Hodder and Stoughton, 1881.

Dasgupta, Saumitra Sankar, Subhro Sekhar Sircar, and M. Justin Moses, eds. *Serampore College: Gems from the Past: A Collection of Old Writings*. New Delhi: Christian World Imprints, 2018.

Douglas, David. *History of the Baptist Churches in the North of England From 1648 to 1845*. London, 1846.

Estep, William R. *The Anabaptist Story; An Introduction to Sixteenth-Century Anabaptism*. Grand Rapids: Wm. B. Eerdmans Publishing Company, 1996.

[Fawcett, John Jr.]. *An Account of the Life, Ministry, and Writings of the late Rev. John Fawcett Who Was Minister Of The Gospel Fifty-Four Years, First At Wainsgate, And Afterwards At Hebdenbridge, In The Parish Of Halifax; Comprehending Many Particulars Relative To The Revival And Progress Of Religion In Yorkshire And Lancashire; And Illustrated By Copious Extracts From The Diary Of*

The Deceased, From His Extensive Correspondence, And Other Documents. London, 1818.

George, Timothy. *Faithful Witness: The Life and Mission of William Carey.* Birmingham, AL: New Hope, 1991.

Gleadle, Kathryn, and Sarah Richardson, eds. *Women in British Politics, 1760–1860: The Power of the Petticoat.* Houndmills. UK: Palgrave Macmillan, 2000.

Grudem, Wayne. *Systematic Theology; An Introduction To Biblical Doctrine.* Grand Rapids: Zondervan, 2000.

Hall, Robert, Jr. *A Short Statement Of The Reasons For Christian, In Opposition To Party Communion.* London: Hamilton, Adams, & Co., 1826.

Haykin, Michael A. G., ed. *The British Particular Baptists 1638–1910.* Vol. 2. Springfield, MO: Particular Baptist Press, 2000.

_____. *The God Who Draws Near; An Introduction To Biblical Spirituality.* Darlington, England: Evangelical Press, 2007.

_____. *One Heart and One Soul: John Sutcliff of Olney, His Friends and His Times.* A Welwyn Biography. Darlington, England: Evangelical Press, 1994.

Hof, Ulrich Im. *The Enlightenment.* Translated by William E. Yuill. Oxford: Blackwell, 1994.

Holcomb, H. Helen. *Men of Might in India Missions.* New York: Fleming H. Revell, 1901.

How, Samuel. *Sufficiencie of the Spirits Teaching, without Humane-Learning.* London, 1692.

Johnson, Arthur L. *Faith Misguided; Exposing the Dangers of Mysticism.* Chicago: Moody Press, 1988.

Kinghorn, Joseph. *Arguments Against Mixed Communion, And In Support Of Communion On The Plan Of The Apostolic Church; With Preliminary Observations On Rev. R. Hall's Reasons For Christian, In Opposition To Party Communion.* London, 1827.

_____. *Baptism, A Term of Communion at the Lord's Supper.* 2nd ed. Norwich, 1816.

Bibliography

Lovegrove, Deryck W. *Established Church, Sectarian People: Itineracy and the Transformation of English Dissent, 1780–1830.* Cambridge: Cambridge University Press, 1988.

Lovett, Richard, *The History of the London Missionary Society, 1795–1895.* Vol. 2. London: Henry Frowde/London Missionary Society, 1899.

Marsden, George M. *Jonathan Edwards, A Life.* New Haven, CT: Yale University Press, 2003.

Mason, J. C. S. *The Moravian Church and the Missionary Awakening in England.* Woodbridge, Suffolk, UK: The Boydell Press, 2001

Nettles, Tom J. *The Baptists: Key People Involved in Forming a Baptist Identity.* Vol. 1. Fearn, Scotland: Christian Focus Publications, 2005.

_____. *By His Grace and for His Glory; A Historical, Theological and Practical Study of the Doctrines of Grace in Baptist Life.* Rev. ed. Cape Coral, FL: Founders Press, 2006.

Newman, W. *Rylandiana: Reminiscences relating to the Rev. John Ryland.* London, 1835.

Noll, Mark A. *The Rise of Evangelicalism: The Age of Edwards, Whitefield and the Wesleys.* Downers Grove, IL: InterVarsity Press, 2003.

O'dell, J. *Century's Story of Baptist Church, George Street, Hull.* 2nd ed. London, 1904.

Owen, John. *The Death of The Death Of Christ in the Death of Christ.* 1684. Reprint, Edinburgh: Banner of Truth, 2007.

_____. *The Works of John Owen, D.D.* Vols. 2 and 10. Edited by William H. Goold. Edinburgh: T. & T. Clark, 1851.

Packer, J. I. *A Quest For Godliness; The Puritan Vision Of The Christian Life.* Wheaton, IL: Crossway, 1990.

Paine, Thomas. *Rights of Man: Being An Answer to Mr. Burke's Attack On The French Revolution.* London, 1791.

Payne, Ernest Alexander. *The Church Awakes: The Story of the Modern Missionary Movement.* London: Edinburg House Press, 1942.

_____. *The First Generation: Early Leaders of the Baptist Missionary Society in England and India*. London: Carey Press, 1936.

Pearson, Hugh. *Memoirs of the Life And Correspondence of the Reverend Christian Frederick Swartz. To Which Is Prefixed, A Sketch of the History of Christianity, In India*. 1st American ed. New York: D. Appleton & Co., 1835.

Perkins, William. *A Golden Chaine or the Description of Theologie Containing the Order of the Causes of Saluation and Damnation, According to God's word. A View Whereof Is to Be Seen in the Table Annexed*. Cambridge, 1660.

Potts, E. Daniel. *British Baptist Missionaries in India 1793–1837: The History of Serampore And Its Missions*. Cambridge: Cambridge University Press, 1967.

Rinaldi, Frank W. *Studies in Baptist History and Thought*. Vol. 10. *The Tribe of Dan: The New Connexion of General Baptists 1770–1891: A Study in the Transition From Revival Movement to Established Denomination*. Eugene, OR: Wipf and Stock Publishers, 2009.

Simpson, W. O. Introduction to *A View of the History, Literature, and Religion of the Hindoos: Including A Minute Description Of Their Manners And Custome, And Translations From Their Principal Works*, 1-12. 5th ed. Madras: Law Bookseller and Publisher, 1863.

Smith, A. Christopher. *The Serampore Mission Enterprise*. Bangalore, India: Centre for Contemporary Christianity, 2006.

Smith, George. *The Life of William Carey, D. D.: Shoemaker & Missionary*. London: John Murray, 1885.

_____. *The Life of William Carey: Shoemaker & Missionary*. Rev. ed. London: J. M. Dent & Sons, 1909.

Spurgeon, C. H. "Exposition of the Doctrines of Grace." *The New Park Street And The Metropolitan Tabernacle Pulpit; Containing Sermons Preached And Revised By The Reverend C.H. Spurgeon, During The Year 1861*. Vol. 7. London, 1862.

Stanley, Brian. *The History of the Baptist Missionary Society, 1792–1992*. Edinburgh: T & T Clarke, 1992.

Bibliography

Starr, Edward Caryl. *A Baptist Bibliography: Being a Register of Printed Material by and about Baptists; Including Works Written Against the Baptists.* Vol. 24. Philadelphia: Published by the Judson Press for the Samuel Colgate Baptist Historical Collection, Colgate University, 1976.

Swaine, Stephen A. *Faithful Men: Or, Memorials of Bristol Baptist College, And Some of Its Most Distinguished Alumni.* London: Alexander & Shepheard, 1884.

Taylor, Adam. *Memoirs of the Rev. Dan Taylor.* London, 1820.

Venn, Henry. *The Complete Duty of Man; Or A System of Doctrinal & Practical Christianity; To Which Are Added, Forms of Prayer And Offices Of Devotion For the Various Circumstances In Life.* New Brunswick, NJ: J. Simpson and Co., 1811.

Walker, F. Deaville. *William Carey, Missionary Pioneer And Statesman.* London: Student Christian Movement, 1926.

Ward, W. R. *Religion and Society in England 1790-1850.* London: Batsford, 1972.

Wesley, John. *The Journal of John Wesley.* Chicago: Moody Press, n.d.

Wenger, Edward S. *Missionary Biographies.* 4 vols. MSS. Carey Library and Research Center, Serampore College.

_____. *The Story of the Lall Bazar Baptist Church; Being the History of Carey's Church From 24th April 1800 to the Present Day.* Calcutta: Edinburgh Press, 1908.

Young, C. M. *Pioneers and Founders or Recent Workers in the Mission Field.* 1871.

Articles

American National Biography. Edited by John A. Garraty and Mark C. Carnes. Vol. 3. Oxford: Oxford University Press, 1999.

Balasundaran, Franklyn J. "Ward, William." In *A Dictionary of Asian Christianity*. Edited by Scott W. Sunquist. Grand Rapids: Wm. B. Eerdmans Publishing Co., 2001.

Benigni, Umberto. "Sacred Congregation of Propaganda." In *The Catholic Encyclopedia*. Vol. 12. New York: Robert Appleton Company, 1911. Accessed December 7, 2018. http://www.newadvent.org/cathen/12456a.htm.

The Blackwell Dictionary of Evangelical Biography 1730-1830. Vol. 1. Edited by Donald M. Lewis. Oxford: Blackwell Publishers, 1995.

Carlyle, E. I., and Brian Stanley. "Ward, William (1769-1823)." In *Oxford Dictionary of National Biography*. Vol. 57. Edited by H. C. G. Matthew and Brian Harrison. Oxford: Oxford University Press, 2004.

Chun, Chris. "The Greatest Instruction Received from Human Writings: The Legacy of Jonathan Edwards in the Theology of Andrew Fuller." PhD diss., University of St. Andrews, St. Mary's College, 2008.

Clary, Ian High. "Throwing away the Guns: Andrew Fuller, William Ward, and the Communion Controversy in the Baptist Mission Society." *Foundations* 68 (May 2015): 84-101.

Daniel, J. T. K. "Ecumenical Pragmatism of the Serampore Mission." *Indian Journal of Theology* 42, no. 2 (2000): 171-77.

Finn, Nathan A. "Robert Hall's Contributions to Evangelical Renewal in the Northamptonshire Baptist Association." *Midwestern Journal of Theology* 6, no. 1 (Fall 2007): 19-34.

Ford, Samuel H., ed. "Abraham Booth; The Great And Learned Weaver." *The Christian Repository and Home Circle* 67, no. 3 (April 1889): 241-45.

Haykin, Michael A. G. "Particular Redemption in the Writings of Andrew Fuller (1754-1815)." In *Studies in Baptist History and Thought*. Vol. 1. *The Gospel in the World: International Baptist Studies*, edited by David Bebbington. Carlisle, Cumbria/Waynesboro, GA: Paternoster Press, 2002.

Bibliography

———. "'With Light, Beauty, and Power': Educating English Baptists in the Long Eighteenth Century." In *Challenge and Change; English Baptist Life in the Eighteenth Century*, edited by Stephen Copson and Peter J. Morden, 177-203. Didcot, UK: The Baptist Historical Society, 2017.

Hill, Andrew. "William Adam." In *Dictionary of Unitarian & Universalist Biography*. Edited by Barry Andrews, et al. Accessed November 28, 2018. http://uudb.org/articles/williamadam.html.

Himbury, D. M. "Training Baptist Ministers." *Baptist Quarterly* 21, no. 8 (October 1966): 341-43.

"Memoir of Rev. William Ward, One of the Serampore Missionaries." *The American Baptist Magazine*. Vol. 5. Boston: Baptist Missionary Society of Massachusetts, 1825. 1-12.

Neill, Stephen C. "The History of Missions: An Academic Discipline." In *The Mission of the Church and the Propagation of the Faith*, edited by G. J. Cuming, 149-70. Cambridge: The University Press, 1970.

"Obituary: Rev. W. Ward." *The American Baptist Magazine and Missionary Intelligencer*, 4:231-32. Boston: James Loring, 1823.

Obituary of The Rev. William Ward: One of the Serampore Missionaries. London: J. Haddon, 1823. Taken from the same title in *Friend of India* monthly series (April 1823).

Oxford Dictionary of National Biography. Edited by H. C. G. Matthew and Brian Harrison. Vol. 4. Oxford: Oxford University Press, 2004.

The Oxford Encyclopedia of the Reformation. Edited by Hans J. Hillerbrand. Vol. 2. Oxford: Oxford University Press, 1996.

Payne, E. A. "The Evangelical Revival and the Beginning of the Modern Missionary Movement." *Congregational Quarterly* 21 (1943): 223-36.

[Payne, Ernest?], "The Serampore Form of Agreement." *Baptist Quarterly* 12, no. 5 (January 1947): 125-38.

Pennington, Brian K. "Reverend William Ward and His Legacy for Christian (Mis)perception of Hinduism." *Journal of Hindu-*

Christian Studies 13, no. 6 (2000): 4-11. Accessed January 21, 2019. https://digitalcommons.butler.edu/jhcs/vol13/iss1/6/.

Potts, E. Daniel. "The Baptist Missionaries of Serampore and the Government of India, 1792-1813." *Journal of Ecclesiastical History*, 15 (1964): 229-46.

_____. "'I Throw Away the Guns to Preserve the Ship': A Note on the Serampore Trio." *The Baptist Quarterly* 20, no. 3 (July 1963): 115-17.

_____. "The Indian Press and Missionaries." *The Baptist Quarterly* 23, no. 2 (April 1969): 73-76.

_____. "Missionaries and the Beginnings of the Secular State in India." In *Essays in Indian history, in Honour of Cuthbert Collin Davies*, edited by Donovan Williams and E. Daniel Potts, 113-36. London: Asia Publishing House, 1973.

_____. "Ward, William." In *The Blackwell Dictionary of Evangelical Biography*. Edited by Donald M. Lewis. Oxford: Blackwell Publishers Ltd, 1995.

_____. "William Ward: The Making of a Missionary in the 18th Century." In *Bicentenary Volume: William Carey's Arrival in India 1793-1993, Serampore College 1818-1993*. Serampore: Serampore College, 1993.

_____. "William Ward's Missionary Journal." *The Baptist Quarterly* 25, no. 3 (July 1973): 111-14.

"The Reverend William Ward of Serampore." *The Bengal Obituary*. Calcutta: W. Thacker and St. Andrew's Library, 1851. 343-45.

Reynolds, Matthew M. "Jonathan Edwards' Influence on the Formation of the Particular Baptist Missionary Society." *Indian Journal of Theology* 60, no. 1 (2018): 105-23.

Sarkar, Mrinal Kanti. "Ward, William." In *The Oxford Encyclopaedia of South Asian Christianity*. Vol. 2. Edited by Roger E. Hedlund. New Delhi: Oxford University Press, 2012.

Schirrmacher, Thomas. "Be Keen to Get Going." In *William Carey; Theologian-Linguist-Social Reformer*, 109-52. World of Theology Series 4. Bonn: Verlag für Kultur und Wissenschaft, 2013. Ac-

Bibliography

cessed October 16, 2018. https://www.bucer.de/fileadmin/dateien/Dokumente/Buecher/WoT_4_-_Thomas_Schirrmacher__Ed.___-_William_Carey_-_Theologian_-_Linguist_-_Social_Reformer.pdf.

Serampore Missionaries. "Sketch of the Character of the Late Rev. Ward." *Friend of India 8*, monthly series. (1825): 571-82.

Smith, A. Christopher. "The Legacy of William Ward and Joshua and Hannah Marshman." *International Bulletin of Missionary Research* (July 1999): 120-29. Accessed January 28, 2019. http://www.bu.edu/missiology/missionary-biography/w-x-y-z/ward-william-1769-1823/.

_____. "Mythology and Missiology: A Methodological Approach to the Pre-Victorian Mission of the Serampore Trio." *International Review of Mission* 83, no. 330 (July 1, 1994): 451-75.

_____. "A Tale of Many Models: The Missiological Significance of the Serampore Trio." *Missiology: An International Review*. 20, no. 4 (1992): 479-500.

_____. "Ward, William." In *Biographical Dictionary of Christian Missions*. Edited by Gerald H. Anderson. New York: Macmillan Reference USA, 1998.

_____. "William Ward (1769-1823)." In *The British Particular Baptists 1638-1910*, vol. 2, edited by Michael A. G. Haykin. Springfield, MO: Particular Baptist Press, 2000.

_____. "William Ward, Radical Reform, and Missions in the 1790s." *American Baptist Quarterly* 10 (1991): 218-44.

Strong, Douglas M. "Ward, William." In *Evangelical Dictionary of World Missions*. Edited by A. Scott Moreau. Grand Rapids: Baker Books, 2000.

Swann, Derek. "Jonathan Edwards & the 1744 Concert For Prayer." *Foundations* 3 (November 1979): 10-21.

Wallis, A. A. "A Sketch of the Early History of the Printing Press in Derbyshire." *Derbyshire Archaelogical and Natural History Society Journal* iii (1881): 150.

"Ward, William." In *The Encyclopedia of Missions; Descriptive, Historical, Biographical, Statistical*. 2nd ed. Edited by Henry Otis Dwight, H. Allen Tupper, Edwin Munsell Bliss under the auspices of the Bureau of Missions. London: Funk & Wagnalls Company, 1904.

"Ward, William (1769–1823)." In *Historical Dictionary of the Baptists*. 2nd ed. Lanham, MD: The Scarecrow Press, 2009.

Ward, W. R. "The Baptists and the Transformation of the Church, 1780–1830." *Baptist Quarterly* 25, no. 4 (1973): 167-84.

Dissertations

Robison, Olin C. "The Particular Baptists in England, 1760–1820." DPhil thesis, Oxford University, 1963.

Vandever, William Tolbert, Jr. "An Educational History of the English and American Baptists in the Seventeenth and Eighteenth Centuries." PhD diss., University of Pennsylvania, 1974.

West, James Ryan. "Evangelizing Bengali Muslims, 1793–1813: William Carey, William Ward, and Islam." PhD diss., The Southern Baptist Theological Seminary, 2014.

Index

A

Act of Uniformity, 103, 145
Activism, 13, 17, 64
Adam, William, 124, 137, 138, 263
Affections, 21, 39, 81, 86, 100, 120
America, 36, 60, 61, 93, 110, 147, 202, 227, 251
American Sunday School Union, 255
Anabaptists, 162
Anglican Church. *See* Church of England
Antinomianism, 75, 119
Arminianism, 65, 66, 67, 71, 72, 75, 83, 256
Asiatics, 36, 38
Axell, John, 167

B

Backsliding, 47
Balukram, 108
Baptism, 16, 38, 41, 46, 47, 49, 79, 97, 140, 148, 149, 150, 152, 166, 167, 168, 169, 177, 213, 218, 219, 221, 223, 238, 239, 241, 243
Baptist Missionary Society, xiii, 1, 18, 19, 23, 52, 79, 83, 132, 251, 252, 253, 254, 255, 260, 261, 263, 264

Battle of Plassey, 173
Baxter, Richard, 103, 114, 115, 223
Bible Society, 153, 161, 162, 163, 202
Biblical Spirituality, 80, 81, 258
Biss, John, 47, 52, 124, 126, 179, 240, 243, 244
Böhme, Anton, 174
Bonaventure, 82
Book of Common Prayer, 67, 145
Booth, Abraham, 31, 219, 262
Boston, Thomas, 115
Brainerd, David, 110, 115
Brine, John, 68, 72
Bristol Baptist Academy, 13, 18
Brown, David, 19, 55, 76, 116, 117, 132, 144, 146, 147, 148, 150, 151, 152, 153, 154, 155, 156, 157, 159, 160, 161, 162, 163, 164, 165, 166, 167, 184, 185, 186, 187, 198, 199, 203, 204, 205, 209, 218, 222, 235, 239, 243, 256
Brundsdon, Daniel, 48
Brunsdon, Daniel, 19, 24, 26, 27, 104, 124, 127, 130, 186
Buchanan, Claudius, 50, 116, 143, 144, 145, 153, 154, 160, 161, 164, 165, 167, 192, 199, 203, 204, 205, 206, 208, 209, 222, 239

Bull, William, 67
Bunyan, John, 114, 115, 218, 223

C

Calvin, John, 83
Campbell, John, 143
Captain Christmas, 27
Captain Wickes, 27, 124, 125, 143, 144, 150, 152, 218, 221
Carey Baptist Church, 50, 149, 254, 255, 256
Carey Jr., William, 45
Carey, Dorthy, 142, 159
Carey, Eustace, 37, 124
Carey, Felix, 32, 34, 36, 43, 48, 49, 127, 134, 135, 175, 177, 240
Carey, Jabez, 47
Carey, Jonathan, 44, 47
Carey, William, 1, 14, 15, 22, 23, 24, 25, 27, 29, 30, 31, 32, 37, 41, 42, 44, 50, 55, 59, 62, 66, 67, 69, 75, 78, 79, 114, 116, 123, 125, 126, 127, 128, 130, 131, 133, 137, 138, 139, 140, 141, 143, 146, 150, 152, 154, 159, 161, 165, 166, 168, 171, 173, 174, 175, 177, 181, 186, 191, 195, 200, 201, 206, 212, 216, 218, 219, 222, 223, 229, 253, 255, 256, 257, 258, 260, 261, 264, 265, 266
Caste, 41, 176, 177

Chamberlain, John, 19, 47, 52, 59, 124, 130, 134, 142, 168, 179, 180, 193, 256
Charles II, 145
Chater, James, 124, 134
Chater, John, 156, 157, 179, 193
Church membership, 148, 152
Church of England, 12, 20, 65, 67, 114, 143, 144, 152, 167, 259
Clarkson, Thomas, 12
Clive, Robert, 28, 173
Closed communion, 142, 149, 217, 218, 220, 221
Closed communion., 218
Colonel Bie, 28
Confucius, 207, 208
Corrie, Daniel, 147, 188
Creeshnoo, 37, 41, 44, 45, 49, 104, 117, 165, 175, 183
Criterion, 9, 26, 27, 103, 104, 111, 116, 124, 144, 150, 218, 220, 221, 231, 233, 236
Cromwell, Oliver, 145
Cruz, Da, 149

D

Deism, 71
Discipleship, 36, 44, 142, 231
Dissenters, 12, 32, 37, 67, 144, 148, 155, 158, 162, 174, 179, 180, 236
Doctrines of grace, 26, 83, 84, 86, 97, 106, 120, 169
Doddridge, Philip, 102, 114, 115, 222

Index

Drewry, John, 10
Duncan, Jonathan, 181

E

East India Company, 27, 29, 41, 55, 123, 142, 147, 154, 159, 160, 172, 173, 174, 180, 182, 193, 198, 228, 255, 257
Ecumenicalism, 63, 67, 68, 80, 94, 116, 117, 142, 147, 148, 149, 152
Ecumenism, 21, 101, 102, 160
Edmonstone, Neil, 180
Edwards, Jonathan, 64, 70, 71, 74, 77, 115, 253, 259, 262, 264, 266
Election, 70, 77, 78, 83, 89, 91, 92, 96
Erasmus, Desiderius, 128, 129
Erskine, Thomas, 14
Evangelical Calvinism, 25, 34, 63
Evangelical Revival, 67, 263
Evangelicalism, 20, 21, 25, 27, 34, 38, 39, 50, 55, 63, 64, 65, 66, 80, 98, 102, 120, 123, 142, 143, 145, 146, 153, 157, 159, 160, 168, 176, 180, 198, 202, 203
Evangelism, 36, 37, 68, 151, 215, 231
Evans, Caleb, 13

F

Fawcett, John, 18, 19, 20, 21, 22, 23, 65, 66, 68, 258

Fernandez, Ignatius, 140, 235, 257
Fernandez, John, 31, 44, 140, 158, 235, 240
Fernandez, John Lewis, 47
Fletcher, Ann, 9
Foreign Bible Society, 202
Forsyth, Nathaniel, 147, 148, 149
Fort William College, 42, 138, 152, 154, 165, 182, 186, 203, 208
Fountain, John, xv, 31, 47, 48, 51, 55, 57, 58, 104, 123, 124, 130, 200, 257
Fox, George, 82
Francke, August Hermann, 29
Frederick IV, 28
Freemason's Hall. *See* Union Chapel
French Revolution, 11, 28, 260
Friendship, 58, 59, 60, 86, 100, 101, 125, 131, 157, 165, 168, 204, 212
Fuller, Andrew, 2, 15, 23, 24, 25, 55, 67, 70, 72, 76, 77, 90, 96, 102, 104, 108, 109, 126, 127, 129, 132, 133, 135, 136, 139, 150, 155, 159, 163, 179, 180, 197, 200, 202, 204, 213, 217, 218, 219, 221, 223, 224, 227, 254, 262

G

General Baptists, 66, 260
Gill, John, 68

Gokal, 44, 45
Gokol, 130, 176
Governor Krefting, 186, 188, 189, 192, 193, 194, 196, 199
Grant, Charles, 55, 132
Grant, William, 26, 27, 124, 130, 152
Great Awakening, 20, 64, 67
Grimshaw, William, 20, 21, 25, 65, 145

H

Hall Jr., Robert, 13, 219, 220
Hall Sr., Robert, 70, 72, 73, 74, 76
Harris, Howel, 64
Hasseltine, Anne, 97
Hasted, Francis, 44
Hasted, Jonathan, 44
Hastings, Warren, 174
Henry, Matthew, 64
Hill, Rowland, 238
Hinduism, 142, 191, 264
Hindus, 34, 38, 39, 40, 41, 42, 45, 47, 61, 80, 116, 117, 152, 173, 176, 177, 180, 191, 195, 204, 208, 264
Holy Spirit, 25, 26, 45, 69, 70, 79, 80, 81, 85, 86, 89, 93, 94, 233, 234
Hyper Calvinism, 68, 69, 70, 71, 72, 74, 77, 79

I

Irresistible grace, 86

J

Jay, William, 143
Jesuit Missionaries, 210, 215
John of the Cross, 81
Johns, William, 124
Johnstone, Patrick, 78
Judson, Adoniram, 97, 98, 149, 256
Junior missionaries, 48, 49, 126, 137

K

Kiffen, William, 218
Kinghorn, Joseph, 219, 220, 259
Komol, 49

L

Lal Bazaar Chapel, 37, 38, 50, 116, 134, 148, 159, 255
Lassar, Johannes, 203
Lawson, John, 37, 124
Leyden, John, 195, 206
Liberalism, 64
Limited atonement, 83, 91, 92, 95
London Missionary Society, xiii, 50, 132, 147, 149, 153, 158, 259
Lord's Supper, 12, 69, 102, 145, 149, 150, 151, 171, 217, 218, 219, 220, 221, 222, 223, 224, 225
Lord's Day, 22, 26, 30, 31, 32, 36, 38, 44, 46, 49, 104, 108, 114, 115, 116, 117, 120, 126, 133, 146, 147, 148, 158, 159, 163, 167,

Index

168, 177, 183, 184, 185, 188, 190, 191, 193, 208, 209, 210, 213, 216, 224, 235, 236, 238, 239, 240, 241, 242, 243, 244, 251
Lord's Supper, 116
Loveless, W., 158
Luther, Martin, 128, 129

M

Mack, John, 60
Mardon, Richard, 19, 52, 124, 135, 206, 240
Marrow controversy, 115
Marshman, Hannah, 26, 57, 104, 124, 182
Marshman, John Clark, 10, 44, 46, 47, 51, 66, 69, 83, 124, 128, 143, 145, 197, 207, 209, 214, 255
Marshman, Joshua, 1, 6, 11, 16, 26, 27, 29, 31, 37, 40, 42, 46, 47, 50, 51, 52, 55, 59, 60, 61, 62, 67, 79, 83, 98, 99, 100, 101, 105, 106, 109, 116, 118, 119, 123, 124, 125, 126, 127, 128, 129, 130, 131, 132, 133, 134, 136, 137, 138, 139, 140, 141, 142, 144, 146, 147, 150, 155, 157, 161, 164, 166, 168, 169, 171, 179, 180, 182, 187, 188, 193, 195, 196, 197, 198, 201, 202, 203, 205, 206, 207, 208, 209, 211, 212, 213, 214, 216, 220, 223, 224, 226, 228, 236, 237, 240, 244, 253, 255, 265

Martyn, Henry, 117, 146, 147, 159
Merton, Thomas, 82
Methodism, 10, 12, 15, 20, 21, 65, 66, 67
Missiology, 33, 121, 215, 216, 265
Mission Press, 9, 35, 40, 42, 50, 152, 163, 181, 184, 191, 199, 251, 252, 255, 256, 257
Mohun, 46, 140, 240
Moore, William, 52, 124, 213, 245
Moravians, 28, 29, 92, 107, 114, 115, 195, 259
More, Thomas, 63
Müller, George, 149
Muslims, 38, 41, 42, 46, 47, 154, 156, 159, 173, 184, 187, 189, 238, 242, 266

N

Newton, John, 25, 67, 143, 144, 256
Northampton Association, 69
Northamptonshire Association, 73, 150, 262

O

Open communion, 102, 142, 149, 151, 217, 219, 220, 221
Open Communion, 222
Owen, John, 69, 70, 95, 259

P

Paine, Thomas, 11
Pal, Krishna, 52, 175, 176, 177, 251
Particular redemption, 95, 96
Peacemaking, 33, 100, 103, 104, 171, 199
Pearce, Samuel, 120, 136, 256
Pearce, William, 124, 136
Penney, James, 124
Perkins, William, 89
Perry, James, 14
Perseverance of the saints, 88
Persian Pamphlet Controversy, 116, 171, 181, 188, 198, 209, 216, 244
Petumber, 101, 104, 116, 183
Petumber Jr., 101
Phillips, Richard, 14
Pitt, William, 11
Plütschau, Henry, 29
Pope Urban VIII, 164
Postmillenialism, 79
Prasad, Krishna, 52
Prayer, 32, 34, 44, 45, 49, 52, 53, 78, 79, 98, 104, 108, 109, 110, 111, 112, 113, 115, 116, 117, 118, 126, 143, 146, 151, 157, 158, 159, 165, 166, 192, 199, 228, 235
Puritans, 39, 64, 67, 68, 69, 70, 84, 89, 115, 118, 120, 260

Q

Quakers, 9, 82, 141

R

Remonstrants, 84
Rennell, James, 29
Rippon, John, 15, 147
Robinson, Robert, 66
Robinson, William, 37, 59, 124, 134, 142, 156, 157, 179, 193, 244
Roman Catholicism, 28, 140, 155, 239
Roop, 46
Rowe, Joshua, 52, 124, 193, 244, 245
Ryland Jr., John, 18, 67, 75, 132, 135, 206, 219, 224
Ryland Sr., John, 69, 78, 174, 218

S

Sandys, John, 31
Schwartz, Christian Frederick, 28
Second wave of missionaries to Serampore, 124, 132
Sedgwick, William, 251
Serampore Controversy, 51, 105, 135
Serampore fire, 153
Serampore Mission, 30, 32, 40, 42, 43, 48, 50, 54, 55, 63, 82, 105, 123, 125, 135, 140, 149, 163, 165, 171, 181, 193, 194, 199, 200, 202, 215, 217, 227, 229, 260, 262
Serampore Trio, 103, 123, 161, 217, 221, 228, 264, 265
Shah Alam II, 173

Index

Slavery, 12
Socinianism, 26, 119, 120
Socinus, Faustus, 120
Soldiers, 38, 92, 166, 167, 173, 178, 198
Spurgeon, C.H., 91, 149, 261
Stennett, Samuel, 10, 19, 36, 38, 83, 84, 98, 127, 237
Sutcliff, John, 19, 23, 67, 68, 132, 258
Synod of Dort, 84

T

Taylor, Dan, 67, 261
Taylor, John, 146, 158, 261
Teresa of Avila, 82
Test and Corporation Acts, 12
Thelwall, John, 16, 17
Third wave of missionaries to Serampore, 125
Thomas, John, 27, 47, 55, 79, 123, 124, 130, 142, 201, 255
Thomason, T.T., 153, 255
Total depravity, 25, 83, 84, 85, 86
Turner, Daniel, 218, 223

U

Udny, George, 55, 161, 181
Union Chapel, 50, 61, 149, 169
Unitarianism, 120, 138
Unna, 130
Usefulness, 15, 16, 21, 32, 37, 38, 39, 83, 98, 116, 118, 120, 121, 185, 199, 216, 226, 227, 228, 230, 233, 235, 236, 241

V

Vellore Mutiny, 156, 186
Venn, Henry, 20, 21, 25, 65, 68, 261

W

Wallin, Benjamin, 68
Ward (née Tidd), Mary, 55, 56, 124
Ward, John, 9
Ward, Mary, xv
Ward, Thomas, 9, 68
Ward, William
   accepted as missionary with BMS, 24
   activism, 13, 16, 17
   as a counselor, 58
   as a father, 55, 57
   as a friend, 58
   as a husband, 55
   as a mentor, 43
   as a Methodist, 12
   as a peacemaker, 103, 105, 171, 193, 227
   as a printer, 10, 16, 23, 32, 33, 36, 40, 48, 182, 237
   as an author, 2, 50, 82
   as co-pastor, 37, 133
   baptized, 16
   becomes a Baptist, 15
   call to ministry, 17
   catechism of children, 48
   childhood, 9
   death, 3, 59, 61, 62, 83, 105, 106, 115, 117, 121, 169, 215, 228

embarks for India, 26, 103
his doctrine, 83
his ecumenism, 7, 102
his legacy, 215, 228
his theology, 34, 111, 113
his wit, 237
international tour, 61
journey back to England, 227
life at Serampore, 30
marriage, 55
on open communion, 150, 151, 218, 221, 225
on open membership, 223
opposition of the British government, 26, 172
ordained as a deacon, 31
roles in Serampore Mission, 32
studies at Ewood Hall, 18

Waring, Scott, 153
Waste, Joan, 168
Watts, Isaac, 49, 114, 115
Wesley, Charles, 66
Wesley, John, 20, 64, 65, 66, 261
Whitefield, George, 20, 25, 64, 65, 66, 68, 259
Wickes, Benjamin, 26, 143
Wilberforce, William, 11, 12, 25, 143
Wilkins, Charles, 181

Y

Yates, William, 124

Z

Ziegenbalg, Bartholomew, 29

www.ingramcontent.com/pod-product-compliance
Lightning Source LLC
Chambersburg PA
CBHW021054080526
44587CB00010B/250